THE REMINISCENCES OF
Admiral Robert L. J. Long
U.S. Navy (Retired)

INTERVIEWED BY
Paul Stillwell

U.S. Naval Institute • Annapolis, Maryland

Copyright © 1995

Preface

Because Admiral Long's active naval service spanned more than four decades, his oral memoir covers a wide range of topics. His time in uniform began with his service as a midshipman prior to World War II and ended with duty in the 1980s as Commander in Chief Pacific, one of the most senior positions in the U.S. armed forces. In between he was in combat as a member of the crew of the battleship Colorado during World War II. Afterward he began a series of billets in the submarine service, both diesel and nuclear. He went through the nuclear-power training program under Admiral Hyman Rickover, whom he discusses in candid terms. In the early 1960s Long was the commanding officer of the gold crew of the USS Patrick Henry, the Navy's second Polaris-armed ballistic missile submarine. He later worked in the Special Projects Office that ran the technical end of the ballistic missile program; indeed, this oral history is particularly useful for its Polaris focus.

In the pages that follow one can read about Long's growth as a naval officer, including a tour as a student at the Naval War College, command positions, duty as executive assistant to Under Secretary of the Navy Robert Baldwin, technical service in the Naval Ship Systems Command, and Commander Service Group Three. As a vice admiral he was at the pinnacle of the submarine warfare ladder, First as

Commander Submarine Force Atlantic Fleet, later as Deputy Chief of Naval Operations (Submarine Warfare). As a four-star admiral Admiral Long was Vice Chief of Naval Operations and Commander in Chief Pacific.

In those high-level billets he came to appreciate that military matters are inextricably linked with political and economic ones. Armed services are not ends in themselves. A vivid illustration came in the bombing of the U.S. Marine barracks in Beirut, Lebanon, in 1983. The Marines were sent to Lebanon for one purpose but got caught in the tangled web of Mideast politics and suffered at the hands of terrorists. Admiral Long headed the commission that investigated the bombing.

Both Admiral Long and I have made changes to the original transcript in the interests of clarity, smoothness, and accuracy. A few things have been moved to improve the continuity and chronological sequence of the narrative. The version that follows, including the annotating footnotes, has Admiral Long's concurrence.

                                              Paul Stillwell
                                              Director, History Division
                                              U.S. Naval Institute
                                              May 1995

ADMIRAL ROBERT LYMAN JOHN LONG
U.S. NAVY (RETIRED)

Robert Lyman John Long was born in Kansas City, Missouri, on 29 May 1920, the son of Trigg Allen and Margaret (Franklin) Long. He attended Paseo High School, Kansas City Junior College, and Washington University in St. Louis, Missouri. He was then appointed to the U.S. Naval Academy, Annapolis, Maryland, which he entered in 1940. As a midshipman he participated in athletics--squash and lacrosse. He graduated with distinction on 9 June 1943, at which time he was commissioned an ensign in the U.S. Navy. He was a member of the class of 1944, which had a three-year course because of the war emergency.

After graduation from the Naval Academy in 1943, he had two months' duty in the Naval Air Operational Training Command, at Naval Air Station Jacksonville, Florida. From September of 1943 until December 1945, during the latter part of World War II, he was at sea in the USS Colorado (BB-45). As a fire control division officer and assistant gunnery officer of that battleship, he participated in the Gilbert Islands operation; the Marshall Islands operation (occupation of Kwajalein, Majuro, and Eniwetok); the capture and occupation of the Marianas (Saipan, Tinian, and Guam); the landings in the Philippines (Leyte, Mindoro, and Lingayen Gulf); and the occupation of Okinawa. He was awarded the Bronze Star medal for meritorious service as plotting room officer in the Colorado.

From December 1945 to June 1946 he received instruction at the Submarine School, New London, Connecticut, and was awarded the L. Y. Spear prize upon graduation. For five months thereafter he was assigned to the office of the Supervisor of Shipbuilding, Electric Boat Company, Groton, Connecticut, to assist in fitting out the USS Corsair (SS-435). He served in various capacities in that submarine from her commissioning in November 1946 until August 1949, including communications officer, commissary officer, gunnery and torpedo officer, operations officer, and navigator. In September 1949 he was assigned to the Naval Reserve Officer Training Corps unit at the University of North Carolina, Chapel Hill, where he served as instructor of ordnance, administrative aide, and executive officer until June 1951.

Long next had two years at sea as executive officer of the USS Cutlass (SS-478). Instruction at the Naval War

College, Newport, Rhode Island, from July 1953 until June 1954 preceded service afloat for two years as commanding officer of the USS Sea Leopard (SS-483). Upon his detachment in August 1956, he was ordered to the Office of the Chief of Naval Operations, Washington, D.C., where he headed the Submarine Weapons Readiness Section until July 1958. During this time he was commended by the Secretary of the Navy for his work with fleet ballistic missile systems. He then reported as flag secretary to Commander Submarine Force Atlantic Fleet.

From July 1959 until June 1960 he had instruction in the Office of the Director for Naval Reactors, in the U.S. Atomic Energy Commission, Washington, D.C. He continued instruction at the Navy Guided Missiles School, Dam Neck, Virginia. On 1 August 1960 he assumed command of the gold crew of the USS Patrick Henry (SSBN-599), which was commissioned 11 April 1960.

In August 1963 he returned to the Naval Guided Missiles School, Dam Neck, for further instruction and in October 1963 assumed command of the blue crew of the USS Casimir Pulaski (SSBN-633). He had duty in connection with the Fleet Ballistic Missile Project in the Bureau of Naval Weapons (later with the Naval Material Command), Washington, D.C., from July 1965 to July 1966, then became executive assistant and naval aide to the Under Secretary of the Navy. For his service in the latter capacity he was awarded the Legion of Merit.

In September 1968, following selection for flag rank, he reported as Commander Service Group Three, serving in that capacity until the following year and receiving a gold star in lieu of a second Legion of Merit. In November 1969 he became Deputy Commander for Fleet Maintenance and Logistic Support, Naval Ship Systems Command, Washington, D.C. While there he received a gold star in lieu of a third Legion of Merit award.

He was promoted to vice admiral in June 1972 and assumed command of the Submarine Force, U.S. Atlantic Fleet. He had additional duty as submarine operations adviser for Polaris/Poseidon operations, Atlantic Command and Supreme Allied Command Atlantic; and as Commander Submarines, Allied Command and Commander Submarine Force, Western Atlantic Area. In September 1974 he was assigned as Deputy Chief of Naval Operations for Submarine Warfare. For exceptionally meritorious service in these two assignments, he was awarded the Navy Distinguished Service Medal.

In July 1977 Long was promoted to the rank of admiral and became Vice Chief of Naval Operations; he remained in that position until September 1979. Admiral Long was awarded a gold star in lieu of his second Navy Distinguished Service Medal for exceptional service to the U.S. Government.

Admiral Long became Commander in Chief U.S. Forces Pacific on 31 October 1979. He was the 11th naval officer to hold the position. As the senior U.S. military commander in the Pacific and Indian Ocean areas, he headed the largest of the unified commands and directed Army, Navy, Marine Corps, and Air Force operations across more than 100 million square miles--more than 50% of the earth's surface. The pacific Command extends from the West Coast of the United States to the East Coast of Africa, from the Arctic to the Antarctic. He was responsible to the President and the Secretary of Defense and was the U.S. military representative for collective defense arrangements in the Pacific. These include the U.S.-Japan Treaty of Mutual Cooperation and Security; the Mutual Defense Treaties with the Republic of Korea and Republic of the Philippines; the ANZUS Treaty among Australia, New Zealand, and the United States; and the U.S.-Thailand defense relationship under the multinational Manila Pact.

Personal Data

Born: 29 May 1920, Kansas City, Missouri

Parents: Trigg Allen Long and Margaret Franklin Long

Married: 28 August 1944 to Sara Helms

Children: Charles Allen Long, born 3/15/47
William Trigg Long, born 12/22/49
Robert Helms Long, born 1/15/60

Dates of Rank

Rank	Date
Midshipman	18 June 1940
Ensign	9 June 1943
Lieutenant (junior grade)	1 September 1944
Lieutenant	1 April 1946
Lieutenant Commander	1 January 1954
Commander	1 February 1958
Captain	1 July 1963
Rear Admiral	1 July 1969
Vice Admiral	29 July 1972
Admiral	5 July 1977

Chronological Transcript of Service

June 1940-June 1943	Midshipman, U.S. Naval Academy
June 1943-August 1943	Naval Air Station, Jacksonville, Florida
September 1943-December 1945	USS Colorado (BB-45)
December 1945-June 1946	Submarine School, New London, Connecticut
June 1946-November 1946	Supervisor of Shipbuilding, Groton, Connecticut, for outfitting Corsair (SS-435)
November 1946-July 1949	USS Corsair (SS-435)
July 1949-June 1951	NROTC Unit, University of North Carolina
June 1951-June 1953	XO, USS Cutlass (SS-478)
July 1953-June 1954	Student, Naval War College Newport, Rhode Island
June 1954-August 1956	CO, USS Sea Leopard (SS-483)
August 1956-July 1958	Submarine Weapons Readiness Section (OP-311), OpNav
July 1958-July 1959	Staff, Commander Submarine Force, Atlantic Fleet
July 1959-June 1960	Nuclear power training, Atomic Energy Commission
June 1960-August 1960	Guided Missiles School, Dam Neck, Virginia
August 1960-August 1963	CO (Gold), USS Patrick Henry (SSBN-599)
August 1963-September 1963	Guided Missiles School, Dam Neck, Virginia
October 1963-June 1965	CO (Blue), USS Casimir Pulaski (SSBN-633)
June 1965-October 1965	Bureau of Naval Weapons Washington, D.C.

October 1965-July 1966	Naval Material Command Washington, D.C.
July 1966-September 1968	Executive Assistant and Naval Aide to the Under Secretary of the Navy
September 1968-November 1969	Commander Service Group Three
November 1969-June 1972	Deputy Commander, Fleet Maintenance and Logistics Support, Naval Ship Systems Command
June 1972-September 1974	Commander Submarine Force, U.S. Atlantic Fleet
September 1974-July 1977	Deputy Chief of Naval Operations (Submarine Warfare)
July 1977-September 1979	Vice Chief of Naval Operations
October 1979-July 1983	Commander in Chief Pacific
1 July 1983	Retired from active duty

Authorization

The U.S. Naval Institute is hereby authorized to make available to individuals, libraries, and other repositories of its choosing the transcripts of three oral history interviews concerning the life and career of the undersigned. The interviews were recorded on 25 January 1993, 26 February 1993, and 5 March 1993 in collaboration with Paul Stillwell for the U.S. Naval Institute.

The undersigned does hereby release and assign to the U.S. Naval Institute all right, title, restrictions, and interest in the interviews. The copyright in both the oral and transcribed versions shall be the sole property of the U.S. Naval Institute. The tape recordings of the interviews are and will remain the property of the U.S. Naval Institute.

Signed and sealed this _11_ day of _Nov_ 1994.

_____
Admiral Robert L. J. Long, USN (Ret.)

Interview Number 1 with Admiral Robert L. J. Long,
U.S. Navy (Retired)

Place: Admiral Long's home, Annapolis, Maryland

Date: Monday, 25 January 1993

Interviewer: Paul Stillwell

Q: Admiral, to begin at the beginning, I wonder if you could start by talking about your boyhood, your parents, and some of your family background.

Admiral Long: I was born in Kansas City, Missouri, on the 29th of May, 1920. I was the youngest of six children. I had two sisters and three brothers. My mother and father grew up in that area. My father was Trigg Allen Long. His father came from southeast Missouri. His mother was a longtime resident of Liberty, Missouri, a member of the Allen family. Her grandfather was Colonel Shubael Allen, who was one of the very early settlers in that area. He ran a very famous trading post on the Missouri River. It was called Allen's Landing and was very important in the westward migration of Americans. My maternal grandparents were Franklins. My grandfather came from a German family, farmers. My grandmother was a French Huguenot from the Quest and Fleurnoy families.

I had a rather normal, happy childhood. The family

was close-knit. My two oldest brothers were 10 and 12 years older than I was, so they were almost like surrogate fathers to me. They were wonderful big brothers who did a lot for me and gave me a lot of experiences, some of which I don't know if I would recommend today. [Laughter]

Q: Such as? [Laughter]

Admiral Long: Well, I can remember at 12 years old, I was driving my brother's car. We used to go to a lot of athletic events and hunting. They were wonderful to me, and that close relationship maintained until they passed away years later.

Q: So there was enough age difference you wouldn't have a lot of sibling rivalry.

Admiral Long: The only sibling rivalry I had was with my two sisters. They actually were very good to me too. I think overall I probably was a little bit spoiled.

Q: What sort of work did your father do?

Admiral Long: My father was an insurance agent. I can remember back to the Thirties, in the depth of the Depression. My father was fortunate that he was selling insurance, essentially only property insurance, and he was associated with some companies that were selling it at a cheaper rate than the others. So we did not suffer too much during the Depression.

He always wanted to buy a farm, and so when I was 10 or 12 years old, he bought a farm outside of town. We used to say he made his money in town and spent it in the country. But that was a great opportunity for me to learn about farming: harvesting wheat, corn, raising cattle. We had some horses that I loved to ride. It was a great outlet for a youngster.

Q: Kansas City is a great stockyard area, so that was a popular commodity.

Admiral Long: That's right. The Kansas City stockyards were almost as large as the ones in Chicago. Kansas City also had a wonderful event every year with the American Royal, which was for horse shows and grading for cattle and livestock.

Q: So you really had both an urban and rural upbringing.

Admiral Long: Yes. Interestingly, when I graduated from the Naval Academy later on, one of my classmates wrote something to go under my picture in the yearbook. He said

Robert L. J. Long #1 - 4

that I always had the yearning to be a gentleman farmer. That has never occurred yet.

Q: What do you remember about the famous Pendergast political machine and Harry Truman and so forth?

Admiral Long: When I was growing up, Tom Pendergast was a major political force, not only in Kansas City, but Jackson County and the whole state of Missouri.* My father was not a Pendergast supporter. He was very much opposed to him. At one time my father considered running for mayor as an independent, but he decided that would be of little or no value.

There were actually two Democratic factions in Kansas City and western Missouri. One was the Pendergast faction called the Goats, and the other was a faction headed by Representative Joe Shannon, and they were called the Rabbits.** Tom Pendergast owned the Ready-Mix Concrete Company. As a result, Jackson County had more paved roads than any other county in the United States. As a matter of fact, we had so much concrete that we not only paved the roads, but we paved some of the streams. Today Brush Creek runs through the Plaza, probably one of the nicest shopping

---
*Thomas J. Pendergast was the Democratic Party political boss for the Kansas City area. He helped foster the political career of future President Harry S Truman.
**Joseph B. Shannon, a Democrat, served in the U.S. House of Representatives from 1931 to 1943 on behalf of Missouri's fifth congressional district.

areas in town, and it is very nicely paved with concrete. It probably was a very good idea, but at the time I don't think that Mr. Pendergast had that in mind.

Kansas City also became the owner of some marvelous buildings. City hall and the county courthouse were magnificent buildings built at that time, and, of course, they are great assets today. There also was a municipal auditorium that was built with good taxpayer money. As a result of all this, Mr. Pendergast lived quite well, as did some of his lieutenants. He had one lieutenant that gained some notoriety, and that was a man named Lazia, who kept the north end of town under complete control.* There was some speculation about his control of the liquor distribution and his relations with criminals from out of town.

My oldest brother, Allen, became involved at that time in some politics with Congressman Shannon, and it was really through Congressman Shannon that I received an appointment to the Naval Academy.

Q: What was the basis for your father's desire to run for office?

Admiral Long: Well, I think he felt that it was such a

---
*Johnny Lazia, one of Pendergast's chief lieutenants, was a racketeer.

corrupt political system. Pendergast had not only control over Jackson County, but also he had significant control throughout the state of Missouri. One of his political appointees was Harry S Truman. While I was growing up, Mr. Truman was anathema in our household, and it was not until much later that I learned really to respect him. He turned out to be one of the strongest Presidents that we have had.

Q: The irony also is that he also had the reputation for being absolutely incorruptible himself.

Admiral Long: Yes, that's right. Before Truman was a United States senator, he was a county judge, which meant that he was one of the executives of Jackson County, not in a judicial sense. Sort of on a personal side, my brother Charles spent some time at college at Warrensburg, and his roommate there was a young man named Wallace Graham. Wally Graham went on to become a doctor, and eventually he became Truman's doctor in the White House.

My oldest brother was over six feet tall--a big, good-looking guy. He was a football player in high school. The next brother was Charles, who was smaller and had a fiery disposition, a temper. He would fight you at a drop of a hat, and that might have been the reaction of having an older, stronger brother--self-protection. Both of them were good men, hard working. The next brother was William.

We called him Duke, also tall, good-looking, quite the ladies' man--fortunately something that I never had to worry about.

My two sisters are Margaret Valentine, who was born on Valentine's Day. We call her Sis to this day. She was a beautiful girl, looked very much like Carole Lombard, if you can remember back that far.* My next sister was Sally Eleanor. We called her Snooks, and we're still very close friends today. Unfortunately, my two oldest brothers have passed on, and my other brother, who is now 80, is not in good health.

The family is spread out across the country. One sister moved across the state line to Kansas City, Kansas, and that's something that is difficult for some of us to accept, because Kansas was where all the hick drivers came from. Kansas City, Kansas, that state line area, is now one of the loveliest residential spots in the area. My older sister still lives in Los Altos, California. My brother lives in that same area. So it's sometimes difficult to get us all together.

Q: How much part did religion play in the family life while you were growing up?

Admiral Long: My grandparents, particularly my mother's

---
*Carole Lombard, the wife of actor Clark Gable, was a popular movie star in the 1930s and 1940s.

parents, were very strong Baptists. My paternal grandparents were also Baptists, and all four of them were very active in the Baptist Church. It was interesting that when I was growing up, my mother became a Christian Scientist. That had some appeal to me, and in the early days I attended the Christian Science Sunday school and church. There are some very positive things that go on in the Christian Science Church. Some of those things I cannot accept today, but the power of positive thought was a very important part of my thinking. Subsequently, my wife and I both were confirmed and joined the Episcopal Church, so we are Episcopalians today.

Q: What do you remember about values and ambitions that your parents imparted?

Admiral Long: My mother was a very sharp person. She was an avid bridge player. As a matter of fact, we played a lot of cards in my family. We played bridge. We played poker. We played pitch. So I think that was where I learned to enjoy playing cards. My wife and I still play a lot of cards today. My mother was, I'd say, a modern woman. As an example, she won the ladies' driving contest in Kansas City put on by the AAA in 1925 and received a silver loving cup that was about three feet tall.* She

---
*AAA--American Automobile Association.

probably prized that as much as anything. She loved to go, she loved to drive. When we would take trips, my mother would be the one who would drive the car. When I was growing up, the whole family routinely took a few weeks' vacation in the summer. We would go to a place called Birch Lake in Minnesota. It was a very nice time for the family to be together.

My father was shrewd and very pragmatic. I learned a lot from him. He didn't just accept people immediately at their word; he needed to have some proof. And he did a lot of struggling in business. He was very good to me. He was very supportive of those things that I wanted to do. He kept a very close interest in what the children were doing. He was also, I'd say, a rather strict father. With six kids in a house, when he said, "Jump!" we normally said, "How high?"

Q: Do you have any examples of his strictness?

Admiral Long: Well, I can remember when my brother Charles was attending Missouri State Teachers College in Warrensburg. I heard the phone ring once when he called up about midnight. My father got on the phone, and all at once I heard him say, "You did what? Goddamn it! You have really done it now!" My brother had gotten married.

[Laughter] Dad gave him hell for it, but he stood by him. He stood by him. He was a fantastic guy and loving father.

As I say, he gave me a lot of the values of hard work and telling the truth. Another thing that I learned from him is something that I feel very keenly about is respect for people--not only your seniors but your juniors as well. That doesn't mean that you're buddy-buddy with them all, but you respect them. There was a good saying that he had when we were teenagers. When we'd go out, he'd say, "Be smart enough to know when to leave the party." That's something that I have never forgotten, although I haven't left the party quite yet. I realized that at a certain point, people need to step aside, and I see that in some of my activities today on boards, advisory boards and so on. He also didn't tolerate us staying out all times of the night. We had to be home at a certain time, and that was it.

He also was extremely protective of his daughters. I can remember one time when we were up in Minnesota, and my Carole Lombard sister had found this good-looking young guy. I guess he might have been 18 or so. He took her up to the local nightclub, and my dad found out about it and immediately got in the car and went up there and pulled her out of that "sinful place." He was a good father.

Q: Did your parents stress the importance of education?

Admiral Long: No, not really.

Q: Was it taken for granted?

Admiral Long: No. Neither of my parents went to college, and I don't think their parents did, although both of my grandmothers came from very well-to-do, well-respected families. The Allens were one of the first families in Liberty, Missouri, and my other grandmother was a Quest. So not all the children in the family went to college. Of course, this was during the Depression. My oldest brother went for a short period of time. My next brother had, I guess, most of a college education. He went to the University of Missouri and to the Teachers College. He studied agriculture and became a really dedicated farmer. My next brother had maybe only a year of college. My two sisters had about a year of college each.

I really was the first one who decided--I guess principally on my own--that I wanted a full college education. I was a very good student in high school. I attended Paseo High School. One teacher there probably had almost as significant impact on me as my parents did insofar as where I was going in life. Her name was Helen Spencer. She was a Salvation Army worker in France in World War I, and then after that she became a teaching missionary in China. She was a maiden lady, and she taught history. I had her for my freshman year, and I established great respect for her. She used to get absolutely furious at me in class, because I was sort of a wise guy. I can remember one time when I said something I shouldn't, she picked up her keys and threw those keys across the room and hit me in the head. She was absolutely crushed. But she saw something in me that she encouraged, and she was the one that kept me going.

As a result, I ended up as essentially the valedictorian of my high school class. I was class president; I was the head of the student council; I was editor of the school newspaper. I attribute a lot of that to Helen Spencer. She was a wonderful, wonderful gal. After I met Sara, I brought her back to Kansas City because I needed Helen Spencer's "okay." As a result, Helen Spencer was almost a member of our family until she died years later.

Q: Her adventurous spirit was depicted in those trips you mentioned. That can really be an inspiration to you.

Admiral Long: I believe that's right.

Q: And you'd get a love of learning, wanting to know more about these things.

Admiral Long: Yes. Also, I don't believe that people who didn't live through the Thirties have an understanding of how tight money was and how difficult it was to get things.

Q: I'd think especially for a farmer, because you're so dependent on the prices and the markets.

Admiral Long: Oh, yes. But in my senior year in high school, I read in the paper that they were having applications for scholarships to Washington University in St. Louis. On my own, I applied, went down for an interview, and received a $1,000-a-year scholarship for Washington University.

Q: A very prestigious school.

Admiral Long: Very prestigious. One thousand dollars was a lot of money in those days. My dad was delighted, and he picked up the rest of the tab for me to go there. Of course, as you know, to go to a private school at that time didn't cost $25,000 like it does today.

At that time, also, I had as a neighbor a naval officer, who was on duty in Kansas City. He painted this glowing picture of travel around the world and this marvelous life as a naval officer. He completely snowed me that this was a great life, so I decided then that I wanted to go to the Naval Academy. So even though I had this scholarship to Washington University, I did apply through my brother's friend, Congressman Shannon, but he had already promised the appointment. At that time the congressmen received just so many appointments for the Naval Academy, and he promised this to a friend of mine who was a little older than I was--Oliver Payne.* So Payne went that year to the Naval Academy. I was still hopeful that I could go later.

So I went on to Washington University and, as a matter of fact, even joined a fraternity, Sigma Nu. I subsequently found out they were pretty wild. I waited tables in the fraternity house. That didn't bother me at all. It might be degrading to some today, but that paid for my room and board there. I received maybe $50.00-60.00 a month from my dad for other expenses. It was a great opportunity.

I dropped out of Washington University when I thought I had a Naval Academy appointment lined up, but it didn't work out. So I came home and went to Kansas City Junior College, where I finished out the two years of its curriculum. Then in my third year I went to the University of Missouri at Columbia. I made good grades all this time.

---

*Oliver H. Payne, who was born in 1917, graduated from the Naval Academy in the class of 1939 and eventually retired in 1956 as a commander.

Robert L. J. Long #1 - 15

Q: Did you have some intended major, or was this all marking time?

Admiral Long: Well, I really wanted to be a lawyer. I was taking political science and I enjoyed it. As a matter of fact, at the University of Missouri I had a scholarship offer from University of Chicago, which was a really prestigious place insofar as political science. But at that time, the Naval Academy appointment finally came through. So that's the way I got into the Navy.

Q: I remember Columbia as a very lovely town in the Seventies when we lived there. How was it when you were there?

Admiral Long: Oh, it was great. We had two women's schools there. We had Stephens College, and the other one was, I think, a religious school--Columbia College. Here again, I joined up in the Sigma Nu house and things were a little wild. The fraternities probably wouldn't be considered wild today, but they were considered pretty wild at that time.

Q: How much did you keep up with world political developments during the Thirties--the rise of the dictators and the start of the war in Europe?

Admiral Long: I can remember going down to Columbia, Missouri, on 1 September 1939. That was the day Hitler invaded Poland.* I didn't have any idea at that time that we were about to go to war, but that was when the war started in Europe. After that the United States started the draft. So this was the beginning of what I perceived to be a very tough time.

Q: Missouri was an isolationist area really for quite a long time.

Admiral Long: Oh, yes, that's right. That's right.

Q: Did that cause discussions in some of your classes as the prospect of war came?

Admiral Long: No, I don't recall that. I think most of the discussions were with young men that I knew, and they were wondering whether they were going to have to go into the Army. At the University of Missouri I belonged to the ROTC.** This was a field artillery unit, and that was of some value to me later on so my Army friends couldn't snow me. [Laughter]

---
*Adolf Hitler was the German Chancellor from 1933 to 1945.
**ROTC--reserve officers' training corps.

Robert L. J. Long #1 - 17

Q: Also it gave you a little indoctrination in marching and drill and that sort of thing before you came to Annapolis.

Admiral Long: That's right.

Q: How close were you to a degree with all these intermediate studies?

Admiral Long: I was still a good year away from a degree on that end. But I liked political science. I saw it really as a precursor to a law degree. Subsequently, in 1949, I even applied to go to law school, but by that time the Navy had closed off the opportunity for unrestricted line officers to go to law school.

Q: So except for that appointment coming through, you would have had an entirely different career.

Admiral Long: Exactly. If old Joe Shannon hadn't given me that appointment, I don't know what I would be today, but I suspect I would have been a lawyer.

Q: Or shot as a soldier in France. Who knows? [Laughter]

Robert L. J. Long #1 - 18

Admiral Long: [Laughter] That's right! Certainly drafted some way.

Q: How did the transition come about when you started your time at the Naval Academy?

Admiral Long: Well, let's see. After my appointment, I dropped out of the University of Missouri, because it was then January and February of 1940. I decided that I was not that well prepared for the academy, although I'd had two and a half years of college. My great deficiency was in mathematics. I had sufficiently good grades in everything else so that I was not required to take any sort of substantiating examination for the academy, which was required at that time. Essentially, the Navy accepted my college record and said, "You can come in without any examination."

Q: But you didn't have much background in the hard sciences.

Admiral Long: I didn't have very much. Most of my courses were in the bull subjects. A couple of months before entering the Naval Academy in early June, I came to Annapolis and I entered Cochran-Bryan prep school to prepare in the mathematics area.* I guess it worked out all right, because I ended up standing number one in mathematics in my class at the Naval Academy. This was a school run by a couple of retired naval officers out on Franklin Street in Annapolis. I guess there must have been 20 other young men there. It was extremely worthwhile for me to go there.

I think one of the things that was very worthwhile was at that time that I met this family in town: Professor and Mrs. Conrad. He was a professor in mathematics at the Naval Academy, and he had two very attractive daughters.** During my three years at the academy, that was essentially my home away from home. Dave Webster, my roommate at the Naval Academy, ended up marrying one of the daughters.*** The Conrads were a wonderful couple, interested in lots of things. He was formerly at the Naval Observatory in Washington, so he was very much interested in astronomy and space travel. I remember he sat down one day and explained how we would get to the moon in a rocket ship. It turned out almost exactly as he said.

---
*The Cochran-Bryan Preparatory School in Annapolis was operated by Lieutenant Commander Schamyl Cochran, USN (Ret.), a 1908 graduate of the Naval Academy, and Lieutenant (junior grade) Arthur W. Bryan, USN (Ret.), a 1922 graduate.
**Dr. William A. Conrad, associate professor of mathematics when Long was a midshipman, had been on the faculty of the Naval Academy in 1919. He later was promoted to full professor and taught at the academy until 1954.
***Midshipman David A. Webster, USN.

Robert L. J. Long #1 - 20

Q: I hope he lived long enough to see that.

Admiral Long: Well, I guess he's been gone now for 25 years, so it was just about the time that the astronauts got there. Wonderful, wonderful couple.

Q: With the time you'd spent in these various colleges, you were probably older than most of your midshipmen classmates.

Admiral Long: Yes. I had just turned 20 when I entered the Naval Academy.

Q: What was the cutoff limit?

Admiral Long: Oh, I think 21. I'm one of the older members of my class, but not the oldest member. I'd say most of my classmates were around 18, so I was a good two years older than most of them. I graduated from high school when I was 17, so that's about a year earlier than most people.

Q: A little tradeoff there.

Admiral Long: A little tradeoff, that's right.

Q: After all you had been through, was there any difficulty adjusting to the regiment and the discipline at the Naval Academy?

Admiral Long: I was a "very sophisticated" young man, having been to two and a half years of college, and I'll have to admit that I looked upon plebe year and particularly plebe summer as just a lot of nonsense. I quickly add that I still think it's a lot of nonsense, and I think that they have changed. The thing I objected to, and still object to, is that it teaches midshipmen to be contemptuous of their juniors. That's not the way you run any organization, whether it's the military or in business. I think that they have made some major changes in that. I don't object to the difficulty of the training. I think it should be extremely difficult physically, mentally. But I do not condone treating people with the level of contempt that they did at that time.

Q: How was that contempt manifested?

Admiral Long: Oh, the business of physically beating you, the business of causing you to assume completely idiotic positions. For example, when you were eating you sometimes had to get off your chair and sort of sit in space and eat

Robert L. J. Long #1 - 22

square meals. Such things as making you swim over the transit of doors, making you recite absolutely idiotic things that have little or no consequence at all. It was the whole demeanor of the upper class toward the entering freshmen. I'm not suggesting for an instant that that relationship should be one of buddy-buddy, but it needs to be one that is essentially tough, fair, and one based on respect. That's what I have tried to maintain in my relations with juniors and seniors throughout my 40 years in the Navy.

Q: What do you remember about the specifics of the regimen during plebe summer?

Admiral Long: Plebe summer was tough, and I believe it still is tough and it should be tough. Of course, we had no air-conditioning at that time. It was hot. We spent a lot of time drilling. We spent a lot of time at the rifle range. We spent an awful lot of time in whaleboats--rowing, sailing. We spent a lot of time answering ridiculous questions of upperclassmen.

We had absolutely no liberty. I don't have any objection to any of that. As I say, plebe summer and plebe year should be a time when you weed out those that can't take it mentally, physically. It should be a time when you weed out those that are not truly motivated for a career in the Navy. From what I read, I think the Naval Academy has come around pretty well to that now.

Q: Did any of this give you second thoughts about this thing you'd embarked upon?

Admiral Long: Yes, there were times when I asked myself, "Long, what the hell are you doing here?" [Laughter] But we knew that the war was going on in Europe, and it became obvious that it was only a question of time before we would get into it ourselves. Also at that time the draft had started and we were beginning to receive officer candidates at the Naval Academy to go to school.

Q: The Germans were really rampaging through Europe in that spring and summer of 1940. Did that give a sense of urgency to what you were doing?

Admiral Long: Yes, I think so, and there were occasional meetings to explain what was going on. After that summer, I don't think there was any question at all in my mind that I should stick it out.

Q: What do you remember about the beginning of academics?

Admiral Long: I had relatively little trouble with

academics except for one course, and that was mechanical drawing. I think that was the only course that I ever received a failing grade in at the Naval Academy. But I'm not really very neat and artistic drawing all these lines. I can remember asking the instructor questions, and the instructor would always come over with a big black pencil and sort of sketch as to how you should be doing it; then you'd spend the rest of the period erasing all of that. So after a while I learned that you never asked the instructor anything. I think for one quarter I received a failing grade, and that put you on what was called the tree. The tree meant you were failing for that particular period, a week or a month or what have you.

Q: How competitive was the atmosphere?

Admiral Long: I never sensed that there was any great competitive attitude. If anybody was perceived to be highly competitive, he was immediately labeled a cutthroat. There was a lot of peer pressure so that you didn't take unfair advantage.

I had two roommates. One was Dave Webster, a young man from California who had come to the Naval Academy from being an enlisted man in the fleet.* He was hard

---

*Midshipman David A. Webster, USN, who retired in 1975 as a rear admiral.

working, very serious. The other was Joe Lister.* Joe was from Connecticut, and he had considerably more trouble academically than Dave and I had.

At that time the routine at the Naval Academy was very rigorous. Reveille, in my recollection, was 6:15 in the morning. Everyone got out of bed, or you were put on report. Everyone went to breakfast at 7:00 o'clock, no exceptions. You went to class about 8:15 or 8:30, I guess. You marched to class. You came back. You had a formation for noon meal. No exceptions. Everybody was there. You went down and had lunch and then went to class again. In the afternoon you had extracurricular activity, and they had an evening meal formation. No exceptions. We all marched down to dinner, had dinner, came back and studied. At 10:00 o'clock, lights were out. No exceptions. So it was bing, bing, bing.

I think that's significantly different from what they have today. I think you can either go eat or not eat. I know that the way the academic curriculum is at the Naval Academy today, few of them are able to turn in and go to bed at 10:00 o'clock. It's a very rigorous schedule.

Q: I remember when I was in boot camp, the only time I could relax was when I was in bed, and I couldn't even enjoy that because I was asleep. [Laughter]

---
*Midshipman Joseph D. Lister, USN, who died in an airplane crash in 1946 when he was a lieutenant.

Admiral Long: That's right. [Laughter]

Q: What do you remember about the duty officers? Some of them were notorious for their methods of dealing with midshipmen.

Admiral Long: Oh, yes. I used to think that they selected duty officers or company officers or battalion officers--these were in the so-called executive department--by virtue of how much of a character they were. We had names for a lot of these duty officers.

Q: Any that you recall specifically?

Admiral Long: Well, I remember we had one that we always accused of wearing a soft shoe and a hard shoe. You could hear him coming, but you'd only hear the hard shoe. So he was coming a lot faster than he appeared to be. We had names for all of these, and I must admit I can't think of any right now. There were a lot of characters, and I think they enjoyed being characters. I'll have to say that I thought the company officers were fine, fine people.

I had a company officer whose name was Sugarman, and he might have been 32 or 33, "old guy."* During plebe year, he was one of those that breathed some reality and

---
*Lieutenant Charles M. Sugarman, USN, born in November 1909.

some sense into the system. He and his wife lived over in Navy apartments. They would routinely invite some of us over for just relaxing and letting our hair down, and that meant a great deal to me.

When you're there at the academy, you can go ahead and make certain changes in your official record, such as your name. My name is now Robert Lyman John Long, but on my official birth certificate, I'm Robert Lyman Long. The way that was changed goes something like this: my mother named me Robert Lyman Long. My dad didn't like either of those names, so he called me John, and I was John to all my family and my friends.

Q: Everyone except your mother.

Admiral Long: Everyone except my mother. I was always Robert to my mother. When it came time for Congressman Shannon to write my appointment to the Naval Academy, he called up my dad and said, "Trigg, I'm about ready to write John's appointment. What's his full name?"

My dad said, "Robert Lyman Long."

The congressman said, "Trigg, you didn't hear me. I'm talking about John."

So my dad tried to explain all this, and old Joe Shannon said, "Oh, the hell with it. I'm going to make it

Robert Lyman John Long."

Well, I couldn't understand it. Midwestern boys don't have three initials; it sounds like you're British or something. So when I got to the Naval Academy, I put in a request to change my name officially to Robert Lyman Long.

Lieutenant Sugarman got the request, and he said, "I don't think you want to do this." He showed me in the directory of officers that there was another Robert Long, and then he painted a picture of reports and adverse papers getting in the files of the wrong people. He said, "It's a hell of a job getting them out. My advice to you is leave it alone." So ever since then I have been R. L. J. Long.

Q: Is that considered official or legal or just de facto?

Admiral Long: Well, by the Navy's official records, I am Robert Lyman John Long, but I really tried to change it at one time. [Laughter]

Q: Were there some people whom you considered role models when you were a midshipman?

Admiral Long: Yes. There were some such as Sugarman that were role models; he was a wonderful guy. Lieutenant Commander Pressey was a good one.* And one of the real

---
*Lieutenant Commander George W. Pressey, USN.

characters was Beany Jarrett.* I think there are probably more stories about Commander Jarrett than any other. I think he went out of his way really to develop these classic stories about himself.

Q: He was viewed as kind of a father figure or a favorite uncle.

Admiral Long: Yes. That's right.

Q: What do you remember of him?

Admiral Long: I only remember that he was not what you'd say is a traditional naval officer. He would say things and do things that were a little bit unusual, but always, I think, very fair, very square. There were others, and I can't really remember their names, who took sort of a sadistic delight in playing gotcha. I think later on, Paul, I probably learned as much from the bad ones as I did the good ones.

Q: Any of the bad ones you might cite?

Admiral Long: [Laughter] Well, there was one guy who had grown up in the old school, and that is where you really

---
*Lieutenant Commander Harry B. Jarrett, USN.

treat juniors with contempt. We'll get to it later, but the classic guy was the exec of my first ship, the commander. I never will forget him.

Q: Do you remember any of the professors specifically, such as Slipstick Willie?*

Admiral Long: Oh, well, yes. Slipstick Willie and Wet Dream Willie.

Q: I hadn't heard of Wet Dream Willie. [Laughter]

Admiral Long: [Laughter] Yes, there are a few characters there. In the "dago" department, for instance, some of the profs over there were real characters.**

Q: What can you tell me about playing squash and lacrosse?

Admiral Long: Well, I'll have to say I never was a great athlete, but I always enjoyed participating. I played a little bit of second-string football in high school, but I really wasn't good enough for any of those big contact sports. I went out for lacrosse and did not make varsity.

---

*"Slipstick Willie" was the nickname given Professor Earl W. Thomson because of his prowess with a slide rule. He taught at the Naval Academy from 1919 to 1959. For details see Shipmate magazine, published by the Naval Academy Alumni Association, June 1982, page 13.
**This was the department of foreign languages.

Robert L. J. Long #1 - 31

I was what we would call a trial horse--in other words, second team. I finally ended up playing battalion lacrosse. Squash was just getting going, and they built squash courts at the Naval Academy. I took up squash along with a couple of my classmates, and I became addicted to that. I continued to play squash up through the time that I was the Vice Chief of the Navy and loved it. It was a tremendous workout. Brought out some of the more Machiavellian side of me.

Q: In what way?

Admiral Long: When guys got in front of me, I'd warn them once, and then if they didn't get out, I'd whop the hell out of them with either the racquet or the ball. Then they'd come out of those games with huge purple spots on their rear ends. I also got a few beat-ups myself in there, including losing my front teeth.

Q: Did you get hit by a ball?

Admiral Long: Got hit by the racquet. And I picked up a few scars on my head. But learning squash was something that I thought was very important to me. Later on, when I had five years of continuous duty in the Pentagon, I'm convinced that I would not have done as well if I hadn't had that outlet. I used to play squash routinely every day in the Pentagon from 12:00 o'clock to 12:30, and that was a great way to let off steam and stress. So I appreciate that.

Q: I remember talking to Admiral Waller, who used to be the superintendent here, and he said when he wasn't exercising at the Pentagon, he could really feel the difference.*

Admiral Long: Oh, yes. It's almost like a drug. I think that that also set me up for my habits today. Today I have a Nordic Track down in the basement, and if I don't use it, I just don't feel right.

Q: It's a healthy habit to have.

Admiral Long: That's right. I don't know if it does you any good, but it makes me feel better.

Q: What do you remember about the varsity athletics as a fan, going to Army-Navy games and so forth?

Admiral Long: That game was always a big event. We'd go

---
*Vice Admiral Edward C. Waller, USN, was superintendent of the Naval Academy from August 1981 to August 1983.

on the train, except for my last year there. Instead, we took a ferryboat up the Chesapeake and went through the Delaware-Chesapeake Canal and on up to Philadelphia.

Q: West Point had some great teams during those years.

Admiral Long: Yes, and so did Navy. That was a great outlet for us. Of course, the war was under way by then. The war started at the end of '41, during my second year as a midshipman.

Q: What do you remember about getting the news and the reaction in the Naval Academy?

Admiral Long: I think that most of us can remember precisely where we were and what we were doing. My roommate and I were at Professor Conrad's house. We were out there eating away, and the news came in that afternoon that Pearl Harbor had been attacked. I remember that Admiral Willson, the superintendent, called a big meeting.* He told us that the war had started and we needed to hang in there because the Navy needed us.

Q: I have seen a picture that shows Admiral Willson with

---

*Rear Admiral Russell Willson, USN, was superintendent of the Naval Academy from February 1941 to January 1942.

Mountbatten when he visited the Naval Academy in '41.*

Admiral Long: Yes, that's right. He spoke to the midshipmen at lunch, and that's also a memorable event. He had been in a war and his ship was in Norfolk for battle repair. He gave a very, very moving speech. When I heard it, I felt, "Let's go! We're ready to go!"

Q: He had lost several ships and by that time he was given command of an aircraft carrier, and some wag said, "Well, there goes the Illustrious." [Laughter]

Admiral Long: [Laughter] Yes. Quite a character. Quite a hero. Quite a hero.

Q: That would be a real injection of spirit for people who'd been only on the sidelines up to then, to see somebody who had been involved.

Admiral Long: That's right. I don't recall that we had a continuing flow of Americans who had been in the war, even after we got into it. I guess people were too busy fighting the war to come back there.

---
*Captain Louis Mountbatten, RN, a member of Britain's royal family, became commanding officer of the aircraft carrier Illustrious after his destroyer, HMS Kelly, was sunk in the Battle of Crete in May 1941. In March 1942 he was promoted to flag rank when he became Chief of Combined Operations.

Q: Do you remember the compressing of the curriculum when it was determined you'd get out in three years instead of four?

Admiral Long: Yes. I'm not really sure whether that decision was made before we entered or after we entered. My best guess is that that decision occurred after we had arrived, because it accelerated not only my class a year, but the class of '43 a year. The class of '42 went up almost six months, and the class of '41 went up about four months.

Of course, one of the results was that the summer cruises were curtailed. My summer cruises consisted of going out and steaming up and down the Chesapeake in the Jamestown, which was not really a combatant ship.* All the combatant ships were out somewhere else. In the past, summer cruises, particularly youngster cruise and first-class cruise, were on battleships going to Europe. But we really didn't have any summer cruise to speak of. We went to the great town of Norfolk. They used to say they had signs that said, "Dogs and Sailors, Stay Off the Grass." But having lived in Norfolk, I can assure you that it's very much of a Navy town today.

---
*The Jamestown (PG-55) had been built in 1928 as the private yacht Savarona. She was acquired by the Navy in 1940 and redesignated a gunboat, though she had minimal armament.

Q: People there appreciate what the Navy does for the economy.

Admiral Long: Absolutely. Boy, without the Navy there, they'd be dead.

Q: What did you learn on board the Jamestown?

Admiral Long: Well, frankly, Paul, I don't think a hell of a lot.

Q: Not really a good taste of sea life.

Admiral Long: No, but it showed us the routine of being at sea for more than a day at a time, and we had some interface with enlisted men. Of course, we were taught by enlisted men, particularly plebe summer, such things as sailing and seamanship, the rifle range. And there were some very impressive sailors. I was about to say young sailors, but a second-class boatswain's mate at that time might have had 15 to 20 years in the Navy. The enlisted men didn't move up very fast in the Thirties, some of these were really old salts. Some of them were real characters.

Q: Any that you remember specifically?

Admiral Long: Yes, there was one that was a boatswain's mate second class. When we were out there pulling hard, hoisting a boat out of the water or something, and somebody might pass a little wind, his comment was, "Speak again, sweet lips." [Laughter] A real old salt. But those men were very good.

Q: How did the impressionable midshipmen react to being with these old salts?

Admiral Long: I think they reacted favorably. I mean, here was something that was out of the real world and not this sort of glossed over, supercilious rank we were seeing elsewhere.

Q: When I first got exposed to boatswain's mates, they didn't talk the way people I had associated with talked. [Laughter]

Admiral Long: That was an insight into what the real world was like in the Navy.

Q: The Navy was a secure employer during the Thirties, and so it could be very choosy and pick capable people.

Admiral Long: That's right.

Q: Did the experience of going to sea appeal to you?

Admiral Long: Yes, I enjoyed the sea itself. I thought it was endlessly fascinating, and I liked the idea of being on your own. As you know, the sea can be very cruel, and it really teaches you that you never take the sea for granted.

I remember some of these YPs and the larger sailboats.* I remember one time I was out and we ran into a good-size storm. The guy in charge had not taken appropriate precautions, and we goddamn near lost some people overboard. So that teaches you that you never want to be stingy in taking precautions when you're at sea.

Q: Admiral Nimitz put out a famous letter after the World War II typhoons.** In it he made the point that it's better to take precautions that prove unnecessary than the other way around.

Admiral Long: That's right, and that's good advice. The sea is very unforgiving. When the crisis is on you, it's normally too late to take the precautions. Naval officers

---
*YP--a yard patrol craft, used primarily at the Naval Academy for training in ship handling.
**Fleet Admiral Chester W. Nimitz, USN, was Commander in Chief Pacific Fleet from 1941 to 1945.

Robert L. J. Long #1 - 39

need to understand that they have the responsibility for the lives and well-being of the people underneath them, so they shouldn't be stingy protecting those people.

Q: Did you get any command opportunities on board the Jamestown?

Admiral Long: No. My recollection was that I was there strictly as a worker bee. And that's all right, because it gives you some appreciation of what people working for you go through.

Q: You did get command opportunity as a striper at the Naval Academy. What do you remember about that experience?

Admiral Long: My first-class year I had command of the Sixth Company.* I was a three-striper. That's worthwhile, and I think that what I would have liked to have seen--and I think that they are doing it today--would have been to give the first class greater responsibility for leading the brigade. When I was a first classman, we had limited responsibility, but I think that we still looked more to company officers to exercise command and control of the midshipmen under them. I don't think we

---
*A first classman is in his final year at the Naval Academy.

really gave the first class sufficient responsibility when I was there.

Q: In what way was it circumscribed?

Admiral Long: I don't believe we really had that feeling of responsibility for the well-being, the discipline of the midshipmen under us.

Q: Are you saying it was more of a ceremonial-type thing?

Admiral Long: Yes, we were out there marching in front of the company, but that was about it. We could also inspect formations and so on. But I'm talking about sort of the counseling. If somebody had a problem, whether it was an academic problem or a personal one, they should have been able to come in and talk about it. But we never had any of that. We never handled any of the special requests from the underclassmen.

Q: Those would go right to the officers?

Admiral Long: Yes, that's right.

Q: I saw in the <u>Lucky Bag</u> that you were involved with the

Hop Committee.* What did that involve?

Admiral Long: [Laughter] Well, I think that was one of my more serious challenges. I say that kiddingly. The Hop Committee essentially set up the arrangements for the various dances. Liberty was much more circumscribed then than it is today, so the hops over in Dahlgren Hall were big events. Everybody got dressed up in his full-dress bib and tucker and invited these gals down from Baltimore, Washington, New York. It was also a big event for those gals to come. So I was involved in setting up the arrangements for the hops and deciding the agenda, the program. However, it didn't take a lot of time.

Q: Did you have any social life apart from those hops?

Admiral Long: Yes, I met, early on, a very nice gal, who, incidentally, lived at Professor and Mrs. Conrad's house. She was a schoolteacher at Annapolis High, and we had a few very delightful years. Her home was in Glen Burnie, and she subsequently married a farmer up north of here who later on become the Speaker of the House in Annapolis in the state legislature. We have seen them. I think my wife thought it was a grand idea to see them. I was not at all enthusiastic about it. [Laughter] But she was a nice

---

*The Lucky Bag is the Naval Academy yearbook.

girl. Her name was Lillian Hawkins.

Q: Did you feel a real desire to get out and experience some freedom after this cloistered life you had lived for three years?

Admiral Long: Yes. I suspect that there are midshipmen then, and today, that really enjoyed their lives at the Naval Academy and hated to leave. I didn't feel that way. I thought it was an unnatural life, and I was delighted to leave and get on to my first assignment.

Q: What do you remember about the graduation ceremony?

Admiral Long: My recollection is that graduation was in Dahlgren Hall.* Frank Knox, the Secretary of the Navy, spoke.** I'll have to admit that I don't remember a thing he said. I was probably much more interested in where I was going and all the business of moving. After the ceremony, we were then all assembled over in Memorial Hall--Mem Hall--and we were sworn in by the Secretary of the Navy as ensigns in the United States Navy.

Q: It must have been an impressive ceremony.

---

*The class of 1944 graduated on 9 June 1943. Long stood 30th of the 766 graduates in the class.
**Frank Knox served as Secretary of the Navy from 11 July 1940 until his death on 28 April 1944.

Admiral Long: It was. It was. After that the Navy decided to take my entire class and send us to Florida to the Naval Air Training Command. We spent about six weeks going around to the various training sites--Jacksonville, Orlando, Daytona Beach--and flying in various types of aircraft. We were indoctrinated into naval air. At that time, graduating midshipmen could not get into naval air or submarines without having spent, I guess, two years as unrestricted line officers in the surface Navy.

Q: That changed soon after that.

Admiral Long: That changed almost immediately. My recollection is that some of my classmates were able to go directly to submarine school. It was not until later that they lifted the ban on flight training. Several of my classmates were on the ship I was on, and they went into flight training. The indoctrination trip to Florida was most important because that's where I met my wife.

Q: Please describe the circumstances.

Admiral Long: My group, first of all, landed in Jacksonville, Florida. A couple of nights after we

Robert L. J. Long #1 - 44

arrived, the Junior League arranged for a dance at the Women's Club in Jacksonville, and we were asked if we wanted to go. I said, "Sure." Sara Helms had also been asked if she would like to go, and she said yes. So I met her there and dated her all summer. I remember talking to my close friend, Russ Jonson, whom we call "Strangler."* I guess it was after the third date I had with Sara, I turned to Russ and said, "I'm going to marry that girl." At the end of the summer, I asked Sara to marry me and she said yes. I'll have to say I asked her father as well, and he also said yes. So that was a very important trip that I took after graduation.

Q: What was it about her that you found so appealing?

Admiral Long: She had everything that I wanted in a wife. She was a lady; she was beautiful; she was smart. Those were the things I was really looking for.

Q: What was her background?

Admiral Long: Her parents had grown up in southern Alabama. Her father had gone into the Army in World War I, gotten out, had graduated from the University of Alabama. He then joined a large corporation, B. F. Goodrich, and he

---
*Ensign Russell M. Jonson, USN, a Naval Academy classmate of Long.

had moved around various parts of the country. At that time he was the manager in the Jacksonville area. Sara had spent most of her life up to that point living in Jacksonville, but she was born in Kinston, North Carolina. She had also lived in Asheville, North Carolina, and spent some time in Atlanta. She at that time was going to Florida State College for Women in Tallahassee, now known as Florida State, renowned for its football teams. She was an economics major and a very serious student. And it's worked. We were married in August of 1944.

Q: What do you remember about the aviation part of that trip? I'm sure that's not quite as vivid. [Laughter]

Admiral Long: [Laughter] Well, I enjoyed it. A lot of the time we spent in airplanes, which was fun. I can remember the old PBYs that we flew in. They were very "high-speed" aircraft--maybe 100 knots.

Q: You say "high speed" facetiously.

Admiral Long: That's right. We also spent some time at the gunnery range. They had a very interesting course at the gunnery range for teaching you not only how to shoot antiaircraft guns but also how to recognize various aircraft, both enemy and friendly. The Naval Academy hadn't quite gotten around to that yet. But that was worthwhile. We had some interesting times down at Sanford, Florida. We also spent some time at Daytona Beach.

During part of that time I had a very interesting roommate, who is probably one of the finest men I've ever known, John F. Laboon.* He was a big football star and lacrosse player at the Naval Academy. He went into submarines, received the Silver Star, left the Navy, went into the Jesuit priesthood, and probably was as well loved as any of my classmates. Of course, the Laboon was launched last week, and it will be commissioned in a year or 18 months.** A wonderful person.

Q: What qualities did you find so admirable in Laboon?

Admiral Long: Well, there were several, and they're not always what you would associate with a priest. There were times in Florida when he was as wild as you can imagine. But you always had the feeling that here was a person that would help you if you needed help. He was a friend. And, of course, we would see that even more and more after he became a priest.

---
*Ensign John F. Laboon, Jr., USN, was a Naval Academy classmate of Long. He eventually retired in 1980 as a captain in the Chaplain Corps. The guided missile destroyer Laboon (DDG-58) is named in his honor.
**The ship, under construction by Bath Iron Works, is scheduled for commissioning in the spring of 1995.

Another example is the time when he and I were on the staff of Commander Submarine Force Atlantic in the Fifties. He was the fleet chaplain and I was on the staff. We had a baseball team, and Jake played first base. This particular day we were playing the Marines. They had a particularly dirty player who wouldn't hesitate to run into you and knock you down. He was running into first base and ran directly into Jake, knocked him down. Jake reached down and grabbed this guy by his collar and pulled him up and was about to hit him. Then this Marine sergeant said, "Now, Father, remember who you are." [Laughter]

But Jake had a temper. He had very high ideals. So he was the kind of guy that if you needed help, you could count on him. He was intensely loyal to his friends.

Q: Sounds as if he was somewhat like your father in being pragmatic.

Admiral Long: Yes, that's right. Not an idealist.

Q: Did the idea of going into aviation appeal to you at all as a result of that exposure?

Admiral Long: I always wanted to go into submarines, and I guess the reason for that was that I knew quite a few of

Robert L. J. Long #1 - 48

the people in submarines. Probably the closest one was Dick Garvey.* He and I had gone through high school together in Kansas City. He was in the reserves, and he had already gotten into submarines at this time. I had asked to go into submarines, but the service selection on graduation was different than they do today. Now you select by your class standing, but we drew numbers out of a hat. Essentially, if you drew number one, you could have your pick within minutes. I drew something like 750, which was pretty near the bottom. So I was assigned to the Colorado, a battleship in the Pacific.** That meant that I could not go to submarine school right away.

By the time that I arrived in the Colorado, the Navy had changed the policy on entering submarines. If you had the okay of the submarine community and you also had the okay of your commanding officer, you could go directly onto a submarine because of the shortage of officers. So I looked up my good friend Dick Garvey, who was in Trigger at that time, and I went over and met the exec, Ned Beach.*** He said he'd be happy to have me, so I wrote out a request. The submarine community said okay. I then took it back to

---
*Lieutenant (junior grade) Richard S. Garvey, USNR.
**The USS Colorado (BB-45) was commissioned 30 August 1923. She had a standard displacement of 32,600 tons, was 624 feet long and 97 feet in the beam. Her top speed was 21 knots. She was armed with eight 16-inch guns, ten 5-inch broadside guns, and eight 5-inch antiaircraft guns.
***Lieutenant Edward L. Beach, USN, who later became well known as the author of popular submarine novels, including Run Silent, Run Deep.

my ship and went in to see my exec, Commander Bowers.*
He looked at this thing and he said, "Long, how long have you been aboard?"

I said, "One week, Commander."

He said, "You get your ass out of here, and I don't want to see you again for a year."

Well, of course, I was very disappointed, but he saved my life, because Trigger was lost later in the war.**

Q: So you might have still be on board had you gone there.

Admiral Long: Oh, yes. But then I applied for submarines the regular way. I finally received orders, I guess, about August or September of '45.

Q: So it was really Garvey's influence that planted the seed with you?

Admiral Long: No, I had wanted to go to submarines while here at the Naval Academy, but the number I drew out of a hat was so far down the list that I could not get included in the limited number going into submarine school at that time.

---

*Commander William A. Bowers, USN.
**The USS Trigger (SS-237) was lost with all hands on 28 March 1945.

Robert L. J. Long #1 - 50

Q: What was it at the Naval Academy that inspired your interest in submarines?

Admiral Long: Oh, I think just hearing about them and also hearing about the quality of the people that they had.

Q: I've heard others mention that early command opportunity was an appeal. Was that a factor with you?

Admiral Long: I don't think so. I don't think so.

Q: Was it the excitement that appealed?

Admiral Long: Oh, I think so, and it might have also been the extra pay. [Laughter] I think also when I went to my first ship, that reinforced my determination to leave the surface Navy.

Q: This was the tradition-bound battleship Navy as compared with the less regulation submarine force.

Admiral Long: The Colorado represented most of the things that I despise in the Navy.

Q: Was there that sense of contempt for juniors that had bothered you earlier?

Admiral Long: Yes. I never will forget the first day when I reported in to the Colorado. I guess there were six of my classmates, and we were standing up in front, meeting Commander Bowers for the first time. His comment was, "Well, you're the new snotties aboard.* I want you to get one thing straight. You're thicker than the oats in horse shit." To be in my first ship, and to have a senior officer speak like that, I had nothing but absolute contempt for him.

Q: Not very inspirational.

Admiral Long: Not very inspirational. Some of the other senior officers on there were sort of like that also. I don't know whether that was typical of the old Navy or not. But I decided I did not want any part of it.

Commander Bowers was not well liked aboard. Years later I was on duty in Norfolk. We went to the circus and I sat next to this guy that I recognized as Captain Bowers. I didn't say anything to him and he kept looking at me.

Finally he said, "Weren't you an ensign in the Colorado?"

I said, "Yes, sir."

Then he went on to say, "Well, I guess I was pretty hard on you ensigns, but it probably did you a lot of good."

---
*"Snotties" is an old British term for junior officers.

Robert L. J. Long #1 - 52

I said, "Yes, sir, I think it did. It taught me how not to treat junior officers."

Q: How did he respond to that?

Admiral Long: He just laughed.

Q: Do you have any other examples of things he taught you about how not to behave?

Admiral Long: Well, his whole manner to junior officers was really deplorable. He always had a Marine orderly with him. Of course, the socializing area was on the quarterdeck, back on the fantail. Junior officers were not allowed to be on the starboard side. That was for lieutenants and up. Every now and then, an ensign or a jaygee would come over and talk to one of his friends on the starboard side. Commander Bowers would send his Marine back and say, "Get those snotties over on the correct side." I think if I had not gone into submarines, I would have left the Navy as quickly as I could, because the atmosphere in the Colorado was anathema to me.

Q: Did you have any contact with the skipper, Captain Granat?*

---
*Captain William Granat, USN, was commanding officer of the Colorado from September 1943 to August 1944.

Robert L. J. Long #1 - 53

Admiral Long: Captain Granat was an old-time, old-school naval officer, little or no communication with the troops. He was almost an unknown.

Q: So he probably lived up in his sea cabin.

Admiral Long: Yes, that's right. I spent some time as the junior officer of the deck.

I was in the fire control division, which was very much of an elite group. The division officer was a guy out of '40 by the name of Cliff Bundy--very, very sharp guy.* The gunnery officer was a guy named John Henkel, who was very much standoffish.** But then things changed; Bundy was transferred, and Henkel fleeted up to executive officer. We got a new gun boss named Commander Steve Carpenter, who was, I thought, one of the finest officers I've ever served with.*** In less than a year, because of these transfers and casualties, I became the F Division officer, which was a fairly senior job. I guess I had just made jaygee or something like that.

We also had a skipper named Macauley, who was a little Scottish guy that I always thought had a bottle of booze in his sea cabin.**** [Chuckles] But a good skipper. I mean,

---
*Lieutenant (junor grade) Clifford W. Bundy, USN.
**Commander John F. Henkel, USN.
***Lieutenant Commander Stephen W. Carpenter, USN.
****Captain Walter S. Macauley, USN, was commanding officer of the Colorado from August 1944 to September 1945.

Robert L. J. Long #1 - 54

he really knew his business.

Then a couple of things happened. They had a new navigator, whom Macauley didn't think was qualified to be the officer of the deck at battle stations. So I ended up being the officer of the deck at battle stations.

Q: A real feather in your cap.

Admiral Long: Yes. I had that job except when we were firing the main battery, in which case I was down in the main battery plot. But it was really a rewarding experience for me to be F Division officer at that time, because we had six or seven other officers. We had warrant officers. We had maybe four or five chiefs, and we were responsible for not only the fire control of the main battery, but the fire control of all the batteries.

Q: You probably had some of the most talented enlisted men in the ship.

Admiral Long: Absolutely. I can still remember those talented people. One of the most talented was a chief I had, Chief King.* He was the leading chief. He was an old guy. He must have been, oh, 32 or 33.

---
*Chief Fire Controlman Charles L. King, USN.

Robert L. J. Long #1 - 55

The first day that I was the F Division officer, I talked to the men at morning quarters and told them I was their new division officer. After quarters, Chief King came up to me and he said, "Well, Mr. Long, you're the new division officer. I want you to know I'm going to make you a good division officer. The only thing I ask is don't fuck it up." That is the attitude of some of the finest chiefs I've known. That is, they consider that they are the ones that train these young officers to be good division officers. Chief King was, in fact, a great adviser to me.

Q: What were some of things he taught you?

Admiral Long: Well, I'm not the most patient guy going. I remember one time we had a problem with one of the main computers. Of course, the computers in those days were wheels and levers.

Q: Analog.

Admiral Long: Yes, all analog. So we had one of these main battery computers down, and I wanted to get the damn thing fixed. I would come buzzing in there and ask, "What are you doing? What are you doing?"

Chief King took me aside and he said, "Mr. Long, we're working our ass off on this thing. Your coming in here and fussing at us is not doing any good. When this thing is fixed, I'm going to tell you. Do me a favor and how about taking a walk up around on the deck." [Laughter] Always very polite.

Q: It's not going to get fixed any faster from your fussing.

Admiral Long: That's right. I can remember another situation. This one involved a first class whose name was LeMaster.* We'd been out for a long time, and his wife was about to have a baby. We were coming from Seattle to San Francisco to go back out, and Chief King came to me and said, "You know, we ought to let LeMaster meet the ship in San Francisco, because his wife is sick and she's not doing well at all."

I said, "Okay. I'll have to get the exec's permission for this."

I went in to see my buddy Commander Bowers and explained the situation. He said, "What the hell do you think this is, Long, a country club?" He turned me down. But that was Bowers.

But Chief King was just a marvelous guy. We also had

---
*Fire Controlman First Class James W. LeMaster.

a warrant officer on there named Gunner Leahy.* We were friends for a long time. So that was an introduction into being in charge and being responsible, and I'll have to say that those subordinates of mine helped me. They helped me.

Q: I talked to one of your junior officer shipmates in that ship, Tom Mallison.** He said that in a way, ironically, it was unfortunate that the Colorado didn't get hit at Pearl Harbor, because she didn't get the modernization that the other old battleships got when they were repaired. Do you remember an outmoded nature of some of your equipment, particularly in antiaircraft?

Admiral Long: Well, antiaircraft, there were 5-inch/25s, Mark 33 directors. You're pressing me.

Q: And the other ships had gotten 5-inch/38s.

Admiral Long: Yes, they were modern, and they had fire control radars. See, we had no real main battery radars at that time. I think we had SC radar or something like that. The main battery fire control was done with something like the Mark I range keeper. It did have a stable element, which is a thing about as big as this table, and gyros on that and so on. It was extremely antiquated equipment. Of

---

*Chief Gunner Roger B. Leahy, USN.
**Lieutenant William Thomas Mallison, USNR.

course, there were optical rangefinders in the turrets.

We also still had the 5-inch/51 broadside guns. This was all just hand-load down there. They did have 40-millimeter and 20-millimeter, but it was not until after the Marianas when we were badly banged up that we came back and we got the more modern fire control computers. We also got the Mark 8 radar, which was marvelous. When you were down in main battery plot, you could watch the radar and see these 16-inch shells go out. You could spot from down there. I mean, you could see the splash and the whole thing. So it was a complete eye-opener to me. However, Colorado did very well.

Q: You have a list of the various engagements the Colorado was in during your time on board. I wonder if you could run through your memories of those, please.

Admiral Long: Well, the old Colorado was really quite a ship. It's interesting to note that from '43 to '45 she had some 204 days in the combat area, she received seven battle stars, she shot down 11 Japanese aircraft, and she also received a few hits herself at Tinian. In the Marianas, she received 22 hits by enemy shore batteries. That was on July 24, 1944. We were hit by a kamikaze at Leyte Gulf in November of '44. At Lingayen Gulf she was damaged by shell fire from another ship. That was in

Robert L. J. Long #1 - 59

January of '45. During this period from '43 to '45, we had some 94 killed and some 327 wounded. She shot over 60,155 rounds of ammunition and received all sorts of commendations.

Tarawa was the first engagement I had participated in. We did a big work-up, and we always arrived at dawn at these places and opened up shore bombardment. I was down in the main battery plot, and I think the ship did a tremendous job of preparing the beach for the Marines to go in.

Kwajalein and Eniwetok were in the Marshalls. That was uneventful. We came up at dawn on Kwajalein, and we put our aircraft up for spotting. We opened up with a broadside of 16-inch, and the first spot from the naval aviator coming in was, "Up five miles, right three islands." [Laughter] We picked out the wrong island to bombard there.

Of course, it was at Saipan and Guam and Tinian in the Marianas where we really took some damage. We were off Tinian doing direct fire of batteries on the beach.

Q: How close would you say your range was?

Admiral Long: We were about 2,000 yards off the beach, and we did not realize that there were still active shore batteries. At that time we were hit 22 times with 5- and

6-inch, which really took a terrible toll on the topside. It was a result of that that we went back to Bremerton for repairs and, I might say, some very, very welcome modernization of the ship's batteries.*

When the ship got there in early August, I called Sara up and said, "I'll be down in two days. Can we get married?" She said yes, so we were married that week in Jacksonville. Sara's dad's company, B. F. Goodrich, came to all stop for a week preparing for that wedding. After that we began our honeymoon.

We took a train to Kansas City, my home town, for just a short visit, and then got on the train again and went across country. I never will forget we arrived at Butte, Montana, in the middle of the night to change trains to go on to Seattle. I walked up to the ticket window and asked if they had any Pullman accommodations available. The ticket agent said, "Yes, the only thing left is a drawing room." If you remember, a drawing room has an upper and a lower and then it has another bunk that sort of acts as a seat, but it can be made into a bunk.

I said, "I'll take it."

Right behind me was a woman with a baby, and she came as I was putting my tickets away. She said to the ticket agent, "Do you have any Pullman accommodations?"

He said, "No, ma'am. This man just got the last."

---
*Puget Sound Navy Yard, Bremerton, Washington.

I looked at her and said, "I have a drawing room. Do you want to share it?"

She said, "Oh, yes. I've got to get this baby some sleep." She was going to visit her husband out at Camp Farragut, a Navy training camp in Idaho. So she got into the lower, Sara got into the upper, and I got on this jump seat. About ten minutes later I climbed into the upper, and off we went. [Laughter] Now, you wouldn't think of doing that today.

Q: That's right.

Admiral Long: But that was wartime and we did that. We then went on to Seattle and across to Bremerton. Then we spent about a week at a place called Obington. It's on Lake Crescent, up on the Olympic Peninsula, where Sara almost lost me. I fell down the mountain, slipped off, and she thought I was gone.

We then came back and rented an apartment right outside the gate at the Bremerton shipyard, a place called the Helena Apartments. This was a nice substantial brick building and we did fine. Last spring I went out to Seattle to speak to the Naval Academy Alumni Association, and one day Sara and I took off and we retraced some of our steps. Sure enough, the Helena Apartments building was still there, although it had a different name. But the clientele, I think, had changed a little bit, because all these girls were hanging out the windows. We struck up a conversation with them. They invited us in and we looked at our old apartment. Our son, who lives in Seattle, was there, and as we were coming out the door, he turned to me and says, "Dad, you've come a long way." [Laughter]

Q: Indeed.

Admiral Long: So we had a marvelous time on our honeymoon there, and then finally Sara went on home. She had just graduated from the Florida State College for Women, and she went to work for the Federal Reserve Bank. During that year, '44-'45, she saved all of her money, and that gave us a little nest egg for when the war ended.

Q: I suspect that was a very difficult parting when you had to go back to sea again.

Admiral Long: That's right. That's right.

Q: I was up in South Dakota last spring and heard a retired schoolteacher tell about a USO canteen at a railroad station for troop trains that passed through there. The USO served, among other things, pheasant salad sandwiches. So the hospitality and feelings toward servicemen were very patriotic and giving during that period. Did you experience that appreciation from the populace at any of your stops along the way?

Admiral Long: Oh, I think at Obington they couldn't have been nicer. They knew that I was in from sea, and they just went out of their way to be hospitable and generous to us. Thinking back over those days, it was a fantastic period of time.

Q: The country was united as it has seldom been since then.

Admiral Long: That's right. I guess the Gulf War is probably the closest to it, but certainly not in the Korean War or the Vietnam War.

Q: What do you recall of the shipyard work itself? Was there a frantic pace to get you back out to sea?

Admiral Long: I don't recall, Paul, that it was frantic. I do have a recollection that the shipyard workers in Bremerton were a very unique, dedicated group. I remember people whose fathers and grandfathers had been shipyard workers at Bremerton. They were probably about as dedicated as any I've seen anywhere.

Q: I've heard similar things said about the workers at Bath Iron Works in Bath, Maine.

Admiral Long: Indeed. I'm not familiar with the workers there, but Bremerton was a very impressive shipyard.

Q: That had been the traditional battleship yard for years, and they took great pride in that.

Admiral Long: Yes, that's right.

Q: What happened after that shipyard period?

Admiral Long: When we got back out to the war zone, we were in the Battle of Leyte Gulf, where I really saw my first kamikaze. I was standing up on deck during a little lull in the firing. A cruiser was near us, and all at once we saw a tremendous explosion. The next thing I noticed was an airplane coming in on our stern. It looked like the pilot was getting ready to land on us, which he did. It was a Japanese kamikaze. That was the first time we really had seen this.*

---

*On 27 November 1944 the light cruiser <u>St. Louis</u> (CL-49) was hit by two kamikazes. Two more headed for the <u>Colorado</u>, one hitting the port side amidships and the other crashing close aboard.

Robert L. J. Long #1 - 65

Q: How close were you to the point of impact?

Admiral Long: About 100 feet.

Q: How did you survive?

Admiral Long: Well, I think you need a little luck, Paul. You need a little luck.

Q: So there must not have been a big explosion after it hit.

Admiral Long: No. It knocked one of the turrets out. It came in on the fantail. Then we went on to Mindoro and Luzon. It was at Lingayen Gulf on the island of Luzon when I was the officer of the deck at battle stations. I had just been relieved as OOD, and I just had walked off the bridge when a shell from another ship hit us.* Of course, it decimated the bridge. But here again, you know, how did you escape? You need a little luck.

Q: You're right.

Admiral Long: You need a little luck. At Okinawa

---

*The Colorado was hit by a "friendly" 5-inch/38-caliber projectile on 9 January 1945.

kamikazes became very commonplace, and fortunately we avoided those. But that's the story of the <u>Colorado</u>.

Q: I'd be interested in how your sense of morale was transformed. It started off very low. Did it go up as you got these more responsible positions?

Admiral Long: Yes. You know, if you get a good boss, it does wonders for your morale. I have one story to tell you to suggest that Bob Long is not all that pure. Shortly after coming aboard the <u>Colorado</u>, I noticed that we had several safes in the room, supposedly to store classified material in the desk. But after a while it became obvious to me that one of the principal uses for the safes was to store a little booze. Tom Polk was a good friend of mine, and when we were off Okinawa, we learned that his wife just had a baby.* So we thought we needed to celebrate this. We waited until late at night when we thought the danger of air attack would be over, about midnight, and we proceeded then to have a few drinks to celebrate the birth of this new baby, Candy.

We were having a grand time, when all at once we heard bong-bong-bong-bong and, "Man your battle stations. Air attack." Of course, I was the officer of the deck at battle stations, so I made my way to the bridge. The man

---

*Ensign Thomas H. Polk, USN.

who was being relieved as officer of the deck was telling me, "The course is this, the speed's this, the formation axis is this. You've got a bogey out here at this position. You've got another bogey over here at this position." All at once he said, "Are you all right?" [Laughter]

Well, let me tell you. If you ever wanted to know why you don't want to drink at sea, that's a good reason.

Q: You weren't too alert.

Admiral Long: A situation like that sobers you up pretty fast. We got through that okay. But I'm convinced booze at sea is not a good idea.

Q: What do you remember about viewing an air attack from topside?

Admiral Long: Well, particularly at Okinawa, where the air attacks were so frequent, you have to picture in your mind that here you have a formation of ships where you'd have maybe eight battleships on the inner circle, inner ring. Out around that you'd have 12 to 15 cruisers, and then outside of that you'd have 30 to 35 destroyers. One of these kamikazes would come in, and it was just amazing to see this cone of fire that goes up. It would move and, of course, it was also dangerous in that if the aircraft was low on the water, you could get shots coming into other ships. At night particularly it was probably as spectacular a display of fireworks as you'll ever see. It's nice to see it in the movies, but I don't care to see it again in real life.

Q: Did you have a sense of apprehension before going into combat the first time?

Admiral Long: Oh, I think a combination of apprehension and excitement and sort of saying, "I wonder what this is going to be like?" But I think I was eager to see what it would really be like.

Q: Of course, you can't see all that much down in main battery plot. It's sort of vicarious.

Admiral Long: That's exactly right. That's why I was glad that in the later months of the war that I was brought up to be the officer of the deck. I replaced the navigator, who was about 5 feet, 5 inches tall and weighed about 200 pounds. We called him "The Little King," and he conducted himself as the little king.

Q: What do you remember about handling the ship?

Admiral Long: I enjoyed that. There were a few times in rapidly changing situations where you have all of this maneuvering, emergency turns, and so on.

Q: Especially at night.

Admiral Long: Especially at night and darkened ship, where you can just barely see the wake. Sometimes you get pretty close. But fortunately we didn't have any collisions. But it was exciting.

Q: Those old ships had a pretty large turning circle, didn't they?

Admiral Long: Oh, yes.

Q: And not as much power as the later ships that came along.

Admiral Long: No. My recollection was that the top speed of Colorado was maybe 20 knots, something like that.

Q: What were the living conditions like on board on such an old ship?

Admiral Long: Well, they weren't all that bad. Of course, we had a junior officers' mess, and then we had a warrant officers' mess. I'm talking about officers' country. And we then had a wardroom. When I first came aboard, I slept in the JO bunk room, and I guess we must have had six, eight officers in there. Shortly thereafter I moved into a two-man stateroom. Of course, when I compare it to living conditions aboard some of the older submarines, it was the Waldorf Astoria.

Also there were times when we would go into places like Ulithi for recreation. Recreation consisted of going over and attending a mile-long bar on the beach. Some of my friends would be on amphibious ships, LSTs or Army, and they would love to come out and visit me where they had hot showers and ice cream and all those luxuries that they did not have on those other ships. So I think it's all relative.

Q: Did the enlisted men still have separate division messes instead of a general mess?

Admiral Long: No, I think it was a general mess. And they had stacked bunks. My recollection was that the bunks were essentially canvas. Living conditions for the troops wasn't all that great. In time of battle, those places were pretty well cleaned out. When we had casualties, I can remember the stacked bodies and the treatment of those wounded down in those places. Pretty primitive.

Q: I've seen some gruesome pictures after that kamikaze hit. What were the emotional reactions on board after losing shipmates and having the ship damaged?

Admiral Long: I think for the kamikaze--I don't think there was any great drop in morale. We did go down to Manus, an island in the southeast Pacific, for some emergency repairs. I think there was a significant impact on the morale after the Tinian engagement, because so many people were killed and wounded at that one. There were some snide remarks about the reason why we took so many hits. Some people complained that the captain couldn't get the ship in gear to get it out of there. But, of course, that was short-lived. We got back to the States, and there was great appreciation to come home for a while. And, as I say, there were also some major improvements in the fighting ability of the ship.

Q: What do you remember about logistic support when you were deployed?

Admiral Long: We occasionally would have underway replenishments, and at other times we would be replenished as in Okinawa in a place called Kerama-retto, which was a little island and it had an anchorage, sort of protected. That's another example of where we almost bought the farm, because we were loading ammunition, 16-inch shells and powder bags. I was on the bridge. Essentially we had the steaming watch set as all of this stuff was coming over from an ammunition ship. When this ammunition was loaded, there was a loading hatch that went down to the magazines. When the powder bags came down to the lower level, men opened a door, put it in, and then shut the door. What happened was that the static charge on one of these cans set the powder off. The first thing I saw was a great mass of smoke and fire coming out of that ammunition loading hatch. If that magazine door had been open when that occurred, it would have blown the front end of the Colorado completely to smithereens.

But most of the time, the operations started from Pearl Harbor. We would go out, conduct the operation, and then come back in a relatively brief period. If you look at the dates for the various engagements, they were normally short-term operations, a couple months, and we normally didn't have all that much replenishment at sea. But later on as we got farther to the west, when we got into the Philippines and certainly Okinawa, they were long, drawn-out operations. We did routinely have some transfer of food and so on.

Q: More likely fuel and food than ammunition at sea.

Admiral Long: That's right.

Q: Do you remember making approaches on an oiler?

Admiral Long: Yes. There were a couple of times when I was the officer of the deck when we were alongside the oiler. When that happened, it was normally an all-hands affair. Of course, I had a much greater appreciation of unreps later on when I was commander of the Service Force of the Seventh Fleet.

Q: What do you remember about communications capability?

Admiral Long: I guess we had VHF on the bridge.* We also used the signal flags a lot. We also used flashing light and also we then had this infrared light for use essentially at night. And there still was an awful lot of use of semaphore flags. The signal bridge was a very active place: signal flags up, executing things, corpens, speeds.

Q: Those were all holdovers from the prewar Navy.

---
*VHF--very high frequency.

Admiral Long: Right.

Q: The Navy was just slowly getting into the radio era.

Admiral Long: The radio era was just coming in. We had a group of reserve officers aboard who were primarily communicators. They spent a hell of a lot of their time on decrypting things. But I'd say that the tactical communications were primarily centered around flag hoists, flashing light, and semaphore--quite different from today.

Q: You've already talked about the fire control radar. What do you remember about the surface search? Did you do station keeping and maneuvering with the surface search?

Admiral Long: Yes. We had a PPI up on the bridge for station keeping and surface search.* My recollection was that radar was an SG, and the air search was an SK. But that's about all I knew about it.

Q: Well, if you had to keep station with darkened ship at night, that could be very helpful.

---

*PPI--plan position indicator, a type of radar that presents essentially a geographical picture with the ship in the center of the scope and surrounding ships, planes, and land areas shown in their respective positions in terms of range and bearing.

Admiral Long: That's right.

Q: Did you face much threat from enemy submarines during all your maneuvers?

Admiral Long: No. I only remember one time when there was a real serious submarine threat, and that was early on, in the Marshalls. There was a submarine that was sighted and it was attacked and was sunk. But other than that, we really did not have a submarine threat that I was aware of.

Q: I think the consensus is that the Japanese didn't use their submarines as effectively as they might have.

Admiral Long: Right. It could have been an entirely different story if they had been aggressive in their submarine warfare. Knowing what I know today about the effectiveness of some of those sonar systems, I wouldn't give you an awful lot on that.

Q: Anything else to mention on the *Colorado*?

Admiral Long: Well, as I said, the *Colorado* really participated all the way from Tarawa to Tokyo Bay, and I participated all the way from Tarawa to Tokyo Bay, and I was aboard all that time. Shortly thereafter, I left and went on to submarine school.

Q: Did you get ashore in Japan?

Admiral Long: Yes.

Q: What are your recollections of that?

Admiral Long: It was almost unreal. Here we had been in a fight to the death with this country, but when I went ashore, I felt absolutely no threat to myself. The people were courteous, friendly. The stores were open. It was just like going there and nothing had ever happened. It was a sensation that I don't think I'd ever had.

Q: The Emperor had put out the word.

Admiral Long: Right. In other words, that was it.

Q: Was this at Yokosuka?

Admiral Long: Went to Yokosuka, and then we also went to Tokyo, rode up on the train. We saw heavy crowds. That was the first time that I observed the Japanese tendency on trains. When the door is open, you'd better move or they're going to run over you. But, as I say, Paul, it was so bizarre to me that here we had just been at a huge war with them, and they were completely accepting of us, courteous. It's an experience that I had never seen.

Q: You remember the Japanese as friendlier than some of the other men I've encountered. They remember them as standoffish and cautious about initiating relationships.

Admiral Long: When I say friendly, I should say that they were not hostile. They weren't up slapping you on the back, but courteous insofar as deferring to you, but not warm--certainly not warm. No, the Japanese are slow to be warm to you, and having lived there years later, we came to realize that very quickly.

Q: Did you see scenes of devastation in your travels?

Admiral Long: Not in Yokosuka. Some in Tokyo, but not any great amount. We spent only a few days there, and, of course, during that I guess I got ashore maybe twice. So I didn't have a great deal of time to be a tourist.

Q: What is your recollection of learning about the surrender and the reaction on board ship?

Admiral Long: Of course, this occurred while we were at Okinawa. We started the campaign at Okinawa on April Fool's Day, and we stayed and stayed. It was a very bitter campaign with lots of kamikazes at sea and a lot of fighting on the beach. That was one of the examples of where we did a lot of replenishment. Of course, we had continuing reports of ships out on picket duty that had been kamakazied, and it was rather routine almost every day that we had some air attack. So the men in the Colorado were absolutely delighted with the news. There was also some skepticism as, "Is this for real or is this some sort of a trap?" I'll never forget steaming into Tokyo Bay and wondering, "Is this going to turn out all right?" It's one of those experiences that you just will never forget.

Q: You were far from alone in having that sense.

Admiral Long: Yes. You just couldn't picture this happening in the United States. You'd never get that kind of conformity.

Q: Discipline was absolute.

Admiral Long: Absolutely. So it was a very unusual event. After the surrender, the Colorado then returned to the

United States and it embarked on a series of trips between San Francisco and Hawaii called Magic Carpet.* I left after a few of those.

Q: What do you remember about the Magic Carpet rides?

Admiral Long: Deadly dull.

Q: How crowded was the ship?

Admiral Long: Very crowded. Most of the crew and certainly the passengers couldn't have cared less about the ship or anything military. All they wanted to do was get home. This was the end of the war, and most of them had their points to get out, and so it was not a very inspiring time.** When I was finally released from the Colorado, Sara came out, and we had an apartment in San Francisco for a short period of time. Then, in December 1945, we took the train on to New London, Connecticut, for submarine school.

---
*Magic Carpet was the program in which overseas troops who were eligible for discharge were brought back to the United States on board Navy ships.
**For the demobilization of the U.S. armed forces after World War II, the services had a point system to determine individual priorities for leaving the service. Points were awarded for length of service, overseas service, battle stars, decorations, and dependent children. Those with the highest number of points were the earliest discharged.

Robert L. J. Long #1 - 80

Q: What was the mechanism by which you finally got to get into submarines?

Admiral Long: Put in my request.

Q: Did you have a new exec by then?

Admiral Long: Yes, that's right. [Laughter] New exec and new skipper. And they very nicely presented me with the Bronze Star medal for all of that.

Q: New London was obviously a very different environment from what you'd known on the Colorado. What do you remember of that experience?

Admiral Long: I remember, first of all, arriving in New London by train, and, of course, we had to find a place to live. The place we finally found was a little cottage behind a chicken house, and the chicken house was a little bit nicer than the cottage we rented. [Laughter] So we didn't stay there very long. But then, along with two other couples, we started the first commune. We rented a large house on the beach, a place called Ocean Beach in New London. It belonged to a former congressman. And we paid $125.00 a month for this.

Robert L. J. Long #1 - 81

Q: That was pretty stiff in that era, wasn't it?

Admiral Long: Oh, yes. As a matter of fact, it was so stiff that three months later, the rent control board came in and said that we were being overcharged so that we got $25.00 a month back. But the other two couples were a classmate of mine named Art Gillis and his wife, Laura, and a shipmate of mine that had been on the Colorado with me, Tom Polk, and his wife Ginny.* They had a baby, and that was the baby I referred to before that we were celebrating on the Colorado.

Once we started to school, it soon became rather obvious that we couldn't have cocktail parties every night and survive the course, so we laid down some rules on cocktails and proceeded to get through the course. The course was really the first six-month course at submarine school, and the head of the school was Fearless Freddy Warder--Captain Frederick B. Warder. I subsequently worked for him twice more.

Q: Those who have worked for him admired him.

Admiral Long: Yes. Freddy Warder was a submariner's submariner. Very successful wartime skipper in Seawolf. We also had some other great submariners that were on the

―――――――――
*Lieutenant (junior grade) Arthur W. Gillis, USN.
Lieutenant (junor grade) Thomas H. Polk, USN.

staff of the submarine school.

Q: Whom else do you remember?

Admiral Long: Hank Munson was the exec of the school, you know, several Navy crosses.* Jim Calvert was there, a much younger officer.** He was in charge of teaching the TDC, the torpedo data computer, which is the fire control system for the submarine. I remember Commander Blish Hills, who was in charge of FC training.*** We also had the diving trainers. We had to learn all of this stuff, including how to dive.

We went to sea quite a few times on the so-called school boats that were in New London. It was a very good course, and it was, I thought, quite realistic on the approach and attack part. The people who were teaching us how to conduct torpedo approaches had been doing that at sea in the real world just a few months before My recollection is that we had about 35 people in the course. I was honored to stand number one in the class and got a very nice watch, which I subsequently lost.

Q: Were there any other incentives? Before the war it had to do with post-school duty assignment.

---
*Commander Henry G. Munson, USN.
**Lieutenant James F. Calvert, USN.
***Commander Blish C. Hills, USN.

Robert L. J. Long #1 - 83

Admiral Long: Yes. My recollection is that the higher you stood, the more you'd have to say about your next duty assignment. Of course, standing at the top of the class and liking New London, I chose a new-construction submarine that was building at that time at Electric Boat at Groton. It was the <u>Corsair</u>.

Q: Before we get to that, I'd welcome some more discussion on the curriculum and methods of training and so forth. What do you remember about the classroom experiences?

Admiral Long: The classes were small and involved a lot of individual training. I particularly liked that they had very good attack teachers. There were trainers where you'd have a simulated submarine conning tower with periscopes, and you'd have all of the fire control equipment and plotting boards. You'd essentially go through a very realistic drill, actually looking at targets and zigzags and changes in course, speed, and range in a very realistic way. The diving trainers were also realistic, with the noise and the angles it would take, very responsive. So those were very good trainers before you went to sea.

I also had some very good courses on damage control and also on engineering. I'd say that the primary emphasis was on the operational side of the submarine--torpedo approaches and diving.

Q: Engineering?

Admiral Long: We didn't have as much on engineering as on the weapons part, but there was certainly training on engineering. So I think that when I reported to my first submarine, I felt fairly comfortable with the entire submarine.

Q: Do you remember a lot of emphasis on memorizing systems and functions?

Admiral Long: Paul, I'd say that that is clearly part of the submarine training. There was heavy emphasis on learning systems and the ability to operate those systems yourself. That philosophy is carried over even today. Certainly at that time, there were very rigorous submarine qualification procedures and standards. Knowing the systems and knowing how to operate those systems was critical if you were to be qualified in submarine. We had a lot of hands-on tests.

Q: Do you remember as a by-product indoctrination in what it means to be a submariner, the ethic of going to sea in these boats?

Robert L. J. Long #1 - 85

Admiral Long: You're going to have to explain that a little bit.

Q: Perhaps it was something along the lines of, "This is an elite force that does something special. We take you only if you're good enough and you prove that you're good enough."

Admiral Long: Well, there were rather rigorous exams. I'm not talking just physical exams, but there were other exams that I would say bordered on psychological exams. One of the great tests in going through this process of entering submarines came when they put you at the bottom of 100-foot column of water. They would flood this compartment and increase the pressure up to the equivalent to 100 pounds of water. Then they would tell you to go ahead and get in that column of water and go to the top. If you have any sense of claustrophobia, that will show up at that point.

Q: What do you remember of that experience? Did you have a breathing device?

Admiral Long: No. I had a life preserver on. We were breathing in air at something like 44 pounds per square inch over atmospheric. When you get into the free ascent, you exhale the entire time that you're going to the surface. If you hold your breath, you could rupture your lungs, because you have all that pressure inside of you. So that was one of the tests. Of course, we'll talk later on about the FBMs, when they had some head shrinkers that would come and visit us after each patrol.*

Q: Was there any screening for aggressiveness in submariners?

Admiral Long: I don't think there is in an explicit way. I think that most submariners have to have the ability to operate as team members and part of a submarine crew. You know and I know that there are all different types of submarine officers as there are surface officers, aviators, and businessmen. Some of them are much more aggressive than others. But I think within the broad perspective, they still have to have the ability to lead, to communicate. One of the examples that I cite when I talk about leadership to, say, the midshipmen is, "Don't get the idea that there's just one type of leadership. There are all different types. They have certain things in common."

For instance, I tell them, "We had a submarine skipper

---

*FBM--fleet ballistic missile, the Polaris submarine program that came along in the early 1960s.

named Slade Cutter.* The story goes that when he took command of his submarine, assembled the crew and he says, 'My name is Slade Cutter. I'm your new commanding officer. I want you to know I'm your commanding officer in every sense of the word. If any of you disagree, we're going to take our coats off, we'll go back here, and we'll settle it right there.'" I said, "You know, I can't imagine that I would ever take such a position. I'd get clobbered." But there are all different types."

Q: He was a varsity boxer, so he didn't have anything to worry about.

Admiral Long: That's right. [Laughter] Well, that's Slade.

Q: What a great guy he is.

Admiral Long: Yes, and he continued that reputation throughout. I can remember one time a bunch of submarines put in up at Newfoundland, and we all went over to the club. There was a young officer, jaygee, on the Sirago, one of the boats.** He and Slade got into a big argument,

---
*Commander Slade Cutter, USN, commanded the USS Seahorse (SS-304) in a number of highly successful war patrols in the Pacific. The oral history of Cutter, who retired as a captain, is in the Naval Institute collection.
**Jaygee--lieutenant (junior grade).

and Slade just really sort of wiped the deck with him. When he was winding up on this guy, about that time a French-Canadian waiter came through the swinging doors with this big tray of drinks and Slade missed this jaygee and hit the waiter. All the drinks went up. [Laughter] But to show you sort of what sort of a guy Slade is, the next morning Slade went down to the *Sirago*, just calling to see how this jaygee was. No hard feelings. There are all different types of leaders.

Q: He has mellowed since then, so I have not seen that side of him.

Admiral Long: He used to be pretty feisty.

Q: Was there a sense of competition among officers trying deliberately to be number one in that submarine school class?

Admiral Long: Paul, I may be pretty naive, but I never recognized it if there was a sense of competition. I never sensed it in the two of my classmates that I lived with.

Q: How demanding was the regimen on your off-duty time as far as studying?

Admiral Long: We did some studying at night, but it wasn't all that rigorous. It was heavy emphasis during the day, but we had things to study at night. Of course, that's one of the reasons why we curtailed the cocktail period. I was doing fine, but my two house mates were on the verge of flunking out. So we said, "Hey, we've got to stop this."

Q: So at least for them it was a pretty demanding course.

Admiral Long: Pretty demanding. That's right.

Q: What do you remember about the approach practices?

Admiral Long: I think those practices covered approaches that were developed and proven to be effective in wartime. Just looking at history a little bit, there were some significant changes in the approach tactics in the war. Before the war, people would shoot way out from the target, so the hit rate was very, very low. These tactics always emphasized trying to get yourself in the position where you would optimize the success rate. It included such things as getting in close enough to prevent the target from maneuvering to avoid, and also putting yourself in a position so that you have the optimum target aspect.

Q: On the beam, if possible.

Admiral Long: Right. Try to avoid down-the-throat shots where the target's coming directly at you, because that way it's very easy to avoid. So getting with the broad beam and getting close. Also very heavy emphasis on the performance of the approach officer, his ability to estimate target course, speed, and, I'd say, great reliance on the sonar operator. Of course, this was just about the time when we started just using sonar bearings only. That was something that was still very much an unknown.

My first job on that submarine was as the operations officer. I was the communicator and ops officer when I got to the Corsair.* Traditionally, the exec was the navigator, and then the next senior guy was normally the weapons officer or the gunnery officer in charge of torpedoes and the deck gun. The next officer normally would have been the engineer, and then you've got the ops officer or the communicator, and then you've got first lieutenant and down the line, assistant engineers and so on.

The Corsair was one of the last submarines that was constructed in World War II. There was the Corsair and the Sarda, and they were different from the ones that went before. There was then the recognition that fire control

---

*The USS Corsair (SS-435) was commissioned 8 November 1946. She was 312 feet long, 27 feet in the beam, and displaced 1,570 tons. She had a top speed on the surface of 20 knots and was armed with ten 21-inch torpedo tubes.

was going to improve, sonar was going to improve, and so they were built with a long conning tower, and this permitted the submarine to have a much more modern torpedo data computer, TDC. The conning tower had better sonar up there and also had a little plot. So this was a big improvement.

Q: Could you describe the role that the TDC played in making a successful approach?

Admiral Long: It was an analog computer, and it was where you put in your own course and speed. This went in automatically, and then you cranked in the target's course and speed, and this was the thing that computed the gyro angle on the torpedo. That was sent down to the torpedo room, and it went into the torpedo. So it was the thing that generated the necessary information for the torpedo to have in order to go out and hit the target. It was a key part of the approach.

Q: I would suspect, though, that the whole procedure is somewhat like driving. You do it over and over and over again until your reactions are almost automatic.

Admiral Long: That's correct. And there was a very rigid, disciplined way of doing that, particularly at the time of firing. The normal sequence was the approach officer got on the periscope, took one last bearing, and his command was, "Final bearing and shoot." Then the TDC operator would match that bearing, would correct into the computer, and then the next guy over there would say, "Set." The next guy, who was watching the output, would say, "Shoot." When the firing key operator pushed it, he'd say, "Fire." So it went bing, bing, bing.

Q: Who was your skipper in the <u>Corsair</u> and what do you remember of his leadership?

Admiral Long: He was a World War II skipper right at the end of the war. His name was Al Fuhrman.* I thought he was an outstanding skipper. He practiced those things that I believed in, including respect for both seniors and juniors. He had a lovely wife. Unfortunately, he has now passed on.** He was out of the Naval Academy class of 1937.

The exec was also a fine guy, a real gentleman--Jim Zurcher.*** We still see Jim Zurcher and his wife Marilyn. They go to Hawaii the same time we do every year, and they share an apartment with another submariner and his wife,

---
*Commander Albert S. Fuhrman, USN.
**Fuhrman, who resigned from the Navy in 1950 as a commander, died in 1986.
***Lieutenant Commander Clarence James Zurcher, USN.

Ken and Lucky Lindstrom.* The gunnery officer was also a very close friend of mine, Bob Kunhardt.** He's out of the Naval Academy Class of '43. He served in submarines in World War II. He and his wife, Shorty, were very close friends of ours. Shorty and Sara had babies about the same time, along with Marilyn. In other words, they were all pregnant about this time.

The engineer was a classmate of mine, Bill Prigmore.*** He was a character, but he wasn't as much of a character as his wife Becky. I never will forget an event before the submarine was commissioned. We were having a wardroom party at the Fuhrmans' house. We didn't know each other all that well. Everybody was talking away, and all at once we heard a voice rise above the rest. This gal said, "Al, I think you're a son of a bitch. None of your officers will tell you, but I'll tell you that. I think you're a real son of a bitch." She then said, "But a nice son of a bitch." [Laughter] So after that, wardroom parties really wouldn't get going good until Becky called somebody a son of a bitch.

Q: In what other ways was she a character?

Admiral Long: Smarter than hell. She was just a marvelous

---
*Captain Kenith V. Lindstrom, USN (Ret.)
**Lieutenant Robert M. Kunhardt, USN.
***Lieutenant (junior grade) William B. Prigmore, USN.

gal. She was smart, kind, but very outspoken.

Then we had some more junior people on there. But we put the ship in commission and we took her on shakedown. This was now early '47. We went to Rio.

Q: Not too hard to take.

Admiral Long: No. Absolutely great. We were there sort of in the preparations for Mardi Gras, and we stopped in Trinidad and Panama on the way down to Rio. Al Fuhrman ran the boat well, and it operated beautifully. We got back just in time for all the wives to have babies. I guess I was back just a couple of weeks before Sara had our first baby, Charlie.*

So we stayed on there, and I became qualified in submarines and qualified for command of submarines. I mentioned earlier that I had wanted to be a lawyer. At that time, unrestricted line naval officers could also go to law school. As a matter of fact, several of the JAGs, the judge advocate generals, in the Navy at that time were submarine officers. A guy who had been SubPac was the JAG.

I had been delayed a little bit in putting in my request. Since I had arrived in submarines a little late, I did want to get my qualification out of the way, and I did want to get qualified for command. Then I finally put

---
*Charles Allen Long, born 15 March 1947.

in my request, and just about the time that I sent it in, the Navy came out with a policy that said, "We're not going to take unrestricted line officers anymore. We're going to take graduates of law school directly and put them into JAG." So that stopped that.

Q: What can you tell me about that shakedown cruise. That sounds like a fascinating experience.

Admiral Long: Well, I think it was really uneventful except for the time in port.

Q: What do you recall of those in-port stops?

Admiral Long: Well, I don't know if I really want to specify all that. You know, Sara may read this some day.

Q: Well, I think the statute of limitations has probably expired. [Laughter]

Admiral Long: Panama was very interesting to me, seeing it for the first time, but it was also of great value to me later on when I was the Vice Chief and we then were faced with the Panama Canal Treaty. My involvement in that, which was really as the Navy representative, and I was the one who testified before the Congress on the Panama Canal

Treaty. But we also stopped in Trinidad and, here again, this was something foreign to me. I had no idea that a place like that existed--a beautiful anchorage, harbor.

Q: Very clear water.

Admiral Long: Very clear water, right.

Q: A combination of hot sun and rum that was not too healthy. [Laughter]

Admiral Long: [Laughter] After that we went on to Rio. We had some interface in New London with the Brazilian submarine people. When we arrived in Rio, they were very hospitable and showed us around their submarine bases and around the whole city. Of course, a real experience was to go see some of the night life there, which is very, very colorful. It goes on for all night long. All of us young officers in the wardroom really enjoyed that. Fortunately, the demands on us were not so great the next day.

I'll have to say that I had no political assessment of Brazil at that time such as I probably would make today, because we really were not operating at that level.

Q: How were the North Americans received by the Brazilians?

Admiral Long: Very friendly. Very friendly. And particularly the Brazilian Navy. We were received very warmly.

Q: What was the tactical role of the Corsair during that period?

Admiral Long: Well, if you remember during World War II, the principal role of submarines was to sink enemy surface ships. Right at this time, Corsair was assigned to an outfit called Submarine Development Group Two. The first skipper of that group was Roy Benson.* They formed Project Kayo, and that was the beginning of U.S. submarine interest and involvement in ASW.** We then tried to develop tactics and doctrine that involved submarines looking for submarines. Looking back at that, you know, some of those were very crude, rudimentary type of things.

Q: Do you remember specifics in that regard, from the tactics?

Admiral Long: Well, just the kind of sonar that they had was very, very crude as compared to the very sophisticated

---
*Captain Roy S. Benson, USN. The oral history of Benson, who retired as a rear admiral, is in the Naval Institute collection.
**ASW--antisubmarine warfare.

Robert L. J. Long #1 - 98

passive sonar. You know, such things as we have today are towed arrays. We had none of that at that time. We also have today big bow arrays, and we had none of that. We just sort of had things on hydraulic cylinders that we lowered down into the water, and they were very ineffective. Also the computing ability was sort of in your own head. But that was the beginning.

I'll have to say that Ensign Benson--Ensign Benson, as he was called--still will sing the song for you if you ask him, Ensign Benson.

Q: I guess the one word I would use best to describe him is enthusiastic.

Admiral Long: Yes, he was. But he and his wife Vida lived up there outside the submarine base. He was a great innovator. As I say, this got the submarine force pointed in the direction of antisubmarine warfare.

Q: Do you remember any specific exercises in that regard?

Admiral Long: Those that I do remember, Paul, were not terribly effective, but the main purpose of those exercises, looking back, they pointed the way to requirements for improved equipment and to pursue the

Robert L. J. Long #1 - 99

technology that has made submarines today the most effective ASW unit we have.

Q: So in part, it was a way of finding out what you couldn't do.

Admiral Long: That's right. It was really to explore what we could and could not do. Of course, I was with them for two years, I guess it was, and we had some fleet exercises where we used these submarines in an antisubmarine role. They were not terribly effective. Of course, that was also the time where just as I left, they went up to the Arctic under the ice, and that's where they lost one of our submarines.

Q: The Cochino.*

Admiral Long: So it was a time of innovation, and I'm always proud of the submarine force for that innovation. Of course, today there is a question of why we need submarines, and, of course, the truth is that submarines can do in the future what they have done in the past. There has been emphasis on different things in the past. The thing that submarines can do now much better than they

---

*The USS Cochino (SS-345) was lost after battery explosions in the vicinity of Norway in August 1949. For a detailed account of the event, see the oral history of Rear Admiral Benson, who was the officer in tactical command.

couldn't do before is conduct strikes. You have modern missiles. You have the stealthiest platform we have. Here we're dealing with a situation where you do not want attrition and where you now have a platform that can conduct strikes with minimum attrition of aircraft and ships and manpower. So I think that we need a real spokesman for that today.

Q: In a way, what you were doing in that period was keeping the torch burning in the submarine force, because the mission that had existed up until 1945 suddenly disappeared.

Admiral Long: And that is analogous to what we face today. Here we've had submarine force oriented primarily toward the Soviet submarine force. Some people say, "Well, that force really is no longer a threat, so why do we need submarines now?" So it's the same kind of thing today as what we had then.

Q: What do you remember about the administrative organization in which the Corsair operated?

Admiral Long: I guess there were technically two submarine squadrons in New London--Squadron 2 and Squadron 8. Later we got Squadron 10, plus the development group. The development group was not officially a squadron, but it was a squadron for all real purposes. The regular squadrons normally were made up of two or three submarine divisions. The squadron commander also spent a lot of time at sea with his ships. I think he took his job as training very, very seriously, and normally for a fleet exercise or a big exercise you would see the squadron commander embarked. The division commander certainly would be.

At that time I was very much interested and concerned at getting my qualification done, and qualification was a very rigorous process.

Q: What was involved in that?

Admiral Long: Well, there were two aspects. One had to do with the practical aspects. You had to know hands-on how to operate the various systems aboard. In addition, you had to certainly know how to dive the submarine. You had to be able to conduct torpedo approaches. You certainly had to be a qualified officer of the deck. But then there was also the academic side, where you had to draw many sketches and write up systems and explain them--big notebooks and all the rest of it.

I never will forget the time when I had just completed a huge drawing. I think it was the high-pressure air system. We had a one-year-old son, and the one-year-old somehow or other got hold of this sketch and crumbled it up. So there was Sara ironing this thing out. [Laughter]

Q: The life of a Navy wife.

Admiral Long: Yes. Well, at some point I want to talk about that too.

Q: Did you have a snorkel in the Corsair?

Admiral Long: No, no. This was still basically just a World War II submarine.

Q: The Guppies came along shortly after that.*

Admiral Long: Shortly thereafter. The next submarine I went to, the Cutlass, had, in fact, just recently been Guppyized.

Q: What do you remember about the enlisted men in the Corsair?

---

*The Guppy program got its name from the acronym for Greater Underwater Propulsive Power. The modifications to the World War II fleet boats included streamlining, more powerful batteries, and snorkels.

Admiral Long: When I think of the F Division I had on the Colorado, I'd say those men closely approximated that submarine crew insofar as smarts and really knowing their jobs. But the thing that really impressed me in submarines was the quality of the people that I was dealing with. They were volunteers. They were carefully screened. They were well trained. They were really an impressive bunch.

Q: And at that point they were probably virtually all combat veterans.

Admiral Long: Yes, that's right, particularly the first class and chiefs.

Q: Anything else about that boat to put on the record?

Admiral Long: Well, you know, you've triggered me concerning the crew. Normally--not always but normally--the chief of the boat is a very outstanding guy, and this was no exception in the Corsair. Chief Smith was the chief of the boat, which is a unique job in submarines. He is the senior enlisted man, and he speaks for the crew. His boss is the exec, and the exec normally gives orders and direction for the crew through the chief of the boat. The crew looks to the chief of the boat for direction and guidance. He's sort of a father/mother figure. In every submarine that I have served on--the Corsair, the Cutlass, the Sea Leopard, Patrick Henry, Casimir Pulaski--all of those chiefs of the boat have really been outstanding, and they've been good friends of mine.

Q: As you say, there is no comparison to other parts of the Navy.

Admiral Long: That's right. I think one of the reasons why there's such a normally good feeling between the crew and officers and the commanding officer is that they all understand that their well-being depends on each other. Any one of those guys can really screw it up for everybody. Therefore, if you don't feel that a certain guy is trustworthy, that's a bad situation, and you'd better get rid of him.

Q: Well, literally everybody's in the same boat.

Admiral Long: In the same boat. That's right.

Q: In recent years, the Navy has established the master chief petty officer of the command, which I think is an approximation of the chief of the boat.

Admiral Long: That's right. That's an approximation.

Q: Did you have any real characters in your enlisted crew in the Corsair?

Admiral Long: Well, I later became the gunnery officer. I had a fire control striker on there, and I forget his name, but subsequently he became the chairman/CEO of a large electronic outfit outside.

Q: That says something about the talent you had.

Admiral Long: Yes, that's right.

Q: Did you use the deck gun very much?

Admiral Long: No. Occasionally we would shoot it, but it really was completely sort of superfluous to the new roles and the mission of the submarine force. When they were Guppyized, the guns were removed, and, of course, the new submarines don't have guns. What they have now is Harpoon, which is a hell of a lot more effective than going after an enemy ship with a 5-inch gun.

Q: That really was a vestigial organ from the time that submarines were submersible torpedo boats.

Robert L. J. Long #1 - 106

Admiral Long: You're right. The old submarines were essentially surface ships that would submerge occasionally. Of course, now they spend most of their time submerged.

Q: How did your next tour of duty come about after the Corsair?

Admiral Long: I mentioned my unsuccessful attempt to become a Navy lawyer. I also had a request at that time from my old gun boss in the Colorado, who was then working at Sandia. He wanted me to come out there and get into the nuclear weapons business. But I thought that I really should spend some time at home. We had our second one on the way. At that time, Sara's family had moved to North Carolina from Jacksonville, Florida. Also, the Navy was saying how important it was for younger naval officers to have some association with the ROTC units. So I asked to go to the NROTC unit at Chapel Hill, the University of North Carolina.

Q: What sorts of experiences did you encounter down in North Carolina once you got into NROTC?

Admiral Long: One of the first things you want to do is get yourself settled. We had some good advice from a lady down there, where not to settle or buy. We finally found this house in a good part of town, 7 Cobb Terrace. I think we paid something like $9,000 for it, several thousand of which we had borrowed from Sara's parents. It was a Sears & Roebuck prefab house from World War I. It had been owned by this college prof. He and his wife had sort of fixed it up, so we moved in there.

When Sara and I passed through that area just two years ago, we stopped in at Chapel Hill. We went by, and there was that same house. It was occupied by a young lawyer and his wife, and they had two babies, just as we did. It hadn't changed. It was a great house. We bought it for something like $9,000 and sold it for $10,000. So we made a lot of money.

We really enjoyed our tour in Chapel Hill, because it was really the first time that we had settled down. That was the place where Sara and I decided to join the Episcopal Church. In our confirmation class was one of the most famous people in North Carolina, and that was the football star at the University of North Carolina--Choo Choo Justice.

We also had some wonderful people that were attached to the NROTC unit at the university. The exec was a great guy named Bill Manning, a surface guy.* He married his landlady's daughter while we were there. Another guy was a young lieutenant named Elmo Zumwalt.** He and Mouza lived

---
*Commander William J. Manning, USN.
**Lieutenant Elmo R. "Bud" Zumwalt, Jr., USN, who later served as Chief of Naval Operations from 1970 to 1974.

Robert L. J. Long #1 - 108

with two babies over in student housing--poor as church mice. We had a Marine who was a great Marine, and we also had a naval aviator.

Q: Zumwalt looks back on that period very fondly.*

Admiral Long: Yes, and so do we. We became very close friends.

Q: What do you remember of him from that period?

Admiral Long: He was probably as close to being an all-American boy as I could imagine.

Q: How do you mean that?

Admiral Long: Well, smart, very high standards, ideals. In his dealings with the midshipmen, he demonstrated all the attributes of a great leader. He had a strong sense of loyalty, of course, to Mouza. He met Mouza in Shanghai, married her, brought her over. Mouza also had an aunt and an uncle there. Bud brought them over and set Auntie up in business in the Cafe Mouza, which went belly up. He never complained. He was always the little boy looking for the

---

*Admiral Zumwalt has been interviewed as part of the Naval Institute's oral history program.

pony. Just a very solid kind of a guy.

Q: He has a reputation as a workaholic. Did he demonstrate that at that time?

Admiral Long: No, but I'd have to say candidly, Paul, that the work was not all that onerous. I mean, we went to work, we did our preparation, but it wasn't like working in the Pentagon.

Q: Did the Navy families tend to socialize with each other frequently?

Admiral Long: Yes, and with the university people also. The Navy was very well accepted by the university. North Carolina was the place of the big V-7 school during World War II.* The head of the university and the head of the athletic department were just great friends of the Navy, and so we were very well accepted there. The skipper was a Captain Cooper. He was pretty conscientious, but he was sort of one of those old-time surface guys. But he was fine.

I remember Bud very, very favorably at that time, and, of course, we were friends from then on. Subsequently,

---

*V-7 was a Naval Reserve officer training program in which individuals with enough college education (normally a bachelor's degree) were trained as deck officers for surface ships.

when he became the CNO, he and I did not always agree on policy. Part of that time I was ComSubLant and he was the CNO. Of course, some of those rather revolutionary ideas just wouldn't fly in the submarine force. But, as I say, even today he and I are good friends.

Q: A name he mentioned from that period, was a retired officer named Swede Hazlett.* Did you encounter him?

Admiral Long: Yes. My recollection is that Swede had retired there, and he was a friend of Eisenhower.**

Q: Right. They had been boyhood friends.

Admiral Long: That's right. The Hazletts were a very fine couple, and we used to socialize with them. We also knew a few other people there, including Dr. and Mrs. McKnighter. Sally McKnighter grew up there, and so she went out of her way to be hospitable, because she was sort of in our age group. She dated one of the officers, Lieutenant Ed French, who was a member of the staff.

That's also the place where we had our second baby, Bill.*** One midnight Sara decided that this was the time

---
*Commander Edward E. Hazlett, Jr., USN (Ret.).
**General of the Army Dwight D. Eisenhower, USA, later President from 1953 to 1961.
***William Trigg Long, born 22 December 1949.

Robert L. J. Long #1 - 111

to have the baby. We had to go to Duke Hospital in Durham, because Chapel Hill did not have a hospital at that time. So I called up Bud, and Bud came over and spent the night with our oldest, Charlie. So we enjoyed going back there and seeing that place.

Q: What was involved in your duties with the midshipmen and the classroom training and so forth?

Admiral Long: I was there for two years. I think one year I taught seniors. The first year I taught ordnance and gunnery, and, as I say, it was sort of fun. They were a pretty impressive young bunch.

Q: And impressionable, also, so you have an important obligation as a role model.

Admiral Long: That's right. That's right.

Q: Did you do any evangelizing for submarines?

Admiral Long: I'm sure I did. I'm sure I did. [Laughter]

Q: How conscious were you at the time in the larger Navy of the big squabble going on over roles and missions and the fight with the Air Force and what have you?

Admiral Long: Paul, I don't think that I really was aware of that at that time. I had some indication that this thing had grown out of the Key West Agreement. I knew that there was some disagreement, but I had no real awareness of it. It was too far removed from me. It was not until later that I became very much aware of it.

Q: Did you enjoy the classroom interaction with the students?

Admiral Long: Yes, I enjoyed that. I think I'm a natural pontificator, anyway, and I enjoy teaching. We also had a good golf course there, and most of us played golf. I don't think Bud played, but some of the rest of us. The Marine played, the aviator played, I played, and Bill Manning played. So we had a lot of golf. It was a great interlude in our life.

Q: And a chance to be with your family all the time.

Admiral Long: That's right. And, of course, one of the reasons that we went there was because Sara's family lived in Charlotte at that time. Just before we left, they moved to Kansas City.

Q: This was at the time when the armed services were integrated racially. I would suspect that it was slow to take in Chapel Hill.

Admiral Long: That's right. That's right.

Q: How would you compare the rigor of that NROTC program with what you had known at the Naval Academy?

Admiral Long: Oh, no comparison. I think it was true then and it's true today that the Naval Academy produces a product that is better trained and better indoctrinated to be a naval officer than the ROTC product. What this does for you is give you a standard of excellence that is terribly important for the first few years in an officer's life. I think that this helps the ROTC or OCS guy come up to a certain standard.*

Now, after three or four years, I really don't think it makes any difference where that officer came from. Initially you've taught him sort of how to use his knife and fork, and from there on it really depends upon the judgment that that officer shows. It depends upon the initiative, the work ethic. Those are the things then that start to show up. But I think that initially, an academy graduate brings that standard of excellence that, if it

---
*OCS--Officer Candidate School.

were eliminated, would have a very negative impact on the entire officer corps over the long run.

Q: Another interesting phenomenon is virtually all the three- and four-star admirals are Naval Academy graduates. There's certainly a vast preponderance.

Admiral Long: Paul, I think your perception that three- and four-stars were almost totally academy graduates was correct in the past, but I submit that if you look at the situation today where you have the Chief of Staff of the Army, I think, is a non-academy, the Chairman of the Joint Chiefs of Staff is not a non-academy.

Q: I think it has been more so in the Navy than in the other services.

Admiral Long: The officer who is CinCLant, Paul David Miller, is non-Naval Academy.* The officer who is CinCUSNavEur, Mike Boorda, is non-Naval Academy and so on. Admiral Jeremiah is non-Naval Academy.** I don't have any problem at all with that, because, as I said before, after

---

*Admiral Paul D. Miller, USN, Commander in Chief U.S. Atlantic Command/Supreme Allied Commander Atlantic.
**Admiral Jeremy M. Boorda, USN, Commander in Chief U.S. Naval Forces Europe/Commander in Chief Allied Forces Southern Europe. In 1994 Boorda became the first non-Naval Academy graduate as Chief of Naval Operations.

the first few years the individual officer's inherent characteristics start coming out.

Q: When you were a midshipman, you had the pleasure of going over to visit an officer's home and having a chance to relax. Did you do that in reverse when you were at Chapel Hill, invite some of the midshipmen into your place?

Admiral Long: No, we didn't invite the midshipmen in, but we invited their dates to stay with us, and so we saw the midshipmen then. Many times we would have one or two gals stay with us when they came down for the weekend.

Q: That was a very convenient service, I'm sure.

Admiral Long: Yes, it was.

Q: What other recollections do you have of the local community there?

Admiral Long: Well, I mentioned the McKnighters, and we also had some wonderful neighbors. Our neighbors across the street--this was really sort of a one-way loop, Cobb Terrace--were Tom Nixon and his wife, Margaret, and he was a Naval Academy grad out of class of '37.* He had been

---

*Lieutenant Thomas J. Nixon III, USN, retired from active duty in March 1945.

aboard one of the carriers when it was sunk during the war. He was on pile of those believed to be dead, but he moved and later recovered. But then the Navy sent him to University of North Carolina to get a law degree. He was retired, but he was still having a little trouble mentally. He and his wife were just great neighbors.

Even though he sometimes was very forgetful, he had a great sense of humor. I remember one time we went ahead and planted a bunch of sweet peas, and Sara and I would look out our big kitchen windows every morning to see if those things were blooming yet. Then one morning we looked out there and they were just covered with sweet peas. We ran out, and then we looked across the street and here was Tom and his wife Margaret, and they were standing there just laughing away. They had taped all these sweet peas on the vines. [Laughter]

There were also academics who lived in that neighborhood. It was just a very warm, warm community. As I say, the college administration was very friendly to the Navy.

Q: Fit right in with the idea of traditional Southern charm and hospitality.

Admiral Long: Yes. There's a famous book called <u>Southern Part of Heaven</u> that was written about Chapel Hill.

Robert L. J. Long #1 - 117

Q: Did you have any sense of reluctance in leaving there?

Admiral Long: Yes, I'd say so. We enjoyed it, and I'd have to say my next assignment was somewhat unnerving. I had orders to go to the executive officer of a brand-new antisubmarine submarine, the K-1, which, incidentally, Jimmy Carter was also assigned to.* But then my orders were changed to go to be the exec of Cutlass.** That boat had gone through two or three skippers in one year and two or three execs in one year. So it was a real problem. And it was at Key West, Florida, where there was no real housing to speak of. So we were less than enthusiastic about, one, going to a place where housing was difficult and, two, going to a submarine that was screwed up.

So, anyway, we went and arrived down there, with two babies, and no place to live, mosquitoes that almost could carry the children away. We moved into a motel. It was Sunday, so I went down and walked aboard Cutlass. All the officers were there, including the skipper, Charlie Styer.*** The officers were all sitting in the wardroom while the exec was reading the deck logs aloud to make sure

---

*Lieutenant (junior grade) James E. Carter, USN, a graduate of the Naval Academy in the class of 1947, later President from 1977 to 1981.
**The USS Cutlass (SS-478) was commissioned 5 November 1944. She was 312 feet long, 27 feet in the beam, and displaced 1,570 tons. She had a top speed on the surface of 20 knots and was armed with ten 21-inch torpedo tubes.
***Lieutenant Commander Charles W. Styer, Jr., USN.

that they were properly worded. I said to myself, "Well, that doesn't look very good to me." Then I went in to see the captain, Charlie, who was a very close friend of mine.

He said, "Bob, we're going to sea tomorrow for two weeks, and I'd like to have you go with us."

I said, "Captain, I just arrived here. I don't have a place for my family. They're sitting in a crummy motel out here. I'd prefer not to."

He says, "Well, I really want you to go. We'll make some time available to you when we get back."

Well, I was so mad, I went back to the motel, sat down, and wrote out my resignation from the Navy. I said, "If this is the way the Navy treats its people, I don't want any part of it." Fortunately for me--or maybe unfortunately--Sara got on the telephone to her father and said, "I don't think Bob should do this." He was a guy I really respected, a great guy, and he talked me out of it.

Q: What were his arguments?

Admiral Long: He said, "Hey, this is a temporary thing. My observation is that you are ideally suited for the Navy. You have a lot to offer. Don't let this one incident destroy that." So, anyway, I went aboard.

Robert L. J. Long #1 - 119

Q: How did you make arrangements for your family's housing?

Admiral Long: They stayed there. Then I came back and bought this little Sunshine House, as they called it. Later on they built Navy housing down there, but not for us. We lived down there for a year and then the home port of the ship was shifted to Norfolk. I might add that we lost money on it. When they opened up Navy housing, the price of the rest of the real estate went down.

But Charlie and I were, I think, a good team on there. When we left, we put the "E" on the ship.* Here again, we had the chief of the boat who was just marvelous--Boyton. We turned that crew around.

Q: I'm sure you knocked off the Mickey Mouse, things like reading the log aloud.

Admiral Long: That's right. I said, "I'm not going to run it that way." But you learn something from every guy you work for, something to do or not to do. Of course, Charlie was desperate. They had already gone through, I think, three skippers.

Q: So his requirement for you to go on that cruise was

---
*The E is an annual award for excellence given to the top-performing boat in a division or squadron.

based on desperation.

Admiral Long: Right. He, in effect, was saying, "Hey, I've got to have you." Well, he was a good skipper and he essentially left the running of the crew to me.

Q: What qualities in him did you admire?

Admiral Long: Well, he knew how to handle the ship well, but I guess the quality I admired the most and that is he let me run it. [Laughter] And I don't mean that in a pejorative way. He had good instincts. He had high standards.

Q: He obviously had confidence in you.

Admiral Long: Right. He trusted me, and he told me what he wanted. They were reasonable things. I could talk to him. You know, I'd say, "Captain, that doesn't make sense." He was amenable to listening. I'd say the chief of the boat was probably as important as anyone, because he was new and he knew how to handle the crew.

So we got through that, and then we were both relieved in the space of about two weeks, which was a disaster. The skipper was relieved by a guy that had very little operational experience. I was relieved by a guy who was extremely arrogant and overbearing and disloyal to his skipper. It resulted in the skipper being relieved. I continued to receive letters from the chief of the boat, and if it wasn't so pathetic, it would have been humorous. But, you know, it was almost like an Abbott and Costello kind of a thing.*

Q: You said you turned the crew around. What sort of changes needed to be instituted?

Admiral Long: Well, I think it was the fundamental business of setting some standards, telling them what you wanted, making it reasonable. We cut out the Mickey Mouse stuff, demanded high performance, rewarded it when we got it. We'd tell them, "Hey, that's a great job," or, "Hey, we don't want to do it that way. That's not right." In other words, we let them know one way or another, but in a reasonable way. I think most people respond to that.

The crew developed a very close relationship. We had a lot of beer ball games, and there were some characters in the crew that really performed well, acrobats and so on. One of the guys was named Dick Harris, a former big football player--about your size.** He was the chief

___
*Bud Abbott and Lou Costello were two popular comedy actors in the movies of the 1940s and 1950s.
**Lieutenant Richard A. Harris, USN.

engineer, and let me tell you, he was as solid as a rock. He came aboard the same time I did. Bob Blount, who was the ops guy, came aboard just before I did.* They were the solid foundation of that crew, plus this chief of the boat. So you can't do it all by yourself. You've got to have good people. And there were good people there. And, you know, Bob Blunt, Charlie Styer, Dick Harris, and I are all still close friends.

Q: You said that this was one of the early Guppy boats. How would you compare it with the <u>Corsair</u> in capability?

Admiral Long: Oh, submerged endurance significantly improved. Submerged speed. You know, you're talking here 18 knots versus eight. We had the ability to stay submerged, using the snorkel. Here you're talking days, as opposed to hours. So we gained advantages in mobility and speed. I'd say it made it an entire new weapons system. Of course, it had the same armament--torpedo tubes, and torpedoes.

Q: Were you getting a better sonar by this time?

Admiral Long: Yes, the sonar had improved. The radar had improved. So it was a better fighting machine. These were

---
*Lieutenant (junior grade) Robert H. Blount, USN.

the Guppies. I think the guy who actually converted Cutlass was Walt Small.*

Q: How was this boat used in operations?

Admiral Long: It was still used principally as an antisurface ship weapon system, not too much as an antisubmarine weapon. We deployed. We went to the Mediterranean and operated with the Sixth Fleet. That was the first time I'd ever really been to the Mediterranean.

Q: Please tell me about some of the ports you visited.

Admiral Long: The first one, and the big one, was Cannes, France. We had taken out a presidential pay commission, and the chairman of it--I forget his name--was a good friend of Florence Gould, who was Jay Gould's daughter-in-law.** Jay Gould's son was an invalid and lived there in Cannes. So when we arrived in Cannes, Charlie Styer called on Florence Gould. Well, we essentially had a home there. [Laughter]

Q: Probably a pretty nice one too.

Admiral Long: Oh, you bet. The parties went on, and she

---
*Commander Walter L. Small, USN.
**Jay Gould was a noted American financier.

had speed boats and we water skied. That's sort of the way it should be. We went to other ports as well. One of the more memorable ports was Izmir, Turkey. We went in there the same day that a submarine was lost--one of those that we had transferred to Turkey.*

Turkey was very foreign to me. That's the first time I've ever been on a wild boar hunt. The Turks were very friendly. I sometimes wonder why the Turks are so friendly, when you look at how poorly we treat them. You know, they and the Greeks don't get along. We do everything for the Greeks and do very little for the Turks.

Q: What was your role in operating with the Sixth Fleet?

Admiral Long: Acting as the enemy. We had not yet developed the concept of a submarine in direct support of a carrier battle group. It took the submarine force a long time to accept that philosophy. Submariners said, in effect, "Don't put us back to that role we had before World War II, where we sort of were the scouting force and tied directly. We want to be independent."

Q: That's where that term "fleet boat" came from.

---

*The Turkish submarine Dumlupinar, formerly the USS Blower (SS-325), was lost in the Dardanelles on 4 April 1953, when she was rammed by the Swedish freighter Naboland.

Admiral Long: Yes. So now we are much more serious about operating directly in support of carrier battle group commander.

Q: I can understand why that would be psychologically difficult to accept, because they had been the lone rangers in World War II.

Admiral Long: Also, if you get too close, you don't know when you're going to get a friendly torpedo or a friendly depth bomb. So there is some understandable concern. But with the C^3I architecture that's available today, you can put a submarine out there and have him essentially responsive to an operational commander, and that's what is required.* If the submarines are going to survive, they have to be something more than antisubmarine warfare platforms.

Q: How effective were the ASW measures that were used against you during those exercises?

Admiral Long: Not very effective.

Q: Sounds as if they were not yet able to cope with this Guppy capability.

---
*C^3I--command, control, communications, intelligence.

Admiral Long: No. I think the surface Navy and the air Navy, along about that time, started building in much more effective sonars and radars. The P-3 is a tremendous improvement with the sonobuoys.* So those things have improved, but even so, the ability to detect, locate, and destroy a quiet submarine, say a diesel submarine, is very, very limited today. It's tough. It's tough.

Q: So they must have been very frustrated in those screens that were operating with the carriers.

Admiral Long: That's right.

Q: Did you get together for critiques afterward to compare moves and so forth?

Admiral Long: Paul, I think that that probably was a significant deficiency. There wasn't an awful lot of critique. There were reports written. But looking back, I don't think that there was a great deal of analysis of fleet exercises, not to the same degree that has been done recently. The idea was just to do the exercise, get the report in, and then we'd get on with the next one. So I think that that was not done as well as it is today.

---

*The P-3 Orion is a land-based antisubmarine patrol plane.

Q: I could see where that deployment would have a great effect on the crew. On the one hand, all these good liberty ports, and on the other hand, the smugness of evading detection in the exercises. Both of those would build morale.

Admiral Long: But one of the principal purposes, I'd say, of the Sixth Fleet, then and now, is to show the presence of the United States. I think that is important.

Q: That was the reason it started, and it's continued ever since.

Admiral Long: Right.

Q: And, of course, the ability to respond in a crisis, which it has also done on a number of occasions.

Admiral Long: Right. If you lose that, why, you might as well stay home. That's sort of like deploying the F-15s to Saudi Arabia during the Carter Administration without any ammunition.* That's not deterrence.

Q: The Korean War started during this period. Was that anything that affected you, or something you just monitored?

---
*F-15s are Air Force fighter planes.

Admiral Long: The Korean War was of little or no impact on us in the Atlantic submarine force. Of course, I'd read about it in the paper, but, quite candidly, it was not of any great import to the submarine community. North Korea has some submarines today, but I'm not aware of any submarines that they had at that time. I'm unaware of any real submarine activity in the Korean War. There could have been some for reconnaissance, surveillance, but I'm just not aware of it.

Q: What else did the boat do during that period?

Admiral Long: Well, we left Key West and went to Portsmouth, New Hampshire, where we spent maybe four or five months, and had a good overhaul. Then we shifted our home port to Norfolk, Virginia. I guess this was also the time when we went to the Mediterranean.

Q: Any specifics you remember about Portsmouth? That's certainly one of the old yards in the Navy.

Admiral Long: Portsmouth is a good yard. It's sort of like Bremerton. People had been there for years and years, following their fathers and grandfathers. I moved the whole family up. The crew lived on a barge, which is no fun at all. My recollection is that there was not a lot of modernization. It was just strictly an overhaul every three or four years. It was uneventful. I think the crew had a good time. I remember we had a lot of lobster pots right off the barge, so we had lots of lobster to eat. We then came back to Norfolk and lived in an apartment there for a while before we then went off to Newport, Rhode Island, to the War College.

Q: I wanted to mention one other thing about your wife and the resignation decision. It certainly takes a special lady to hang in there under those circumstances, because had she reinforced your frame of mind at the time, you would have been gone.

Admiral Long: Absolutely. Well, let me tell you, I think I would be remiss if I did not recognize the job that Navy wives do. I mean, this at-sea period with Cutlass and when I had command of Sea Leopard and command of Patrick Henry, Casimir Pulaski, and particularly during the Patrick Henry time, Paul, when we operated out of Holy Loch, Scotland. I'd be gone three and a half months, back two and a half months. Three kids. Let me tell you, that's a challenge, and a lot of wives can't do it or won't do it. So I'm very, very grateful to my wife for her going through all of that.

Q: You certainly gave her an indoctrination to it when you disappeared right after the honeymoon. [Laughter]

Admiral Long: That's right. [Laughter]

Q: When you were in the *Cutlass*, what kind of family support services were there? Probably nothing comparable to the ombudsman and things that are available today.

Admiral Long: That's correct. Of course, in those submarines, I'd say that the family support really centered around the wardroom, the chiefs, their wives. The key players there had to be the skipper and the exec's wife. If somebody needed help with the boat gone, what normally happened was if this word got to the exec's wife or the skipper's wife, I think they did a good job of making sure that this was taken care of. Later in the FBMs we had what we called familygrams, which were messages that would go out to the submarines at sea. But we didn't have those kind of things before then.

Q: Was there kind of a paternalistic attitude that the officers' wives would take care of crew's wives if problems came up?

Robert L. J. Long #1 - 131

Admiral Long: Yes, and the wives would many times get together. My sense was that the skipper's wife and the exec's wife had that feeling of responsibility to make sure that if there was a problem, somebody would take care of it.

Q: And I think you implied that with working wives now they may not have the time to do as much of that as in the past.

Admiral Long: That's right. So it's changed.

Q: After the *Cutlass*, you went to Newport. Was that another pleasant interlude as Chapel Hill had been?

Admiral Long: Yes, it was. I went to the command and staff course at the Naval War College. Admiral Conolly was the president of the war college.* In his opening remarks was something I've quoted many times, "There's one thing I want you officers to understand when you finish this course, and that is that your damn fool ideas are just as good as the next guy's damn fool ideas." [Chuckles]

But it was a time of opening new doors. I think the most important thing that I got out of the war college was

---
*Vice Admiral Richard L. Conolly, USN, served as president of the Naval War College from 1 December 1950 to 2 November 1953.

the opportunity to meet and to know officers of different service--naval aviators, surface people, Air Force people, Army people, Marines. Those contacts were very helpful to me later on.

Q: Do you recall any examples?

Admiral Long: Well, I think it just enhanced my appreciation that not all Air Force officers are bad.

Q: Not all of them. [Laughter]

Admiral Long: Not all of them. [Laughter] I also gained a better appreciation of some of the Army's problems. Some of those officers that I met and knew there, I still see today. So it was an opportunity to get me out of this very closed community and give me a better appreciation of what the rest of the military looked like. So that's a very important thing.

Q: It gives you insight into how the other services think and how they approach problems.

Admiral Long: Yes. Well, we'll get to that later. It was very helpful to me when I recently chaired a study for the Chairman of the Joint Chiefs of Staff on officers' education at the more senior level. The message of that study to the Chairman was that you need to restructure the curriculum at the National Defense University, the National War College, and the Industrial College of the Armed Forces and ensure that senior officers are educated not only in the military factors of national security, but also the political, economic, and cultural aspects, because you can't separate them out. All of the services have been rather parochial in their thinking over the years, and I'd say particularly the Navy. The Navy has been quite reluctant to accept jointness. I think we're now doing a good job of accepting jointness, but you cannot look upon military operations only in isolation. The war college opened my eyes to some of that.

Q: In what ways? What kinds of things did you get into?

Admiral Long: Well, we were very much open to lectures by Foreign Service people. We had Foreign Service people in the course. We also had lectures on economics. We also had lectures about how various foreign countries did business. Those things made me start thinking about military operations in a much broader way. Now, do you really want to increase the curriculum at the Naval Academy to start expanding that? Yes, somewhat. But you primarily want to teach them how to be good professional division officers when they graduate. But this is part of the continuing education of military officers. You want to make sure that when they reach certain points that they're broadened even further. Jointness is just one aspect. But I submit certainly as a CinC, you'd better know something about the political situation.* I don't mean Republican/Democrat; I'm talking about geopolitical. You need to know something about the economics of the theater, and you really need to know something about the cultural attitudes within the theater.

Q: Again, with hindsight, we did not understand the Vietnamese culture when we were fighting a war there.

Admiral Long: You're damn right. That's right. So this was the beginning of opening that up.

Q: What sorts of things did the curriculum get into in terms of, say, staff studies and planning and that sort of thing?

Admiral Long: Well, we did some very interesting war games which brought out these points. We also studied joint operations. Interestingly, the Naval War College was one of the first of the war colleges really to be pushing some

---
*CinC--commander in chief.

joint warfare concepts, although the Navy has been criticized, and criticized fairly, I'd say, for being very reluctant to accept jointness. So those things were terribly important.

Q: What might have been a typical war game, let's say, and what kind of equipment was available?

Admiral Long: Well, of course, the Naval War College has probably been the preeminent institution for war games, where they've actually had the facilities set up. Those facilities have been greatly modernized, and there are many places where you can play war games today. You can even play war games aboard ship, where they have these very fancy communication networks where I can sit on my flagship down in Norfolk and I can play a war game that would involve CinCLant, CinCLantFlt, a whole series of commands. But at that time, this was sort of state of the art. Some of the things we looked at were such things involving, say, a conflict in the Mediterranean. Another was, I think, an operation against North Cape.

War games were not universally accepted. When I was CinCPac, I set up the first war games as a unified CinC. We could play war games at CinCPac. So those new ideas are terribly important for someone if you want to grow, and I thought the Naval War College just was a super place to

Robert L. J. Long #1 - 136

help me grow.

Q: Especially when the president says there's not necessarily a staff solution, let your mind explore new ways.

Admiral Long: Right. And I guess that's also confirmed my thinking that probably one of the worst concepts there is in the military and that's completed staff work, where somebody does a lot of thinking and puts it down on paper and then presents it to you, and you either sign it or wait another six months to get another answer. That's not Bob Long.

Q: How demanding was the pace in that course?

Admiral Long: It was full, but it was not hectic. We had times for square-dancing, we had time for the theater. As a matter of fact, that's where I debuted in the theater.

Q: Please tell me more.

Admiral Long: I participated in a play called the "The Man Who Came to Dinner," and I played the part of one of the juveniles, or the young men. That went all right except that after the play somebody came up and asked Sara, "Who was that guy playing the juvenile that had the bald spot on the back of his head?" [Laughter]

We also had time for a lot of squash. Several of my classmates were there. Dave Bagley, who is a very dear friend, was there.* George Talley.** Howard Greer was there with his first wife.***

Q: Talley was a bright guy, from what I've heard.

Admiral Long: Yes, he was OP-06 when I was the vice Chief.**** Howard Greer was ComAirLant, also a very bright guy.***** So those contacts are very good. We lived in housing up there, a place called the Anchorage, which has since been torn down. But we had a great time.

Q: Did you write a thesis as part of that course?

Admiral Long: No. This was also before they permitted students to get a master's degree. I thought it was a mistake when the master's degree was allowed, because that detracted really from the war college.

Q: Dilutes your attention.

---
*Lieutenant Commander David H. Bagley, USN.
**Lieutenant Commander George C. Talley, USN.
***Lieutenant Commander Howard E. Greer, USN.
****OP-06--Deputy Chief of Naval Operations (Plans, Policy and Operations).
*****ComAirLant--Commander Air Force Atlantic Fleet.

Admiral Long: Yes. You know, if you have more time, let's beef up the curriculum. And I'll have to say that when Stansfield Turner went there, that's what he did.*

Q: Like a whirlwind.

Admiral Long: Yes.

Q: Well, we're right near the end of the tape. Any last thoughts on the Newport period?

Admiral Long: Well, that was probably one of the most useful, broadening tours that I had that helped prepare me for higher command, and I'm delighted I went.

Q: Thank you, Admiral, for today. We got off to a great start. I appreciate it.

Admiral Long: All right. Thank you, Paul.

---

*Vice Admiral Stansfield Turner, USN, served as president of the Naval War College from 30 June 1972 to 9 August 1974.

Interview Number 2 with Admiral Robert L. J. Long,
U.S. Navy (Retired)

Place: Admiral Long's home, Annapolis, Maryland

Date: Friday, 26 February 1993

Interviewer: Paul Stillwell

Q: Admiral, it's good to be inside and warm on this snowy Friday morning.

Admiral Long: Yes. Having recently returned from the sunny climes of Hawaii, I must admit this white stuff is a little puzzling to me.

Q: We finished yesterday talking about your time at the Naval War College, and have you ready to take your first command, the USS Sea Leopard. So if we could resume there, please.

Admiral Long: When I left the Naval War College in Newport, I went to Norfolk, Virginia, and took command of the USS Sea Leopard.* That was a converted World War II diesel submarine that had been Guppyized, and it was a fine

---

*The USS Sea Leopard (SS-483) was commissioned 11 June 1945. She was 312 feet long, 27 feet in the beam, and displaced 1,570 tons. She had a top speed on the surface of 20 knots and was armed with ten 21-inch torpedo tubes.

diesel submarine that had been Guppyized, and it was a fine ship. I relieved a friend of mine, a little bit senior to me, Buck Catlin.* This was in the summer of 1954.

The ship was attached to Submarine Squadron Six. The squadron commander at that time was Captain Selby.** I had a great crew. My exec was a part-time lawyer, Lionel Goulet, and we had a few Harvard graduates and a few Yale graduates aboard.*** As a matter of fact, the chiefs became so impressed with the Yale graduates that they hung a sign on the chiefs' quarters, otherwise known as the goat locker, and they indicated they put up the red flag of Harvard to oppose. My division commander at that time was Ebby Bell, who has been a great friend of mine ever since.****

Q: Later a vice admiral.

Admiral Long: Later a vice admiral, commander of the amphibious force. The ship was assigned to a new outfit called Task Group Alfa, which here again was innovative. It was oriented primarily to seeking out enemy submarines.

Q: Hunter-killer group.

---

*Commander Allen B. Catlin, USN.
**Captain Frank G. Selby, USN.
***Lieutenant Commander Lionel J. Goulet, USN.
****Commander C. Edwin Bell, USN.

Admiral Long: Hunter-killer group. The chief of staff of that outfit, Hal Bowen, became a very good friend of mine and still is.* He also retired as a vice admiral. We would exercise in this role in the hunter-killer group. Here again, I think that the tools were rather elementary. We had not really developed some of the sophisticated sensors and analysis systems that we have today. But it was a very good beginning and was a healthy beginning for the Navy faced with the threat of the Soviet submarine threat.

Q: This was early in the time of using the Essex-class carriers as dedicated antisubmarine ships.**

Admiral Long: That's correct.

Q: Were you working up those tactics?

Admiral Long: Yes. However, Paul, even at that time the friendly submarine was not closely integrated into the task group. We were normally kept at some distance, and many times we operated as a target submarine. Of course, that permitted us to maintain our skill in tracking and

---
*Captain Harold G. Bowen, USN.
**The Essex-class carriers were used in an attack role during World War II and Korea. In the early 1950s some ships of the class were converted to the CVS designation to support antisubmarine-type aircraft.

attacking enemy surface ships, and, of course, we had a certain amount of pleasure of putting the carrier in our periscope cross hairs.

Among the things that stick in your mind as you go through your career are those incidents when a few seconds might mean the difference between life and death or tragedy and success. I mentioned earlier that there were a couple of times I had very close calls when I was in the Colorado. Almost immediately after taking command of Sea Leopard, I had another one of those incidents. It happened as all of us sortied from Norfolk.

Of course, the Sea Leopard's role was to go out and wait for the carrier task force to come out and then attack it. I was able to position the submarine so that we had a good approach on the carrier. I was in the process of firing off smoke signals indicating a simulated torpedo attack, when my sonar operator said, "Captain, I have another contact that's very close aboard on the port bow." So I swung the periscope around, and there was a destroyer with a zero angle on the bow. She was literally just a couple of hundred yards away, bearing down on us at about 25 knots. That gets your attention.

I immediately ordered the diving officer to flood the negative tank and take her deep. My estimate is that that ship missed us by just a matter of a few feet. So that also embeds in your mind a necessity to keep a search all the way around when you're in close quarters with those ships.

Q: You get so preoccupied with the target, you lose track of the rest of the ships.

Admiral Long: That's right. Subsequently over a beer, the skipper of the destroyer related his surprise and fright when he saw this periscope dead ahead just a couple of hundred yards, and he was certain that he was going to hit us. So here again, Paul, you need a little luck as you go through life.

Q: What do you remember specifically of your dealings with Captain Bowen?

Admiral Long: Hal Bowen was a "very much older" officer; he must have been in his 40s.* Of course, he was very mature, but he probably was one of the most perceptive officers that I had known, very much an open mind, very easy to talk to. He had the characteristics that I admire: that is, smart, showed great respect for the people working for him, encouraged them to voice their views, rewarded performance. He and I served later together in Washington, and he still maintains those traits today. He's a very

---

*Bowen was born in October 1912.

and he still maintains those traits today. He's a very delightful person.

Q: We talked yesterday about the fact that there wasn't much post-exercise analysis. Had you gotten more by this time with Task Group Alfa?

Admiral Long: Yes. Task Group Alfa was a step change in analysis as compared to the Sixth Fleet. We had wash-ups and we had discussions. It was a major improvement in that aspect of looking at the exercises, taking them apart, and then deciding what should be done better. I attribute much of that to Hal Bowen, who was a very professional person. He maintained that task force. Of course, he was a surface sailor, but he commanded great respect throughout Task Group Alfa--the aviators, the surface people, the submarine people. Just a great guy.

Q: Do you remember any tactical innovations from that period?

Admiral Long: No, I do not.

Q: For one thing, there was a dedicated antisubmarine plane in the S2F, and I imagine that was part of the picture.

Admiral Long: It was at this time that we developed much more effective air tactics--the use of the S2F and also the use of dipping sonar for helicopters. I attribute Task Group Alfa really with setting those requirements and developing the tactics for them. I am not intimately familiar with those tactics in a non-aviator.

Q: Were there any direct support submarines as part of the task force?

Admiral Long: No, we still had not decided within the submarine force community that we wanted to be part of those carrier task groups. That came later.

Q: So you were an aggressor exclusively.

Admiral Long: Yes. Almost exclusively I was considered to be the target.

Q: What was your success rate?

Admiral Long: My recollection was that the ASW capability of the United States Navy still had not achieved a great measure of effectiveness. As a result, Sea Leopard, more often than not, was able to penetrate to the point where we units of the task group.

Q: That's great for the morale of your crew and building a team.

Admiral Long: Oh, yes, yes. Good morale on <u>Sea Leopard</u>. About halfway through my tour, I took the ship to Portsmouth, New Hampshire, for overhaul. We didn't get any significant improvements in capability, but essentially work on the hull, work on the main pumps and valves. That overhaul lasted about three months. This time I did not take my family. We had two children now, and they were in school. So my family stayed in Norfolk and I would commute many weekends.

While at Portsmouth, I took up woodworking as a hobby. One of the things I produced was a small three-legged candle table. I was very proud of this work, so I wrapped it up in a pillow case and got on the train in Portsmouth, going to Boston to take it home to Sara. A little old lady sitting across from me kept eyeing this package, kept looking at it. After about 15 minutes she said, "Excuse me, but what do you have in there?"

And in sort of smart-aleck way I said, "It's a submachine gun."

She immediately threw her nose up in the air and looked out the window. [Laughter]

Q: Did you still have a deck gun in the boat?

Admiral Long: No. They'd all been removed.

Q: By this time, did the submarines have the more streamlined sails?

Admiral Long: Yes. We were Guppyized with snorkel, streamlined, had what at that time was high-speed propulsion. The test depth was not what it is today, but still deeper than the World War II submarine's test depth. It was a great improvement over the fleet boat. It did have the speed. It did have the potential endurance to stay submerged, but it still lacked the great mobility of nuclear power.

Q: This is the time when the Nautilus was coming along. I presume you were following that development closely.*

Admiral Long: Yes. As a matter of fact, Nautilus went to sea during this time. Around January of 1956, Nautilus came to Norfolk and tied up alongside Sea Leopard. Coming

---

*The USS Nautilus (SSN-571), the Navy's first nuclear-powered submarine, was commissioned 30 September 1954. She was 324 feet long, 28 feet in the beam, and displaced 3,533 tons. She had a top speed on the surface of 22 knots and undisclosed higher speed submerged. She was armed with six 21-inch torpedo tubes.

in, Nautilus had made a rather sloppy landing and rammed Sea Leopard, which gave it a good dent. The next morning, several of us went to sea in Nautilus. This was the first time I had been aboard a nuclear-powered submarine. When Nautilus was backing out of the slip, she again hit Sea Leopard and took a screw off. After that we were known as the "USS Bumper." [Laughter]

But that one-day trip in the Nautilus really impressed me with the advantages of nuclear power, the ease with which you could go ahead and increase speed. And, of course, Nautilus was a Model-T version of what we have today, but it was such a dramatic improvement over the old diesel boats that I became convinced at that time that the United States Navy needed to go nuclear for its submarines. The case is overwhelming for submarines, nuclear power.

Q: Hydrodynamically, she didn't have the shape that later proved optimum for the nuclear submarine.

Admiral Long: No, she was not designed to optimize the hydrodynamic shape. Of course, we had built at that time Albacore, and Albacore was in Portsmouth at the same time that I had Sea Leopard there.* I had also put to sea in

---

*The diesel submarine Albacore (AGSS-569) was commissioned in December 1953 as an experimental vessel to test the feasibility of the teardrop-shaped hull. The test was successful, and the hull shape has since become standard.

Robert L. J. Long #2 - 149

<u>Albacore</u>, and she handled just magnificently. That's where we had controls that looked very much like aircraft controls, and the <u>Albacore</u> hull design was, of course, later embodied in <u>Skipjack</u> and subsequent submarines.

Q: I haven't seen her, but I understand she's back up there now as a museum and memorial in Portsmouth.

Admiral Long: I'm not aware of that, but she clearly was almost as important in the development of submarines as nuclear power.

Q: Was Wilkinson still the skipper when the <u>Nautilus</u> rammed you?*

Admiral Long: Yes. Yes. And whenever I see him, I normally remind him of his rather inadequate seamanship.

Q: Oh, he must be delighted to hear that. [Laughter]

Admiral Long: Oh, he has a great sense of humor, and we are still very close friends.

Q: I would hope that that was sort of atypical for him and for the <u>Nautilus</u>.

---
*Commander Eugene P. "Dennis" Wilkinson, USN, who was the first commanding officer of the <u>Nautilus</u>.

Admiral Long: Oh, sure.

One of the principal jobs for the <u>Nautilus</u>, and Wilkinson did it magnificently, was to take visitors to sea in order to demonstrate this nuclear power. I remember one time I was talking to Dennis. I said, "How in the world do you do this? You do it with such grace and hospitality."

He said, "Well, I decided a long time ago that when someone asks me to do something, I look at it to see whether it should be yes or no. If it comes up yes, even though it's not overwhelmingly yes, then I always go ahead and play that like I'm delighted. Then we bust ourselves in order to do a good job. There's no mediocre response. If it's a mushy no, then I go back and I say, 'Absolutely not. We cannot do it.' I mean, there are no in-betweens on that."

Q: You either do a great job or not at all.

Admiral Long: Precisely. And that's not a bad philosophy, because if you're going to do it, you might as well do a good job. Because if you do a half-hearted job, people will know it, and there's no benefit for you putting out all that effort. So that was a good philosophy he had, and it's one that I probably use today.

Robert L. J. Long #2 - 151

Q: Slade Cutter told me he visited the <u>Nautilus</u> also in that period, and the respect that Wilkinson's men had for him bordered on awe.*

Admiral Long: Yes. Well, they probably played poker with him.

Q: I would think he would be too kind to take their money. [Laughter] But he said there was a genuine respect for him throughout the boat.

Admiral Long: Well, I've known him really from that period, and, of course, subsequently I've relieved him twice, first as ComSubLant and then as the DCNO for submarine warfare.** So I have a great respect for him.

Q: Any other insights on his personality?

Admiral Long: I think if you know Dennis, you recognize that he has probably one of the sharpest minds of anyone that you'll ever meet. He's part politician. He knows how to get things done, and that's not said in a derogatory way.

---
*This was covered in the oral history of Captain Slade D. Cutter, USN (Ret.).
**ComSubLant--Commander Submarine Force Atlantic Fleet; DCNO--Deputy Chief of Naval Operations.

Q: That bears on your earlier comment about entertaining visitors.

Admiral Long: Right. Right. He also is a dedicated family man, and we have a great respect and love for Janice, his wife. Interestingly, to show how small the world is, I sat on the St. John's College board in Annapolis and Santa Fe, and his daughter sits on that same board. So he has kept himself busy.

He has truly been a dedicated nuclear-power person. He was the one that set up the nuclear power monitoring office down in Atlanta, Georgia--NPO. That was an organization that the electric utilities funded and set up to act as a watchdog on their own operations. He set that up and it resulted in a much tighter control, a higher level of operation and training, professionalism within the electric utility outfit. It's too bad that this had not been set up and operating strongly at the time of Three Mile Island.* If it had been, we never would have had Three Mile Island. So he has contributed significantly to the nuclear power business. He continues to contribute even today. He lives out in California. I think very highly of him.

---

*In 1979 a partial melt-down occurred in the civilian nuclear power plant at Three Mile Island, near Pittsburgh.

Q: With the Sea Leopard, you were taking command for the first time. What can you say about the satisfactions and the responsibilities and so forth that one feels?

Admiral Long: Well, Paul, I must admit that I like being in charge. Some people do not like to take responsibility. I'm sure you have seen them, as I have seen them. That doesn't bother me. I felt a great sense of satisfaction having this small command and knowing that I had control over not only that ship, the safety of the ship, but also the life and well-being of the crew. It was a challenge, and also it was a great source of satisfaction for me to be able to mold that crew and develop a strong, strong sense of loyalty to each other. We performed, I thought, well as a group.

There are also some unpleasant aspects to any job of leadership. Every now and then someone turns up who is not appropriately a member of that crew, and that's a hard decision in order to disqualify him and get him off, but those instances are few and far between.

Q: You don't need many of those to set an example for everyone else.

Admiral Long: That's correct. Far more instances occur where you have people who are dedicated, who are qualified, who are getting promoted. Those are sources of great satisfaction. Of course, later on in my life in the Navy, to have young people work for me and then subsequently see them do well, it's one of the great sources of pleasure that I've had. When you really look upon those youngsters who are moving up, you see that a piece of yourself is there.

Q: In my discussion with Yogi Kaufman, he saw the advent of nuclear power almost as a watershed in the types of crewmen that served in submarines.* Before that, there was the World War II type, maybe comparable to these boatswain's mates and other sailors that you encountered. And afterward they were better educated, more technically oriented and so forth. Does that square with your own experience?

Admiral Long: I wouldn't put it that strongly, Paul. I think that the submarine community has always been known for its professionalism and high state of training and readiness. Diesel boat submariners also were very highly trained, and what we see in nuclear power is really an extension or a continuation of past submarine history. We are stronger because of the submarine operations in World War II, as an example. So I do not see that the nuclear

---
*Vice Admiral Robert Y. Kaufman, USN (Ret.), coauthor of Sharks of Steel (Annapolis: Naval Institute Press, 1993).

submarine force is a different submarine force than the diesel submarine force. It's all one submarine force. Another example is the Nautilus, which was a different technology than what we have in Seawolf that is about to start operating today. We have different weapons, we have different tactics, we have different missions and roles. I think it's incorrect to look upon the nuclear submarine force as entirely different from a diesel submarine force.

Q: But partly that's probably a matter of perception.

Admiral Long: Yes. But I think that the people who consider that they are not a product of the old submarine force are entirely incorrect.

Q: Certainly one of the Navy's strong points is tradition, and it sells it every day of the year.

Admiral Long: Right.

Q: Did you deploy to the Med in that submarine?

Admiral Long: No, Sea Leopard did not deploy. We went on a variety of fleet exercises, operating primarily with Task Group Alfa. Of course, we made Guantánamo and up and down the coast and all of that, but we did not get to the Mediterranean. I guess that's one of the areas in my career that I'm not all that knowledgeable about. My experience has been Pacific, the Atlantic, but not so much in the Mediterranean.

Q: What do you remember of family life there in Norfolk?

Admiral Long: We bought a home near Ward's Corner, really in the same area that we lived before when I was exec of <u>Cutlass</u>. It was a very nice bungalow. We had gone from our $9,000 house in Chapel Hill and we now were up to about $17,000 or $18,000.

Q: That was big money back then.

Admiral Long: Yes. [Laughter] We had invested--I was about to say wisely, but we just invested--and so we did have enough money to put down on a $17,000 house. I guess this was a good three-bedroom, two-bath house, one-car garage, in a nice neighborhood, and it was close enough that our children could get to school. They went to a little school near Ward's Corner. It was very nice living.

Of course, at this time, going to sea and being away from home, I would have to say again that really puts a challenge to the family. Sara has done that extremely well, and I'll have to say very candidly if it hadn't been for her, I doubt very much if I would have gotten very far myself.

Q: How much of an interest did your boys take in your service?

Admiral Long: They essentially lived submarines. Occasionally we would have opportunities to take the families to sea, and they went to sea a couple of times. I don't think I really convinced them that they should go into submarines. Later on, my number-two son did go to the Naval Academy and did go into submarines and served in <u>Skipjack</u>. But family separation was not for him and his wife, and he subsequently got out of the Navy, went to medical school, and is now a doctor in New York City.

Q: Quite a change. [Laughter]

Admiral Long: So I don't know if his wife sees him any more now being a doctor than she did before.

Q: You mentioned some of the crew members you were with and other submarines. Any that particularly stand out from the <u>Sea Leopard</u>?

Admiral Long: Here again, the chief of the boat stands out, Sam Boyten. My exec was Lionel Goulet, whom we called "Lefty." He and his wife are still very close friends. He put in 20 years and left the Navy and practices law in Chicago. One of my young officers was Christy Emerson. He was a Yale graduate, very fine family from Philadelphia. Here again, sort of an all-American boy, smart, good athlete, fine character. He had a girlfriend in Philadelphia and she would come down. We would see her and she would stay with us. It's interesting that she subsequently then married a lawyer in New York, and he and I sit on the same corporate board. We were flying in a company aircraft, the first time that I had just joined the board, and we were en route to Palm Springs for a board meeting.

This lady came up and she said, "Didn't you have command of Sea Leopard at one time?"

I said, "Yes."

And she said, "I used to visit you." She was the same gal that had dated Christy Emerson. So it's a real small world.

Q: Indeed it is.

Admiral Long: As I say, some of those contacts that you make you keep forever, and they're very good contacts.

Q: How did your ship handling compare with Commander Wilkinson's? [Laughter]

Admiral Long: [Laughter] Well, I'll have to say, Paul, that I was not the best ship handler, but I was normally able to get it in and out of port without ramming anyone. But submarines don't handle all that well.

Of course, when they built the early SSBNs, such as Patrick Henry, they put something on there that was absolutely marvelous. It was sort of an outboard motor that you could lower like a sonar head, and you could train it 360 degrees. It was really a thruster. You could come in at 90 degrees and essentially swing your stern around. So that helped poor ship handlers. But submarine officers don't have the same amount of opportunity to maneuver ships, as you would in, say, a destroyer. You go out at sea for long periods of time, then you come in, and it's an unusual event.

Q: We've talked about the evolution of radar and sonar. Were the torpedoes still essentially the short-range torpedoes of World War II?

Admiral Long: Yes.

Q: So you had to get in very close.

Admiral Long: Yes, that's right. I think it was the Mark 45. They had two speeds, high speed and low speed. The high-speed maximum range was not more than 4,000 yards, low speed maybe almost double that.

Q: And the technology was still a long way from the homing type or wire-guided of today.

Admiral Long: Yes. And, of course, it was about this time that we still had the Mark 18, which was an electric-driven torpedo, very quiet but very slow. We were also at this time developing the nuclear-tipped torpedo. I remember reading about it, and I came across the statement that the probability of significant damage to your own ship if you shot one of these was not much more than 10%. I said to myself, "You mean I have a one in ten chance of sinking myself if I shoot this?" I decided then that I doubted very much if I would ever shoot one.

Q: Right. [Laughter]

Admiral Long: But that was at the time when nuclear weapons were considered the panacea for a lot of things.

Robert L. J. Long #2 - 161

Q: It was only later really that it got into the idea that they were primarily a deterrent. I think the idea in the Fifties was these were to be used.

Admiral Long: Yes.

Q: And probably there was some serious discussion about their use in Korea, for example.

Admiral Long: We'll talk more about nuclear weapons later, since I have been heavily involved in advising the Secretary of Defense on where we should go.

Q: Well, any more on that boat to discuss?

Admiral Long: No, no. It was a very, very delightful, very rewarding experience, and as my first command I was blessed to have people that knew what they were doing, and it was good training for me.

Q: Then you had to do your penance by going to OpNav.*
[Laughter]

Admiral Long: [Laughter] Yes. Here again, that was a fascinating tour for me. We moved the family up and we

---
*OpNav--the extended staff of the Chief of Naval Operations.

didn't have a lot of money. We did sell that house in Norfolk for $18,000. So we made a lot of money--$1,000. But we couldn't find anything in Washington that we could afford, so we decided to rent. We rented a house on Hanover Street in Springfield, Virginia. My recollection is that we paid something like $150.00 a month. I guess at that time I was a lieutenant commander, and we lost money. We could not save any money living in Washington at that time. That was before they made the pay raises.

Q: And you didn't draw submarine pay ashore either.

Admiral Long: No. No. So we moved in there, and I'd say at the end of two years we had dipped into what savings we had. That was not a very encouraging thing if you're looking for the long haul.

Within OpNav, I was assigned to an outfit called OP-311. At that time OP-311 was submarine warfare. Of course, until recently, it has been OP-02, a separate Deputy Chief of Naval Operations. But it was then in OP-03. OP-03 dealt with all fleet operations and readiness headed by a naval aviator, Admiral Combs.* Within OP-03 they had undersea warfare, which included submarines and also ASW, mine warfare, research and development in undersea warfare. OP-31 was headed by an old friend of

---

*Vice Admiral Thomas S. Combs, USN.

mine, Rear Admiral Freddy Warder.*

OP-311 spoke for all submarine warfare requirements. It was headed by a great guy, Pete Galantin, who was captain at that time, and he was subsequently replaced by Captain Frank Walker.** OP-311 was organized very much as a submarine wardroom. We had a captain. We had an exec, who was Fred Taeusch.*** We had a weapons officer. We had an engineer. We had an ops officer. And that's the way we operated.

I, first of all, started out as sort of the ops officer, handling special operations and all that. Bob McWethy, who was the engineer, was out of the class of '42.**** Charlie Rush, who is out of the class of '41, was the weapons officer.***** Charlie left shortly after I got there, and I became the weapons officer. We also had during the time I was there Jon Boyes, who subsequently became Vice Admiral Jon Boyes.****** And Marmaduke Bayne, who was subsequently also a vice admiral.******* So it was a pretty good training ground for future senior officers in there.

---

*Rear Admiral Frederick B. Warder, USN.
**Captain Ignatius J. Galantin, USN. Captain Francis D. Walker, Jr., USN.
***Commander Frederick L. Taeusch, USN.
****Commander Robert D. McWethy, USN.
*****Commander Charles W. Rush, USN.
******Lieutenant Commander Jon L. Boyes, USN.
*******Commander Marmaduke G. Bayne, USN.

Robert L. J. Long #2 - 164

Q: It also sounds as if they picked people that had potential.

Admiral Long: Well, I would like to think so. But I'd say that the principal accomplishment during those two years that I was there was to set the requirements and really start the development of Polaris. During this time that we had Galantin and Walker in OP-311, I was the action officer. Hal Shear was down in the OP-06, which was strategy and plans.* Paul Backus, Pappy Sims, and Worth Scanland were involved.** Some of the things that we did at that time had a profound impact on the subsequent development of Polaris.

Q: Please tell me.

Admiral Long: We had the Polaris office, and that was, of course, Red Raborn, and Levering Smith was the technical director of that.*** When Polaris first started out, it was not embraced by the submarine community, because the planning at that time was still for a liquid-propellant missile. About the time that I got there, we then decided that we could make a solid-propellant missile. That was

---
*Commander Harold E. Shear, USN.
**Commander Paul H. Backus, USN; Commander William E. Sims, USN; Captain Francis Worth Scanland, USN.
***Rear Admiral William F. Raborn, USN; Captain Levering Smith, USN. The Polaris recollections of Raborn are included in the Naval Institute oral history collection.

one thing. Other components were small nuclear warheads and, of course, nuclear power, in order to make the Polaris system possible. We still had to answer a number of questions. How many of these things do we build? What's the operational concept? Do we have three crews, two crews, one and a half crews? What have you.

I can remember meetings that we had with Admiral Burke, who was the CNO, with Freddy Warder and myself, and we had Hal Shear and his boss, and, of course, OP-05.* I can still remember Admiral Burke saying, "Well, I don't know how many of these things we ought to build. It seems to me that maybe 40, something like that. And I think we should be able to do it for maybe, $5 billion. Why don't you go off and look at it."

Well, when we came back to Admiral Burke, we said we should build 41, and we probably could be able to do it for about $5.5 billion dollars. So I don't know which was the chicken and which was the egg there, but Admiral Burke was a very strong supporter. Without his support and that of Secretary Gates, we never would have gotten the system off the ground.** Of course, the President at that time also decided that this was the way to go.***

---

*Admiral Arleigh A. Burke, USN, served as Chief of Naval Operations from 17 August 1955 to 1 August 1961. OP-05 was the Deputy Chief of Naval Operations (Air).

**Thomas S. Gates, Jr., served as Secretary of the Navy from 1 April 1957 to 7 June 1959.
***Dwight D. Eisenhower served as President of the United States from 20 January 1953 to January 1961.

Q: I've heard that Gates had an unusual degree of understanding for a service secretary.

Admiral Long: That's right, he did. He really understood this program very, very well. And, of course, that was caused in large measure because Red Raborn was probably the most effective salesman we had. His job was to sell it. I can remember subsequently talking to Freddy Warder, who said, "Red, I don't know where we're going to get the money for these training facilities and all these things that you're talking about."

And Red said, "Freddy, when this system goes, they're going to give me the keys to Fort Knox." Of course, it turned out pretty well that was true.

Q: He had been given that sort of assurance by Admiral Burke, so he had some sense of backing. [Laughter]

Admiral Long: [Laughter] That's right.

One of the things that we developed in OP-311 was where we were going to operate these things. We did a lot of studies and looks, and we finally decided that because of the limited range of these missiles, we had to deploy them from forward bases. That started the discussions with the U.K., and we finally settled on Holy Loch, Scotland.*

Another major decision was how do we man these things. We went back and forth, and I finally presented a paper which made the case for two crews. The real reason for that was with anything other than two crews, then the question of accountability and who is responsible, you get it lost. If you had a crew and a half, for instance, how do you hold one crew accountable for something that didn't quite go right? There also is a psychological factor, and that is, I'm one crew, you're another crew. I'm not going to turn over something to you that's no good. There is going to be a certain amount of pride in what I turn over to you. And that's what actually happened. The material condition of the SSBNs actually went up over a one-crew ship.

Q: It's a sense of rivalry.

Admiral Long: That's right. I mean, later on when I had command of the gold crew of Patrick Henry, there wasn't any question we were better than the blue crew, we thought.

Q: That's interesting. I didn't get that viewpoint from Admiral Shear.** [Laughter]

---
*U.K.--United Kingdom.
**Admiral Shear, who was commanding officer of the blue crew for the Patrick Henry (SSBN-599), has also been interviewed for the Naval Institute's oral history program.

Admiral Long: I know. [Laughter] But my relations with him, that's also an interesting subject. So Holy Loch, Scotland, two crews, the amount of the patrol time, essentially two months out, one month in, when you turn over the crew, have at-sea trials, upkeep--those were all worked out there. Shortly there we had a squadron commander designated, and that was N. G. Ward, Bub Ward.* We could not have had a better one. I mean, he was innovative. He was tough. God, I would have hated to work for him. But he was smart enough to listen to his skippers, and, as a result, procedures and policies were laid down that have served us well.

Q: Tough in what ways?

Admiral Long: Oh, I mean, if you were on his staff, he was absolutely demanding, and he was demanding really to give the maximum support to those boats alongside. He worked the tender mercilessly. He would say to his staff people, "Don't tell me you can't do that. That submarine needs it. Now do it!" So, as I say, he was an ideal guy for this brand-new weapon system that came about.

We continued through this process of developing the

---

*Captain Norvell G. Ward, USN. Ward, who retired as a rear admiral, has also been interviewed as part of the Naval Institute's oral history program.

requirements and laying down the training procedures, off-the-boat training for the off crew. Those were some major things that we established as requirements for New London. And, of course, the whole concept was that the crews and their families would live in New London. The submarine crew members would be ferried over to Holy Loch, Scotland, in order just to take charge of the boat, to get it ready and take it to sea. And that worked out very, very well.

During this time, Red Raborn and Levering Smith did some of the critical testing. We also had Bob Wertheim, who subsequently became the head of SP.* He was in charge of the missile development itself. So it was also interesting that today if you want to develop and deploy a major weapon system such as Polaris, you should count on at least 15 years.

It's interesting that here we were in 1956 laying down the requirements for this weapon system, and the first one deployed at the end of 1960. Now, that tells you a little something about what's happened to our acquisition system, the amount of time that it takes to develop and produce a major weapon system. You also need to remind yourself that cost is directly related to the time it takes to develop

---

*Lieutenant Commander Robert H. Wertheim, USN. The oral history of Wertheim, who retired as a rear admiral, is in the Naval Institute collection. SP stands for the Special Projects office, which ran the Polaris program.

Robert L. J. Long #2 - 170

something. So the longer it takes for development and production, the greater is the cost. So it seems to me that one of the things that should be done today is to revisit Polaris and see if there are things that we can learn in order to breed life into this defunct acquisition system that we have today.

Q: That was certainly not a business-as-usual process.

Admiral Long: No, it had the highest priority. Highest priority.

Q: Somebody said it depended on a series of miracles being performed in succession. [Laughter]

Admiral Long: [Laughter] Well, subsequently, in my conversations with Levering Smith, whom I greatly respect, we talked about the risk involved in development. The probability of success, for a missile at that time was not considered much better than 80%. In other words, 20 missiles out of a hundred we would expect would fail. And Levering is quite eloquent about the cost and the time involved when you go from an 80% probability of success to 90%. And, of course, it goes up tremendously when you go from 90% to 95%, and it's completely unrealistic to develop a complex weapon system and try to seek 100%. You can't afford it. So that essentially took most of my time.

Q: What was your specific piece of this whole big pie?

Admiral Long: I was the action officer for the submarine community from the standpoint of operational requirements. It was from our shop that we developed the concept of operation. It was our shop that developed the manning of the ship, the training facilities, the location of the squadron. We spoke from the operational side.

Q: Paul Backus has been called one of the unsung heroes in this. What do you remember of his role?

Admiral Long: Paul was, I'd say, more from the technical side. Even today, OpNav generates requirements, sponsors programs, and develops the budget. OP-05 was really the sponsor of the missile budget and the Polaris budget, and from there you had, say, oversight of the development of the Polaris missile and the navigation system and all the rest of that. Where we were primarily concerned was how the system would work. We weren't primarily concerned with whether the missile would be 1,500 miles or 1,400 miles. That was a technical thing. We were told that we would receive a missile that would do certain things, and then we figured out how we were going to use it.

Robert L. J. Long #2 - 172

OP-06, on the other hand, was very much interested in the strategic application--the targeting and that kind of thing.* So probably today you would have a different set of responsibilities of the various OpNav codes. But at that time the missile was considered part of the aviation budget. Of course, the cruise missiles were sponsored down there--Regulus I, Regulus II. We also had a third cruise missile that was being developed before Polaris came on the scene, and that was the Triton. We had submarines dedicated to those cruise missiles. Pappy Sims, who subsequently had command of Theodore Roosevelt--the submarine, not the carrier--worked with Paul Backus on the technical end of the missile development.**

Q: You said Captain Ward was demanding. If anything, Backus has been portrayed as even more demanding.

Admiral Long: That's right. Well, I remember him as extremely supportive of this program. And, of course, he was not a submariner.

Q: But he enlightened me on so many areas that I hadn't thought of, like doing the underwater surveys so there

---
*OP-06--Deputy Chief of Naval Operations (Plans and Policy).
**Commander William E. Sims, USN, was commanding officer of the blue crew when the USS Theodore Roosevelt (SSBN-600) was commissioned in February 1961.

Robert L. J. Long #2 - 173

would be maps of the ocean bottom.

Admiral Long: Right. Sort of those technical requirements for that.

Q: And even getting the survey ships and disguising them in the budget, and then working on communications frequencies and getting diplomatic clearances for other countries and so forth. There were a lot of things that had to be done at the same time.

Admiral Long: Right. This was a time where we had great cooperation between the submarine force and OP-05, the naval aviation community, where we had the sponsorship of the missile itself. The OP-06 people, who were the strategic plans people, and the OP-03 people, who were the operational requirements people, none of this would have worked well, in my opinion, if we had not had the strong personal support of Admiral Burke and Tom Gates.

Q: And it also helped sell it to the aviation community that Raborn was an aviator.

Admiral Long: Yes, I agree with that. I really learned to admire him, because he was such a persuasive, aggressive person. He could sell an Eskimo ice cubes. He was an

Robert L. J. Long #2 - 174

optimist. And, of course, he was the one that set up a management system that in many ways was a model for other programs, not only in the Department of Defense, but in the business community, called the PERT system.*

Q: It's a system of milestones and objectives.

Admiral Long: Yes. I've lived with it for a long time. Of course, later on when I came back to Washington, I spent a year in SP as sort of the operational guy, the requirements guy, over there. So I read PERT.

Q: Did you get to spend time on any other submarine matters, or was this a consuming thing?

Admiral Long: Oh, yes. This was also the time when Nautilus went to the North Pole.** The Skate also went up there. We had some special operations that were going on at that time. Of course, I was sort of the action officer on some of those things. Admiral Don Felt, was the Vice Chief.*** As I said, I was a lieutenant commander, and I used to go up with Admiral Warder to brief the Vice Chief on some of these special operations. My impression was

---
*PERT--Program Evaluation Review Technique.
**On 3 August 1958 the Nautilus became the first ship to go under the North Pole submerged.
***Admiral Harry D. Felt, USN, served as Vice Chief of Naval Operations from 1 September 1956 to 28 July 1958.

that Don Felt loved to eat rear admirals for breakfast.

Q: And then picked his teeth with lieutenant commanders. [Laughter]

Admiral Long: Right. [Laughter] I remember he loved to needle Freddy Warder. We'd go in there, and Admiral Felt would say, "Well, Freddy, how are your little submarines today?" I could see the red just rise up Admiral Warder's neck. [Laughter] But, of course, later on when I became CinCPac, Admiral Felt was living in Hawaii, and he was the sweetest, gentlest, kindest person you could ever imagine. So people change.*

So that was really, I think, a real high point in my life, to participate in the development of this remarkable weapon system.

Q: Did those special operations involve intelligence-gathering?

Admiral Long: Yes. And, then as now, I believe that they are a tremendous source of readiness and combat effectiveness. Those operations were very successful and highly productive. I don't know what we're going to do with them in the future.

---

*Admiral Felt served as Commander in Chief Pacific from 31 July 1958 to 30 June 1964.

Q: That's certainly the stealthy platform, to go collect information.

Admiral Long: It teaches submarines probably better than any other exercise, and that is how to operate in a wartime condition. I think that's about all I can say on that.

Q: Anything that you remember specifically on the North Pole operations?

Admiral Long: Of course, it had tremendous appeal. If you remember, it was not only <u>Nautilus</u> that went to the North Pole, but we also had <u>Skate</u>--Jim Calvert.* And I guess Dennis had been relieved, and Bill Anderson was now the skipper of the <u>Nautilus</u>.** So it was rather spectacular, and the parades and things really brought nuclear power to the attention of the American people dramatically.

Q: How much coordination did you do with ComSubLant and ComSubPac in that job?

Admiral Long: There were an awful lot of telephone calls to make sure that we were kept informed as to what their plans were for those jobs. By this time, I guess the ops job had gone to Duke Bayne, and he was the one that really

---
*Commander James F. Calvert, USN.
**Commander William R. Anderson, USN.

was following those operations very, very closely. Duke Bayne now lives down in Northern Neck. Do you know Marmaduke Bayne?

Q: I've certainly heard of him.

Admiral Long: A great guy. So that is the summary of my first tour in OpNav, which was a real eye-opener. From there I went on to work for Freddy Warder, who was then ComSubLant up in New London, Connecticut.

Q: This was before the shift down to Norfolk.

Admiral Long: That was before the shift to Norfolk.

Q: Before Joe Grenfell seized power.* [Laughter]

Admiral Long: That's right. The shift made a lot of sense, because the farther away you are from the throne, so to speak, the more difficult your relationship with the boss becomes. So I was assigned to ComSubLant as the flag secretary.

Q: Admiral Warder must have admired your work to take you

---

*Vice Admiral Elton W. Grenfell, USN, was Commander Submarine Force Atlantic Fleet from 1960 to 1964.

up there.

Admiral Long: That was the third time. [Laughter] You would have thought he would have learned better. But went up, and he was a great boss. He was Mr. Submarine.

Q: What made him a great boss?

Admiral Long: Well, he knew submarines. He had a great rapport with the staff. He didn't sit up in this ivory tower. People could come in and talk to him. He had a fiery temper, but at the same time he was a guy that you could talk to. I just thought he was great, having worked with him. He probably wasn't as political as he could have been.

Q: Not as political as Grenfell.

Admiral Long: That's right. He was much more outspoken than some of the other admirals. As a result, sometimes he rocked the boat, and I'm sure that was the reason why he never went on to three stars. He did drink a little bit. I always had a great rapport with him. He had a great chief of staff, Joe Enright, who's still a wonderful friend.* Both of them are.

---
*Captain Joseph F. Enright, USN.

Q: Captain Enright is a genial guy.

Admiral Long: He is. A charming man. But Admiral Warder came in pretty grouchy one morning, and I went in and knocked on the door, which was open. He jumped up and he said, "Goddamn it! Why do you come in here and scare me like that all the time?" [Laughter] He proceeded really to snap at me. So I excused myself and left.

So the next morning, on my desk was this cartoon showing the terrible-tempered Mr. Bang talking to his secretary, "Miss Jones, I don't have ulcers; I give ulcers." So he had a great sense of humor. Well, I felt very close to him.

Q: The kind of guy you really enjoy working for.

Admiral Long: That's right. That's right. You always knew where you stood with him. Just a great submarine operational commander, but he was a little bit out of water, as I say, in the Washington political arena.

Q: And I can imagine that it would be more satisfying for him to be king of his own domain there in New London than listening to Admiral Felt.

Robert L. J. Long #2 - 180

Admiral Long: Yes.

Well, this was also the time when we moved the family up. Admiral Warder lived out in a place called Glen Woods. We lived right on a little pond. We rented a house owned by Molly Garnett, and it was an ideal place for the children, right on the pond. We loved to ice skate and paddle around out there. I guess they were starting high school then. Very pleasant living. Very pleasant living.

But this was also the time when I had my first call to see Rickover, and that meeting did not go well.* He was sort of abusive, and he and Warder were at sword's point most of the time. Without going through a lot of words, I did not pass the interview.

Q: Did you get an indication why not?

Admiral Long: Well, he wanted to get into a conversation about why Admiral Warder was just a no-account son of a bitch, and I refused to get involved in that. So he'd throw me out of the office and bring me back.

He said, "Well, are you willing to admit that what a no-good guy he is?"

I'd say, "No, sir."

"Get out of here!"

So it was one of those things, rather degrading. But

―――――――――
*Rear Admiral Hyman G. Rickover, USN, was head of the Navy's nuclear power program.

Robert L. J. Long #2 - 181

a few months later I was called back. I guess he needed people. [Laughter] So he gave me his blessing at that time. So after a fairly short tour as the flag secretary at SubLant, I went back to Washington, rented another house, put the kids back in school, and then went to school at Rickover's knee along with the other PCOs at that time.*

Q: Where had the impetus come from for the interview by Rickover? Had you volunteered?

Admiral Long: No.

Q: You were drafted.

Admiral Long: Right. I was. And there was really a question in my mind whether I wanted to go back for another interview. Some of the senior members of the SubLant staff--Joe Enright and Dave Bell--encouraged me to go back.** They said, "You know, he's not going to be there forever."

Q: How wrong they were.*** [Laughter]

---
*PCOs--prospective commanding officers.
**Captain David B. Bell, USN.
***Admiral Rickover remained on the job until 1982.

Admiral Long: [Laughter] They said, "It's in the best interest of the submarine force. If you can be in it, you should be in it." So with a little flattery, I went back and accepted.

That period of time was fascinating because it's like no other training that the Navy had. You actually went to class with the people who were designing the nuclear submarine's power plant. You had lectures by the guy who was designing the radiation standard. You had lectures by the guy who was designing the reactor. We were talking there essentially to the horse's mouth. We had some dealings with Rickover, not a great deal. I might add that the organization was an extremely professional organization that I admired greatly and continue to.

Rickover was sort of the political mouthpiece, Machiavellian, smarter than hell, manipulating people within the DoD, as well as the Atomic Energy Commission, as well as Congress. He's the guy that facilitated these power arrangements, as well as the money, but the actual staffs that were responsible for the technical design, the standards of construction and operation, those were good people. In other words, there was not any foolishness about them. I really benefited from those standards and that knowledge that I received from the Rockwells and the Mandils and the Panoffs--they were all very, very professional people.* I admired them then and I still do.

Q: They stayed with him a long time.

Admiral Long: Stayed with him a long time. We spent part of that year's training--on two separate occasions, a month at a time--out at Arco, Idaho. That was at the land-based prototype, where we actually then took hands-on training at the nuclear power plant there.

Q: The Navy's equivalent of Siberia.

Admiral Long: Yes, and it was winter also. [Laughter] I can still see the snow on the ground and the steam pipes running along, with jack rabbits all sitting on top of the steam pipes.

Q: How demanding was that training course?

Admiral Long: Well, we essentially lived right at the site, so we didn't travel anyplace. We cooked our own meals. We lived in a Quonset hut. There were three of us that lived together--Paul Lacy, who later was ComSubPac;

---
*Theodore Rockwell is author of The Rickover Effect: How One Man Made a Difference (Annapolis: Naval Institute Press, 1992). Among the other technical people working for Rickover were Harry I. Mandil and Robert Panoff.

Joe Williams, who's a retired vice admiral, who relieved me at SubLant.* Joe had been a short-order cook when he was a teenager, so he was the cook. Paul was the mess cook, so he cleaned up. I was the business manager, and I kept the accounts and ordered the food. They still razz me about my performance. But, here again, the training was a no-nonsense type of thing, very professionally run, and if you really wanted to train somebody how to appreciate, operate, train, nuclear power plants, that year was just great.

The final period was spent at the Bettis Laboratory run by Westinghouse.** This was a further in-depth look at the design operating characteristics of the nuclear power plant that we were going to. Of course, there's the Nautilus plant; there was the Seawolf plant; there was the Skate plant; there was the Skipjack plant, which was essentially the same as the early Polaris submarines. So there were all those different types of nuclear power plants.

So we went there, and it was about this time that Sara had our third child, Robert, at the Army hospital at Fort Belvoir.*** We had also done a little planning ahead. Fortunately, this time I knew that I was going to command the gold crew of the Patrick Henry, and we had made

---
*Commander Paul L. Lacy, USN; Lieutenant Commander Joe Williams, Jr., USN.
**Bettis Atomic Power Laboratory, near Pittsburgh.
***Robert Helms Long, born 15 January 1960. Fort Belvoir is near Mount Vernon, Virginia.

arrangements to build a house in this Glen Woods area in Gales Ferry, Connecticut.* As a matter of fact, with the help of my father-in-law, we drew up the plans and built that delightful little house. It was so successful that a bunch of these other people who were PCOs also did the same thing.

Q: Did you have franchise operation? [Laughter]

Admiral Long: Well, they accused me of getting 10% right off the top, but it was only 5%! [Laughter] But we had this community up there: Paul Lacy, who had command of Ethan Allen; Joe Williams, who had command of Robert E. Lee; my exec lived right across the street, Harvey Lyon.** So there was a series of us that had homes right up there. I never will forget when we moved up there, Harvey had already arrived and already had the Patrick Henry building. His wife was out in the yard working. So I went over and introduced myself to Marge Lyon, who was a real character.

I said, "I'm Bob Long. Where's Harvey?"

She looked me right in the eye and she said, "He's down on the boat doing the captain's work." [Laughter]

---

*The USS Patrick Henry (SSBN-599) was commissioned 9 April 1960. She was 382 feet long, 33 feet in the beam, displaced 5,900 tons surfaced and 6,700 tons submerged. She was had six 21-inch torpedo tubes and 16 Polaris missile tubes.
**Lieutenant Commander Harvey E. Lyon, USN.

So we then moved in there, and Patrick Henry was about complete. She'd already had her sea trials, and I had gone up for the sea trials with Rickover. Of course, Rickover used to attend all of the initial sea trials. Interestingly, on those initial sea trials we had Edward Teller, and he was really a very influential member of the Advisory Committee on Reactor Safeguards.* Dr. Teller had been opposed to positioning nuclear-powered submarines in U.S. ports. His recommendation was that nuclear submarines needed to be tied up on islands outside the continental United States. We took him to sea in Patrick Henry, along with other members of the advisory committee. At the end of the day, the commission met and voted unanimously to support home-porting these submarines in U.S. ports. That was a very significant event.

Q: What convinced him to change his mind?

Admiral Long: I think principally he was impressed with the quality of the training and performance of the crew. He commented several times that he had never really seen people perform with the professionalism that these people performed. He already knew about the technical performance, he knew about Rickover's team and all that, but the crew, I think, really turned him around.

---
*Dr. Edward Teller had been involved in the development of the atomic bomb during World War II.

Q: How much personal contact did you have with Admiral Rickover during this period, not only training, but then of working up the submarine?

Admiral Long: Admiral Rickover maintained frequent personal contracts with the skippers at that time. The rules required that if anything, anything, abnormal occurred on that nuclear power plant, the skipper was obligated to call Rickover personally, day or night. I'm sure that this rule was followed to the letter by all of the skippers, because at that time he had absolute control over the selection and tenure of skippers. If they didn't follow the rules, he could get them relieved.

He also had a naval reactors representative at the shipyards, and that person was there really to keep Rickover informed of what was going on in the shipyard as well as in the ship building. As I say, Rickover routinely rode along with his key people. He rode every submarine on initial sea trials and put it through its paces and so on, which was fine.

Later on, Rickover started trying to exert greater and greater control over things that were not associated with the nuclear power plant. That's where he and I had some problems. In the case of the Casimir Pulaski's initial sea trials, Rickover rode with me when I was the commanding officer of the blue crew. One of my chiefs did something that was incorrect, and Rickover called me in and demanded that I should fire him and disqualify him, and I refused to do that. I said, "It's an understandable mistake. He's learned his lesson. He's a good man, and I'm not going to do it." Well, that almost became a federal case, but he backed off on that. But that's the kind of intimate detail that he tried to exercise.

Later on, when I was ComSubLant and also when I was the Deputy CNO for Submarine Warfare, he and I had some real knock-down, drag-out fights where he tried to tell me how to do my business. So he was quite a character.

Q: It sounds like he was trying to bully you in that specific example.

Admiral Long: Oh, he was probably the world's outstanding bully. If he could, that just encouraged him to do it more.

Q: On the other hand, if you stood up to him, that would discourage him from doing it more.

I'm interested in how the SSBNs were perceived in the submarine force at the time. Submariners are aggressive, seeking to attack, and this was a submarine that was supposed to go and hide.

Admiral Long: Right. I think it was true then and it is true to some degree today that SSBNs, particularly for skippers, are not considered their number-one choice. I think many officers who are going to command would much rather command an SSN than they would an SSBN. Now, that was particularly true a few years ago where we had the very exciting special operations for SSNs and SSNs also participated in some exercises with the fleet. Now, today I'd say that that situation may be somewhat changing, because the threat for submarines is not all that clear today. It's perceived not to be there, whereas I don't think anyone that is knowledgeable and in some level of authority in Washington would say that the SSBN is unimportant. The SSBN today is clearly proven as the bedrock core for United States nuclear weapons, and I think that this is enhancing the position of the SSBNs because of the greater relative importance of the SSBN.

But your perception is correct that most aggressive young submarine officers, I think, would have preferred to serve on SSNs rather than SSBNs, and that was a problem that some of us certainly recognized when we got into positions of greater authority. That's why we always have that policy of making sure that officers rotate between SSNs and SSBNs, not only because of the excitement or the

Robert L. J. Long #2 - 190

fun of it, but also you don't want to grow a submarine officer community that spends all its time hiding. You want to encourage aggressive behavior on the part of your submarine officers, and so that's why I always insisted that officers should have their fair share of SSN duty and SSBN duty. That's a very important point.

Q: Was it considered a prestigious command?

Admiral Long: Oh, certainly at the beginning, and I'd certainly say it is a prestigious command today. Of course, any nuclear-powered ship in those early days was considered to be very prestigious. Just look at the number of requests for speakers at Rotary or various other organizations. The early skippers had lots of opportunities to get out and speak. As an example, the Marco Polo Club is a very prestigious club at the Waldorf Astoria in New York City. Lowell Thomas was the president of the Marco Polo Club.* In 1961, a certain number of the skippers of those early nuclear-powered submarines were brought down and made honorary members for life. I still am an honorary member of the Marco Polo Club in New York City. Every time I go there, Sara and I normally have a wonderful dinner in this beautiful club, very prestigious club. So it was an exciting time from that point of view.

---

*Lowell Thomas was for many years a radio and television newscaster and narrator for newsreel films.

Q: How much were you able to say on an unclassified basis in those public appearances?

Admiral Long: There were certain things that were not permitted. For instance, we couldn't say much about any depth in excess of 400 feet. We couldn't describe in any detail the nuclear power plant. There were certain restrictions on the nuclear missiles that we couldn't talk about. I don't have the recollection that we were terribly constrained, and it normally was a very interesting talk you could give--in other words, how did the crew live? Can you just go out and shoot those missiles? Of course my answer to that was, "Yes, we could go out and shoot those missiles, but I think if I got up one morning and told the crew that we were going to shoot the missiles today, they'd get a straitjacket and put me in it." But there was a lot of interest, of course, in nuclear power and, of course, this new Polaris system.

Q: A lot of curiosity probably also.

Admiral Long: Yes, that's right.

Q: What measures were used to choose the crew members?

That would require, I think, a special individual, very stable.

Admiral Long: Paul, I don't recall that there were any special screening measures for SSBN crews. At the very beginning, they did have a special medical team formed to follow the crews. For the first couple of years, when we would come in from every patrol, we would be met by these doctors who would come down and talk to the crew. After a while this event came to be a big joke. Some of the crew members would do all sorts of strange things.

Q: Pulling the doctors' legs?

Admiral Long: Pulling the doctor's leg. [Laughter] You know, such things as pulling a stuffed bear or an animal behind them and going along and saying, "Come on. Come on, kitty cat. Come on, kitty cat." I remember we had this one great big machinist's mate. One time the doctor came down the hatch, and this big machinist's mate met him and gave him a great big kiss right on the lips. He said, "I'm so happy to see you." So after a while it became sort of a source of a lot of amusement for the crew. There really wasn't anything to worry about, because the crew, certainly on those early SSBNs, were so busy that they didn't have time for sitting and thinking about being there all that time. Of course, they stood one-third of their time on watch, eight hours a day, and then there was a whole series of drills for all hands. There were lectures. There were qualifications that people had to go through. So they were busy.

Q: And they took their work seriously.

Admiral Long: They took their work very seriously. And that was for all parts of the ship--the missile people, the engineers, the torpedomen, all of them. Of course, in those early days, we really didn't know what the reaction of the Soviets would be, so we took the security of that platform pretty seriously. At that time the SSBNs operated fairly closely to the Soviet Union because of the limited range of the A-1 missile.* Today you can essentially hit targets almost sitting in port. In those early days they were very, very, very, very busy, and I don't recall any real difficulties that were unique to the SSBNs. I don't recall any difficulties with the people.

Now, also there were things that were done on individual submarines. As an example, Commander Pappy Sims, who had command of the Theodore Roosevelt, was a great hydroponics fan. He and his crew grew tomatoes and all sorts of vegetables with this hydroponic business. I

---
*The A-1 version of the Polaris remained in service until late 1965; it had a range of approximately 1,500 miles.

think all of the crews would all have one or two happy hours, you know, where they would actually put on performances. That was always sort of a welcome break.

All throughout the patrol, you would be interrupted at various times when you would have exercise alerts. Then you'd essentially go through the entire process of launching the missiles, except, of course, you wouldn't open the outer doors and you wouldn't shoot them. Those exercises were all carefully written up. We spoke earlier about analysis of operations. One of the things that Levering Smith did at this time was set up at the Applied Physics Laboratory at Johns Hopkins University an intense program to analyze each patrol. That still goes on, and there is an awful lot of payoff from that.

Q: Did these post-patrol analyses by Johns Hopkins entail detailed record keeping during the patrols?

Admiral Long: No. I think we just turned over the various logs that were routinely kept--the sonar log, the ship's log, and, of course, the missile logs. I don't recall that there was any onerous record keeping placed on the crew.

Q: What do you remember about the trials of the Patrick Henry?

Admiral Long: [Laughter] Well, that's another one of those events.

Q: Were both skippers along?

Admiral Long: Yes. Yes. And, of course, the principal event on shakedown was to go to the Cape and shoot what is called a DESO shot--demonstration and shakedown something or other. It was sort of a graduation exercise for the entire ship and crew. The George Washington had previously gone to the Cape and had shot a missile with each crew, and it had gone okay. Patrick Henry Blue shot a missile, and it had gone okay. Then Patrick Henry's gold crew took over around July 1960. We went to sea, and we had more flag officers aboard than we had non-rated men. Chief of Naval Operations Arleigh Burke was on board. We had the Deputy Secretary of Defense. We had the Chief of Naval Personnel. We had ComSubLant and other assorted admirals. Of course, the first missile was heavily instrumented. When we shot the first missile, it went right straight up and then came right straight back down, hit the submarine, broke into pieces. The pieces all came apart up at the surface and started flying around like unguided missiles. One of them put a nice, big dent in the superstructure of Patrick Henry.

So we prepared the second missile to shoot and took about ten hours. We fired it early that evening. That missile went right straight up, and when it got out of the water it exploded in a huge fireball.

Q: Not one of your better days.

Admiral Long: No, and our morale was down around our shoe tops. I never will forget Admiral Burke. He got on the public address system and gave probably one of the finest morale-booster speeches I've ever heard. The thrust of it was that any crew can have good morale when things go well. This crew has worked hard and now it was a challenge for them to maintain their morale when they've had a temporary setback.

So we off-loaded all those senior people and continued on our shakedown. As a tribute to Levering Smith, with all the instrumentation that they had collected, he then came in with what had occurred. Without going into all of the technical details, the instrumentation was at fault. On the first shot, it had prevented first stage ignition signal, so it never received the signal to ignite. They found a similar type thing on the second one. So they corrected those deficiencies, called us back in, and loaded us up with six missiles. We went out into the middle of the Atlantic with Levering Smith and Captain Ward, who was our squadron commander, and Red Raborn. We were escorted by a ship commanded by Elmo Zumwalt.*

We went out there under top secret orders and fired all six missiles downrange. All of them were hot, straight, and normal. So it sort of vindicated not only Arleigh Burke, but it also vindicated Levering Smith's view, and that is that with a development like this, you are learning over time.

Q: You can expect some bugs.

Admiral Long: You can expect some, and if you wait until you get them all worked out, you're going to spend a lot more money and it's going to take you a lot longer. So we had then essentially proven the weapon system. I remember something Bub Ward said on the way in, and this is another characteristic of his. He said, "Now, Bob, tell me. What do you want to change on these things if we're building more of these?"

So I went through and said, "This is no good. We ought to get rid of that," so and so. So we sent in a message, not to ComSubLant, but directly from Patrick Henry to CNO. Well, when we arrived at New London, we were greeted by a representative of ComSubLant, who was Admiral

---

*Commander Elmo R. Zumwalt, Jr., USN, was the first commanding officer of the guided missile frigate Dewey (DLG-14). He was later CNO, 1970-74.

Daspit at that time.* This representative said, "The admiral would like to see you and the Commodore Ward immediately." We then went up and got our fannies chewed out for bypassing this whole chain of command.

He turned to me and he said, "Let me tell you, Long, if skippers weren't so hard to come by, I'd fire you." So, here again, Paul, you've got to have a little luck along the way. [Laughter]

In hindsight, Bub Ward and I were wrong to do that. As I said, Bub was a real supporter of people on the boats, and he sort of had a contempt for those that were outside people. He said, "They don't know anything about it. Why do we fool with them? Let's just send it on to the people that do it." But that's not the way you do business.

Q: He got a little enthusiastic there, carried away.

Admiral Long: That's right. That's right.

Q: Well, you said before that he was demanding and you wouldn't want to work for him. Now you were working for him. What did you find him to be like as a squadron commander?

---

*Rear Admiral Lawrence R. Daspit, USN, served as Commander Submarine Force Atlantic Fleet from 13 January 1960 to 2 September 1960.

Admiral Long: Well, as I said, he was very much demanding on his staff and on those people who were supporting the boats. He went to great lengths to support the commanding officers of the submarines. He thought they were the reason why the staff and the tender existed. So he never really allowed the staff or the tender to complain that they were being worked too hard. This was a typical example when he came to me and said, "What do you want to change?"

Q: But he told me it was a privilege for him to work with such a talented group of skippers.

Admiral Long: Well, he's a great guy, I think. Without exception, his commanding officers had the greatest respect for him.

Q: And because of what he had achieved as a skipper himself. He had a very good war record.

Admiral Long: That's right. That's right.

Q: How much hands-on work did you have to do on the plant, or was that just knowledge so you would know what others were doing?

Admiral Long: Paul, I think it is a fundamental philosophy in the submarine force, and I'd say maybe enhanced in the nuclear submarine force, and that is that for someone to exercise his responsibility, he needs to know what's going on. You can't know what's going on if you don't understand it. Also, I think it is part and parcel of submarine force philosophy and that is that a commanding officer can delegate every bit of authority that he possesses, but he cannot delegate his responsibility. To exercise that responsibility, he must know what's going on. So, as far as I was concerned, I never tried to tell the chief engineer how to do his job, but I expected he would be meticulous in keeping me informed if there were any problems at all developing.

I think most commanding officers believe this, but I never relied on just the chain of command keeping me informed, in other words, the exec or the engineer or the weapons officer or the communicator. I believe that you have to get information wherever you can. Based on that, I was a great believer in walking my ship and talking to the people, taking to the chiefs. I was absolutely careful never to give orders that bypassed that chain of command. If I wanted something changed, I would go to the chief engineer and direct him. But I always felt that I had free license to get information wherever I could. That's the the same philosophy I had when I was the commanding officer of the ship and also as commander in chief of the Pacific theater.

Q: It makes the crew feel good when they see you back in their spaces.

Admiral Long: Yes, I think so. Now, obviously like a lot of things, you can carry that too far. If they're involved in some sort of a complex operation, sort of like Chief King told me in the Colorado, you can sit there and unnerve them to the point where you're looking over their shoulders continuously: "How are doing? How are you doing? How are you doing?" Well, I think you have to show some restraint. But fundamentally, if commanding officers are to be responsible, they have to have some appreciation of how the system works.

Q: What sort of provisions were made for the families of the crew members?

Admiral Long: Jake Laboon, whom I've mentioned before, helped set up the first family support program in New London back in 1960-'61. Guy Leonard, who was also a very famous Protestant chaplain, worked with Jake and really sort of set this thing up.* But we didn't have all of

---
*Lieutenant Commander Guy J. Leonard, CHC, USNR.

that much back then. And, of course, most wives at that time did not work. The situation now is entirely different. Wives work.

Q: What do you remember about the situation going over to Holy Loch, especially with the protesters that were there?

Admiral Long: Well, let's see. I guess it was in March of '61. The blue crew had taken Patrick Henry from New London and had gone on the first patrol. The gold crew flew over to Holy Loch, and I met the ship coming in, way down in the southern entrances to the Clyde estuary, along with Bub Ward. We arrived at Holy Loch alongside the Proteus, the tender. The ship had performed okay, and the gold crew took over.

We were then suddenly engulfed in this huge demonstration, and these were anti-nuke demonstrators. Interestingly, the local people were extremely warm, welcoming, hospitable, yet I sensed that there was some bitter resentment. They had, as they call them, Saxonex, who were from the south, England. We had several incidents where these demonstrators were circling in canoes. We had a wonderful picture of one of them that was able to climb up on the rudder of Patrick Henry; that made the press in a lot of places.

These demonstrations went on for several days. They

were camped over on the hills by us. The local people in Dunoon were very apologetic for this kind of reception. My recollection was that this lasted for several days, but then it really petered out. I don't recall that there were continuing large demonstrations subsequent to that. There were occasional demonstrations by smaller groups of people, but, as far as I know, that was the biggest one that we had. Of course, the Proteus was anchored out in the loch, and we were tied up alongside.* To get to the beach, we had to take a boat to get in.

Q: Did you get involved in the public relations effort of selling the program in the area?

Admiral Long: Yes, not in a heavy way, but I think several of us made calls on the local mayor, who was a wonderful woman, a very strong supporter. And then, of course, I also made calls on the mayor over in Greenoch and Glasgow and some of the other towns.

There were also some very influential people that lived around there. A fellow named David McLean was the British rep in Yugoslavia and was the liaison with Tito.** Of course, he was knighted. He had a beautiful house. We

---
*A painting of the Patrick Henry alongside the Proteus (AS-19) appeared on the front cover of the January 1964 issue of Proceedings.
**Josip Broz, known as Marshal Tito, was President of Yugoslavia at the time.

established very good relations with him. Also the Duke of Argyle lived there right off of Loch Fyne, and several of us used to visit there. They were all very, very hospitable.

Then there was a lady, a widow, who lived in the old McNaughton castle on Loch Fyne. Her name was Margaret Weir, and her father-in-law was Lord Weir, who developed the Spitfire for World War II.* She was a charming lady, and Sara and I visited her. She was a little strange. For instance, she used to tell these silly stories about the ghosts, and then she would say, "But there is something in my bedroom. I'll notice my dog, and he will get very upset, or the cat, and the hair on the cat's back will stand up. And I will feel that there's somebody in that room, and I can feel their presence." But she doesn't believe all the rest of that stuff. [Laughter] We developed some wonderful relationships over there.

Q: Were there any rules about the interaction between the sailors and the local lassies?

Admiral Long: If you looked at the marriage rate, I think that there probably is a good percentage of the submarine wives that are Scottish. As I say, the local people were very, very hospitable, warm.

---

*First Viscount William Douglas Weir. The Spitfire was a well-known British fighter plane.

Q: What do you remember about the relationship with the tender and Captain Laning?*

Admiral Long: Dick Laning is probably one of the brightest, most imaginative naval officers that you'll ever see. My sense is that there was a very good rapport between him and Bub Ward. Between the two of them, they provided outstanding support for those SSBNs. Dick Laning was always available. He would be on the submarine looking to see how his people were doing. I have a tremendous regard for Dick Laning.

Q: Extremely energetic.

Admiral Long: Oh, yes, yes, physically and mentally, particularly mentally. He's got more new ideas in a week than I have in a year.

Q: What was your relationship with your counterpart, Commander Shear?**

Admiral Long: Hal Shear is a wonderful guy. I think if

---
*Captain Richard B. Laning, USN, was commanding officer of the Proteus. He has been interviewed as part of the Naval Institute's oral history program.
**Commander Harold E. Shear, USN, was the first commanding officer of the blue crew of the Patrick Henry.

you just sort of look at that situation where you have a commanding officer of one crew versus a commanding officer of another crew--particularly if one is senior and is there first, like the blue crew--you can easily see that there is a spirit of competition. There also could be a tendency on the part of the senior skipper not to be forthcoming to the junior skipper, and that occurred in some of the submarines.*

But I will say this. Hal Shear bent over backwards to make sure that he treated the blue crew and the gold crew equally well when he had command of both before they split. He offered me every opportunity to bring the gold crew up. There also could be a tendency in that case for the first man to pick the best of the officers. I'll have to say candidly that I thought I had the best pick of the officers. So Hal Shear really set the standard.

Here again, there were no rules, but how were these crews handled? I remember the Robert E. Lee, Reuben Woodall and Joe Williams initially didn't get along very well because they're both very strong-minded people.** Reuben and Joe rode with me on my shakedown, and they witnessed this blue/gold interaction. That, I think, helped change their attitude dramatically. We were plowing

---
*Shear was senior to Long.
**In the USS Robert E. Lee (SSBN-601), Commander Reuben F. Woodall, USN, commanded the blue crew, and Commander Joe Williams, Jr., USN, commanded the gold crew.

new ground, and I think Hal Shear plowed this ground well. The standards were set well by him in that relationship, so I had no problem with him.

Q: Are there any examples you remember of procedures you initiated on doing various evolutions?

Admiral Long: Well, Paul, I think just about everything we did was brand new. [Laughter]

Q: Any examples from those?

Admiral Long: I think just the whole business of establishing procedures for battle stations missile. This was also the time when we had to work out a responsible way to ensure that we acted in accordance with proper authorization from the National Command Authority. How do you handle a valid release message? It was during this time that we actually worked out procedures of getting certain information out of the commanding officer's safe and verifying that with certain people. We went through a process that assured not only the commanding officer that it was valid, but also assured the entire crew that it was valid.

So those were things where we didn't have any rules. As you know, technically there is nothing that will inhibit the crew from actually launching those live missiles. Now, we're probably going to change that as a result of the Kirkpatrick Committee that I served on, but as of today, we do not need any external information to unlock anything, other than a weapon release message.

Q: It's useful, I think, to sketch in the psychological and political background of the era. That was the height of the Cold War. We're talking about the U-2 shootdown and the Kennedy-Khrushchev confrontation in Vienna, the Cuban Missile Crisis.* So people could be very much in the frame of mind that these missiles might be used.

Admiral Long: That's right. Of course, I had command of the Patrick Henry when we did have the Cuban Missile Crisis. At that time, a very high state of readiness was set. We set various conditions of defense, called DefCons. Of course, DefCon One is when you are actually engaged in hostilities. DefCon Two is just minutes or hours before that. While we were in upkeep, DefCon Two was set, and we all went to sea and there was a very high state of readiness. Now, you can speculate as to whether the President would ever have released those nuclear warheads

---

*In 1960 the Soviets shot down a U.S. U-2 photo reconnaissance plane over Soviet territory; at Vienna, Austria, in May 1961 Soviet Premier Nikita Khrushchev bullied President John F. Kennedy; in 1962 Kennedy imposed a quarantine after the Soviets put missiles in Cuba.

or not. Your guess is as good as mine. But I can assure you that the Patrick Henry was ready to launch if we had received orders. That's a pretty scary, pretty scary thing.

Q: I think there was a specific effort to get the ships out of port so they couldn't be targeted, wasn't there?

Admiral Long: That was part of it. But in DefCon Two, automatically the ships go to sea. So it could have been whoever blinked first.

Q: Another thing that was interesting that came out last year on the 30th anniversary was that tactical commanders in Cuba had authority to release nuclear weapons if the island was invaded. So we might have been closer to confrontation than we realized.

Admiral Long: That's right.

I've mentioned before the vital role that senior enlisted people play, and I particularly want to comment about my chief of the boat in Patrick Henry. His name was Sam Bledsoe, called "Cycling Sam."* He was a real character. He was a torpedoman's mate who had conducted maybe eight or nine war patrols, and he was just about as

---
*Chief Torpedoman's Mate Samuel H. Bledsoe, Jr., USN. He eventually retired as a senior chief.

fine a chief of the boat as you can imagine. The crew loved him. He had a great sense of humor. He was very, very tough in standards. He was so good that when I received orders to put the Casimir Pulaski in commission, I asked to take him with me, and he agreed.

We had sort of a typical Sam Bledsoe story as they were sitting there on the outfitting crew for the Casimir Pulaski. We had these partitions, dividing a big room into cubicles for offices. I heard the door open, and I heard Chief Bledsoe say, "What can I do for you, sailors?"

One of them said, "Chief, we're reporting in to Casimir Pulaski."

Chief Bledsoe said, "Like hell you are. You can report in when you get your uniform clean and your hair cut."

A long pause. Finally, one sailor said, "Chief, we don't have any money."

Chief Bledsoe said, "All right, goddamn it. Here's $10.00. Now get the hell out of here." But that was sort of typical Chief Bledsoe.

Q: Where did he get that nickname, "Cycling Sam"?

Admiral Long: He was always in a state of animation. On the Patrick Henry, the chiefs were the diving officers, and he used to have some real experiences when he was the diving officer. He wasn't the most proficient diving officer; he would cycle up to 120 feet, down to 130, and so on. But a great guy. As I said, he went with me to the Casimir Pulaski. Much later on, he died, and the primary enlisted school at the submarine base in New London is named after him, Bledsoe Hall.

Q: That's a high honor.

Admiral Long: Yes, and I dedicated it.

Q: You said you had some very talented officers in that ship. Any of them that you particularly remember?

Admiral Long: In Patrick Henry, at that time we had nuclear-trained officers and non-nuclear submarine officers. I had several of them that were out of Naval Academy class of '53. My navigator was a non-Naval Academy graduate. My exec was Harvey Lyon, and he subsequently made rear admiral. My navigator was Bill Williams, and he made rear admiral.* My chief engineer was Bill Purdum, who made captain, then died shortly after that.** My weapons officer was Art Moreau, and he subsequently made

---
*Lieutenant William A. Williams III, USN.
**Lieutenant William H. Purdum, USN.

four stars.* So that sort of gives you a sense for the quality of those officers.

Q: What are your memories of Moreau as a junior officer?

Admiral Long: He clearly was the most outstanding junior officer that I had, other than Harvey. He loved the theatrical. He loved the Scots, and he would deck himself out in kilts. Very high standards. He ran his department in a very disciplined way.

Q: He was a forceful individual, from my observation.

Admiral Long: He was. He had very high standards. I think that he always resented the fact that he was not chosen as a nuclear officer. But he clearly, I think, among the weapons officers of all of those early crews, he was considered to be the number-one guy. He was the most knowledgeable. He and I had conversations about his future, and early on I said, "Your future is not in the submarine community. My recommendation is get out, establish yourself in the surface Navy. You'll be outstanding there." And that's what he did.

Q: How would you account for him not being chosen for the

---

*Lieutenant Arthur S. Moreau, Jr., USN.

nuclear power program?

Admiral Long: Of course, at that time Rickover was offered up the very best, and blindfolded he could almost just point to that one or that one. Essentially, they were all outstanding, and I think he had to have a certain number that didn't make it. Because I can assure you that as far as Moreau versus some of the nuclear-trained officers I had of the same vintage, Moreau was equal or superior. So it's one of those things. Rickover had to have this mystique that he was somehow a mystic in being able to pick these people. But as I say, if you're sent over the top 5%, it's hard to go wrong.

Q: Admiral Moreau struck me as a very clear example of what's described as a Type A personality, and that may have accounted for his early demise.*

Admiral Long: Possibly. Possibly. But he was a great loss.

Q: You mentioned the exec, Lyon. It's no wonder he did well since his wife said he was doing your work for you.
[Laughter]

---

*Admiral Arthur S. Moreau, Jr., USN, died 8 December 1986 while serving as Commander in Chief Allied Forces Southern Europe. He was 55 years old at the time of his death.

Admiral Long: Harvey Lyon is also an extremely capable officer, very professional. Not a great sense of humor, but hard working. Probably more technical than some. Very loyal. The thing that's interesting about Harvey is his wife. As I told you the story when I first met her, she's a real character, even today, extremely talented. She spends part of her time as a minister, preaches sermons in her church. She also took hula lessons. She took belly dancing. She is a poet. She writes beautifully. We recently had a party. Joe Williams and his wife had their 50th anniversary, and Marge Lyon wrote this magnificent poem describing their lives. She went around and tapped all of their old friends, such as ourselves, to get stories about Joe Williams, and she put all of this in the poetry. She also ran her father's lumberyard after he died in northern Virginia. She's the kind that can look you right in the eye and say, "You're fired." She doesn't flinch.

I remember one time we had a party; in fact, we had a lot of wardroom parties. And she's pretty athletic. She has a great ability to walk on her hands. So I remember a party at our house, and here she comes in leading a parade of two or three other officers in the wardroom, with my pajama bottoms on, walking on her hands. [Laughter] We had some of the crew there who were being paid to sort of help out, and that made her famous in the crew.

Q: She's multi-talented.

Admiral Long: She really is. As I say, she is a real character.

Q: One thing we haven't really talked about would be a typical patrol in the <u>Patrick Henry</u>. How did you go about this business of staying lost, on the one hand, and ready on the other?

Admiral Long: Of course, we would leave the Clyde and take various routes to the patrol area. As soon as we could, we would submerge and essentially stay down for, at that time, about 57, 58 days. It's longer now. We would stay submerged that entire time, and we would immediately go into patrol routine. As I say, men spent eight hours a day on watch, exercising at various drills, such as fire and flooding. Normally we set the clock at a certain time and kept it at that time. We didn't change the clock depending on where we were longitude-wise. But sometimes we did it one way. The crew was a little bit split on that thing. They didn't like having breakfast at midnight.

Most of the patrols were uneventful. Sometimes we would have contacts with Soviet submarines, and that always got your blood pressure up a little bit.

Q: What did you do in a situation like that?

Admiral Long: There were times early on when we really didn't know what was going to happen. We developed procedures for snapshot. Snapshot was where you essentially point one torpedo in a certain direction and shoot--I mean, in a manner of seconds. We exercised at that. There were a couple of times when we had very close contact, and, as I said, we didn't really know what the Soviets were going to do. But if they had taken any hostile action, I think we would have been prepared to fire a torpedo, and we were certainly authorized to do that.

The rest of the patrol was pretty routine, and it was really spent not only in watch standing, but, as I said, in qualification drills and lectures. But I'll have to say that after six patrols or so, I thought it got a little bit boring, particularly if some guy's already qualified and so on. That's why I think we at that time established a policy of purposely rotating a certain percentage of the crew after each patrol. That made a lot of sense, because it prevented us from having to rotate the entire crew after three years.

Q: Did you have the sense that you were detected by the Soviet submarines?

Admiral Long: Never did. Never, never really had any indication that we were detected. We had some pretty close encounters, but we never detected any hostile action on the part of the Soviet submarines.

Q: Why would you be more capable of detecting them than vice versa?

Admiral Long: I think at that time we were quieter, so we had an acoustic advantage. Of course, also at that time, Paul, the operating area was essentially all the way up to North Cape. So those early days were interesting. We were blazing trails.

Q: Did you have any specific measures to fight boredom and loneliness and isolation?

Admiral Long: Of course, I was busy monitoring what was going on and conducting drills. And the crew, as I said, was busy most of the time. They had these entertainment breaks, and they were busy.

Q: Did the doctor and the chief of the boat keep you informed on the state of mental health for the crew?

Robert L. J. Long #2 - 218

Admiral Long: Yes, and in the early days, we carried a medical officer with us. Later on, we shifted to an independent-duty hospital corpsman, who was almost like the chaplain. He was a first class or chief, and he was very sensitive to not just the physical health of the crew, but the mental health of the crew. I don't recall that we had any real problem.

Q: After you had that command, you had another short command, the Casimir Pulaski.* Why did you go from one SSBN to another?

Admiral Long: There was a shortage of more senior submarine officers, nuclear trained, at that point. Also, Admiral Rickover liked to keep those that he had trained as long as possible. He wasn't really interested in their naval careers. He wanted to ensure that he kept them in the nuclear program as long as he could. So having put the Patrick Henry in commission and taken her on several patrols, I then received orders to put the Casimir Pulaski in commission at Electric Boat in New London, Connecticut. And in the summer of '63, I shifted over to Pulaski, and my gold counterpart was Tom Brittain.**

---
*The USS Casimir Pulaski (SSBN-633) was commissioned 14 August 1964. She was 425 feet long, 33 feet in the beam, displaced 7,250 tons surfaced and 8,250 tons submerged. She had four 21-inch torpedo tubes and 16 Polaris missile tubes.
**Commander Thomas B. Brittain, Jr., USN.

The building of the Casimir Pulaski was relatively uneventful. I guess the most significant thing, looking back, and that is that from the time of keel laying until commissioning, it was the shortest building time of a nuclear submarine at EB.* I think it was something like 19 months, so it was done very rapidly. Of course, they were getting to be pretty good at doing this. It was SSBN-633, so that gives you some idea of the number of nuclear submarines that we had built from the 599, the Patrick Henry.

Q: And this was a somewhat new and improved version.

Admiral Long: Yes. This carried a new missile, the Polaris A-3, and it also had improved sonar equipment. It was just a much better submarine. We went through sea trials and shakedown, commissioning, and the ship went on its first patrol. It was then to be operated out of Rota, Spain, and the crew was to be home-ported in Charleston, South Carolina. I never did effect the change of home port. By that time, I was selected for captain, and at the end of my first patrol, I was transferred to the Special Projects Office, and back to Washington we came.

---

*EB--Electric Boat Division, General Dynamics Corporation. The keel for the ship was laid 12 January 1963, and she was commissioned 14 August 1964.

Robert L. J. Long #2 - 220

Q: Do you have any recollections of Rota in comparison with Holy Loch?

Admiral Long: Rota was next to the Rota Naval Air Station, so it was much more accessible then Holy Loch. It also had a tender tied up alongside a pier, so getting on and off the submarine was not the same chore as it was in Holy Loch. I subsequently visited Rota several times, and I have to say I enjoyed the sherry-sampling and I enjoyed the beauty of the place, quite distinct from Scotland, both of them being beautiful. But I came back to Rota several times later on as a member of the Special Projects Office and also as ComSubLant.

Q: Spain has been a sometimes reluctant partner in NATO. How did that factor play in the hospitality and so forth?

Admiral Long: I was fairly well removed from the political aspects of it. The people that I saw were very warm and gracious. But you're correct. Even at that time, there were groups that were opposed to having nuclear submarines and nuclear missiles in Spain, and, of course, as a result of that, plus the increase in the range of SSBN missiles, we subsequently pulled out of Rota, Spain, as a submarine base.

Robert L. J. Long #2 - 221

Q: One of the events in April of the year 1963 was the loss of the Thresher.* What kind of impact was felt in the submarine community from that?

Admiral Long: I think most people believed that Thresher was lost because of inadequate quality control for what we would call the secondary salt water systems. Those were the systems that were not directly under the control of Admiral Rickover and his group. People don't appreciate the tremendous amount of noise and confusion and destruction that can occur with even a very small leak at 400 to 500 feet of depth. A half-inch seawater pipe that is ruptured causes deafening noise and spray and water.

I think that most people have come to the conclusion that Thresher was lost because of failure of one of those auxiliary seawater systems. This resulted in a tightening of quality control for all of those systems, and this has been, I think, a hallmark of U.S. submarine construction, and that is the quality control that goes into the construction.

Q: There was a question about the brazing, wasn't there, on the pipes and how solid that was?

---

*On 10 April 1963 the attack submarine Thresher (SSN-593) was lost east of Cape Code while on a test dive.

Admiral Long: Yes. That deals really with the quality control, the tests that are made on the various pipes and the quality of the procedures. The submarine community has been meticulous in preserving the quality of submarine hulls and seawater systems since that time. There have been several times when the operating depth of submarines has been restricted because of certain questions that have arisen on those systems.

Q: You mentioned you had a better sonar in the Casimir Pulaski. How did that make a difference tactically?

Admiral Long: We were able to hear better. I don't think it really changed anything significantly, other than I think we had a greater confidence that we could hear other ships or other submarines more clearly.

Q: And possibly at greater range, also?

Admiral Long: And also at greater range. Right.

Q: Did you feel a sense of regret in going ashore after being part of this new thing?

Admiral Long: No, I thought that I had been at sea long

enough.

Q: You paid your dues.

Admiral Long: I paid my dues. I thought that if I was going to proceed any further in the Navy that I needed to be doing something else, so I welcomed the opportunity to go back to Washington. It was also an opportunity for me finally to be more at home with my family. As I've said before, they sacrificed a great deal during those seagoing years. Of course, this was now 1965, so essentially I had been at sea quite a bit of the time over the previous 20 years.

So I reported in to SP. Admiral Levering Smith was the Director of Special Projects. I became SP-11, which was Plans and Programs. It was sort of the one that puts the program together, sets us up so that we can get the budget, works closely with OP-02.

I must admit that working with Levering Smith was a real pleasure. He was an extremely intelligent, dedicated person, not terribly aggressive personality-wise, but very strong-willed as far as his own technical views. He had as his deputy Paul Lacy, who was a very close friend of mine and was almost a next-door neighbor for several years in the New London area in Glen Woods where we lived. The technical director at this time was an EDO named Bob

Gooding.* He was a captain at that time. He subsequently became a vice admiral. As a matter of fact, we're going to the theater with him tomorrow night.

But we worked very well as a team. At that time, the Department of Defense promulgated what were called draft presidential memos. Those, in effect, were decision memos, and they really formed the primary guidance for preparing the budget. They were neither draft nor were they presidential, but they were very important.

A principal player in preparing those were the McNamara "whiz kids," the systems analysts.** The person that I worked with very closely was a young analyst called Ivan Selin.*** Ivan Selin was in charge of the strategic draft presidential memo, and he subsequently left the Navy to form a very successful corporation. He later left that and is currently the head of the Reactor Safeguards Commission. But in that draft presidential memo, we essentially laid out where the Polaris program was going, and we were quite successful with Ivan. He was a strong supporter of the Navy SSBN program.

I wasn't in SP too long before I received a call to come over to be interviewed by the Under Secretary of the

---

*EDO--engineering duty officer; Captain Robert C. Gooding, USN.
**Robert S. McNamara served as Secretary of Defense from 21 January 1961 to 29 February 1968
***Ivan Selin served as a systems analyst for the Department of Defense from 1965 to 1967 and as Deputy Assistant Secretary of Defense from 1967 to 1969.

Navy to be assigned as his executive assistant. I never will forget that interview. This was with Under Secretary Robert H. B. Baldwin, and I was to relieve a classmate of mine, Dave Bagley.* The conversation went on for some period of time, and then Bob Baldwin, who subsequently has been a very close friend of mine, said, "Well, Captain, would you like to be the executive assistant to the Under Secretary?"

I said, "Well, frankly, no."

That took him aback a little bit, and he said, "Why? I don't understand."

I said, "I'm working for the best program manager in the Department of Defense. I think I have an awful lot to learn from him, and I'd just as soon stay where I am."

His response was a classic, and he still reminds me of it today. He said, "Wouldn't you like to learn a little something more than that?"

Well, I came back and I told Levering Smith of my interview with Mr. Baldwin. Levering at that time was a heavy cigarette smoker. He took a big drag on his cigarette, blew the smoke out, and said, "Well, I've lost you." Sure enough, within a matter of days I had orders to report to the Under Secretary of the Navy as his executive assistant.

---

*Captain David W. Bagley, USN.

Q: Why did you consider Smith the best program manager there was?

Admiral Long: Well, I guess I had observed him ever since I was in OP-311, and I had seen the result of what he had done. I also saw his office's continuing support. They were not typical bureaucrats. They were absolutely dedicated to putting this program on track and keeping it there. Of course, I'll have to say, in all fairness, that he had the priority, he had the money, he had the people, he had an autonomous organization. He didn't need to look to another organization for his contracting. He didn't need to look to another organization to do his budgeting. He had it all right there. But he was an extremely effective guy.

Q: I've heard him described as "a scientist in uniform."

Admiral Long: That's not a bad description. But I would have one addition to that. Sometimes scientists are interested primarily in research. Levering Smith was a scientist who could go ahead and translate new technical ideas into engineering and production, and I think that separates him from, say, the regular run-of-the-mill scientist.

Q: Let me ask you to draw a comparison, please, with Admiral Rickover. You said that he couldn't have gone wrong because he had all this talent to choose from. Was that a comparable situation for Smith?

Admiral Long: Of course, Smith drew on the same pool of talent that Rickover did. I would submit that some people, even if you gave them the priority and the money, they'd botch it. But that was not Smith. You compare Rickover and Smith, both successful.

Q: You indicated that Admiral Rickover used people. I take it you would not say that about Admiral Smith.

Admiral Long: No. I think they were different personalities, both very effective in getting their jobs done, Rickover having a much more aggressive personality, much more Machiavellian. Levering Smith, of course, having full support of the Navy and the Secretary of Defense and the Congress, didn't have to resort to those things. They interfaced with each other normally at arm's length. I think that they respected each other's turf, but there never was any great warmth or harmony between the two.

Q: It's interesting that you wanted to remain and work for Admiral Smith. I gather that wouldn't have been the case with Admiral Rickover.

Admiral Long: Well, that's true. I had a great respect for Admiral Smith, and even today we still see each other and we still work together. He and I are on a board of advisers at the Applied Physics Laboratory at Johns Hopkins, and he doesn't look a lot different than he looked 25 years ago.*

Q: One of the innovations that Secretary McNamara brought in was the PPBS, the planning and programming system that really changed the way the Pentagon did business financially.** Was your setup a reaction to that initiative when you were working in SP? Did you have to interface with that system?

Admiral Long: Yes. As I said before, the interface was principally with the systems analysis people who were charged with drawing up the draft presidential memos, the so-called DPMs. And I'll have to say that my experience in that job with systems analyst Ivan Selin was a very positive relationship. I think other people didn't have as positive a relationship.

---

*Vice Admiral Smith died shortly after this interview.
**For background on PPBS (Planning, Programming and Budgeting System), see Gordon G. Riggle, "Looking to the Long Run," U.S. Naval Institute Proceedings, September 1980, page 60.

Robert L. J. Long #2 - 229

Q: The Navy, in some cases, had to be dragged very reluctantly into using that system.

Admiral Long: That's right. Of course, later on, you're quite correct, the combination of Paul Nitze and Bud Zumwalt really set up the Navy Systems Analysis Group.* Also, they were the ones that really set up the Center for Naval Analyses as we know it today.

Q: Could you explain just how your planning and programming operation worked? Where did you get the inputs and what kind of a product did you produce?

Admiral Long: Of course, the program is really a continuation of past programs that we continually updated. In those updates we attempted to reflect the requirements, as we understood them, of the Chief of Naval Operations as to those things that he wanted to see in the Polaris weapons system. Those included such things as the number of submarines, the type of missiles, the number of missiles, the training facilities that he would like to see, the depots to put the missiles together, and, of course, those things that would also include the

---
*Paul H. Nitze served as Secretary of the Navy from 29 November 1963 to 30 June 1967. He set up Rear Admiral Elmo R. Zumwalt, Jr., USN, as head of the systems analysis division within OpNav.

sponsorship of the Polaris office itself. That would involve not only supporting the contracts with organizations such as Lockheed or the Applied Physics Laboratory or the variety of other corporations that were involved in the Polaris program, but the entire group. So it was one of continuing that relationship not only within the technical organization, but also trying to capture the requirements in an iterative way with the Chief of Naval Operations and his staff.

Q: Were you already looking ahead to the Poseidon program and its requirements?*

Admiral Long: Yes. At that time, we were looking at updates, improvements to the SSBN system.

Q: There was the ULMS initiative that later led to Trident.** Was that a factor at the time you were there?

Admiral Long: No, that actually occurred a little bit later. I think this occurred during the time when Bud Zumwalt was the CNO, and I was not personally involved in that. I was elsewhere at the time.

---

*Poseidon was the longer-range successor missile to Polaris.
**ULMS--Underwater Long-range Missile System, which became Trident, the successor to Poseidon.

Q: Did you feel at all out of place being surrounded by all these engineers when you weren't one?

Admiral Long: No, not really, because I guess I spent as much time talking to the fleet, as well as OpNav, as I did talking to the engineers. And, having spent that time in Rickover's office, I even came to the conclusion that some engineers are very realistic and make sense.

Q: You were the token operator.

Admiral Long: Yes.

Q: Did you get any special training in financial management? Where did you pick that skill up?

Admiral Long: There was a separate financial management office, so I was not that intimately involved in the juggling of the numbers.

Q: Yours was more a conceptual thing?

Admiral Long: Mine was more programmatic as to where we wanted to go. In rough numbers, how much money are we talking about?

Q: So then it would be a matter of making some priorities and choices.

Admiral Long: Right. And it was terribly important as to where the draft presidential memo put all of those priorities. Of course, they had draft presidential memos for strategic systems as opposed to the general purpose forces, and so we were in competition with other strategic systems, such as the Air Force's and even the Army at that time.

Q: One thing I didn't ask you about from the time you were in submarines was the targeting. Did you have any contact with Omaha and the organization there that specified what targets would be hit?

Admiral Long: We received our targeting instructions really from JSTPS, but it was through the operational commander, who was CinCLant for us.*

Q: So those were essentially orders that you followed, not something that you had any say in?

Admiral Long: That's correct.

---
*JSTPS--Joint Strategic Target Planning Staff, based at Offutt Air Force Base in Nebraska.

Robert L. J. Long #2 - 233

Q: Anything more before we move on to your work with Under Secretary Baldwin?

Admiral Long: No, I think that pretty well covers it.

Q: What do you remember about his personality and style of leadership?

Admiral Long: Bob Baldwin also was a unique individual. He's a guy of tremendous drive, energy, almost a compulsive nature to tell people how to do things. He's the kind of guy that gets in a taxicab and invariably will tell the taxicab driver how to get to the airport. He was the Under Secretary under Paul Nitze, two rather different personalities. Paul Nitze is almost an academic, loves studies, loves to sit and discuss things conceptually.

Q: Very reflective.

Admiral Long: Very reflective. Bob Baldwin, on the other hand, is a hands-on, let's-get-it-done kind of guy. He loves to get into the details, and is extremely effective when he believes in something and can be very antagonistic if he does not believe in it. He didn't always get along with the OpNav admirals. They looked upon him as somewhat too independent at times. He asked a lot of hard questions. He was not one that took everything on blind faith. And sometimes his personality was such that he rubbed people the wrong way just by his rather aggressive personality.

Overall, he was as effective an Under Secretary as any I've seen, though. When he decided that something was worthwhile and needed by the Navy, he was absolutely tenacious in getting it approved through the rest of the system. A good example is here at the Naval Academy. All of those new buildings are essentially the result of Bob Baldwin getting that building program approved.

I established a good rapport with him. I wouldn't say that I'm a terribly aggressive personality, but he and I established a rapport early on which I felt absolutely no compulsion about telling him where I thought he was wrong, and he appreciated that. Obviously, I told him that not in a large crowd.

Of course, at that time McNamara was the Secretary of Defense. It was interesting, when I reflect on the presidential appointees--Paul Nitze, Bob Baldwin, Chuck Baird, Bob Frosch, Jim Bannerman--these were people who had achieved a measure of success outside the government.*

---

*Charles F. Baird was Under Secretary of the Navy, 1967-69; Robert A. Frosch was Assistant Secretary of the Navy for Research and Development, 1966-73; Graeme C. Bannerman was Assistant Secretary of the Navy (Installations and Logistics).

Of course, Paul Nitze was a guy wealthy in his own right. Bob Baldwin was a young, upcoming executive at Morgan Stanley. Chuck Baird was a young executive at Exxon Standard Oil of New Jersey. Chuck Bowsher was with Arthur Anderson, successful there, and Frosch had come from DARPA.*

It was interesting that many of these men were recruited by Tom Gates. Although people will criticize Robert McNamara for a variety of things, one of the things that was a great strength was that he tried to select the very best people he could, regardless of their political affiliation. Of course, as we all know, we don't always do that today. So these people were recruited at that time by Tom Gates, and they came not from congressional staffs, but they came from being successful people on the outside.

Q: It's interesting how many came from the financial community.

Admiral Long: Yes. Of course, when these people left office, Bob Baldwin went back to being the chairman and CEO of Morgan Stanley in New York, probably the most prestigious international investment house in the world. After Chuck Baird left the Under Secretary's job, he went

---

*Charles A. Bowsher was Assistant Secretary of the Navy for Financial Management, 1967-71. DARPA--Defense Advanced Research Projects Agency.

on to become the chairman and CEO of International Nickel. Chuck Bowsher went back to Arthur Anderson, and, of course, he currently is the Comptroller General of the United States. Bob Frosch has also enjoyed continued success. So it was a very impressive bunch of civilians that we had up there.

There were several major decisions that were made during this time. There was always a question as to the relationship between the Material Command and the Chief of Naval Operations. The decision was made at that time that a new position was to be created, the Chief of Naval Material, and he would report directly to the CNO. Of course, during Secretary Lehman's tour, this was changed, and there is now a question as to how the CNO relates to the Material Command.*

There also was a conscious policy, which I thought was a good policy, and that was the level of detail that the Navy secretariat managed within the Navy. It was interesting that the Navy secretariat almost assumed a board of directors' role with regard to the Navy, and that it was ultimately responsible for the decisions of the Navy. But as they were wont to say at times, "The Navy secretariat sets the policy, and it is executed by the CNO and those beneath him." Here again, we see some change in that today, where there is a tremendous amount of detailed

---
*John F. Lehman was Secretary of the Navy from 1981 to 1987.

micro-management that is done by the civilian secretariat.

So those were times when some major organizational and management policies were established. As I said, this was also the time when systems analysis was getting going in OSD.* Paul Nitze was very much interested in the studies, and he then established the Systems Analysis Group in OpNav. Bud Zumwalt headed that up, and the Center for Naval Analyses was really sort of put on the map.

Those were good initiatives. Unfortunately, later on, particularly the Systems Analysis Group was prostituted somewhat and so was the Center for Naval Analyses. They were almost made preachers and subordinates of the budget shop, and that clearly was not a good idea.

Q: Because you don't get independent conclusions.

Admiral Long: That's right. They became the enemy to the rest of OpNav, and as a result, they really were not effective.

Q: I remember that there was quite a community of EAs there that later went on to higher rank, including Jerry Miller, Ike Kidd, and Admiral Zumwalt.** Did you get involved in that community?

---
*OSD--Office of the Secretary of Defense.
**EAs--executive assistants. Captain Gerald E. Miller, USN, was EA for the VCNO; Captain Isaac C. Kidd, Jr., USN, was EA for the CNO; and Captain Zumwalt was EA for Secretary of the Navy Nitze.

Admiral Long: Well, the EAs at that time were somewhat unique, and I guess it all goes to the style of the civilian secretary. But directives and requirements from the civilian secretariat were normally transmitted to the blue-suit Navy by means of executive memos. Executive memos were signed out by the executive assistant to SecNav. They went to the executive assistant of the CNO or the Vice CNO, and they normally read something like, "The Secretary of the Navy desires that the CNO take the following actions. Signed, Joe Smith, Executive Assistant to the Secretary," and this thing was addressed to the Executive Assistant to the CNO. So it was a rather interesting way of doing business. [Laughter] But when you got an executive memo, that really meant that you were being directed by the civilian secretary.

But there were some interesting characters who were executive assistants--Ike Kidd, Dave Bagley, Worth Bagley, Bud Zumwalt.* They all went on to pretty good things.

Q: There was a question whether the job made the man or vice versa.

Admiral Long: Well, maybe a little of both. Of course, I was privileged to be the executive assistant for a while,

---
*Captain David H. Bagley, USN; Captain Worth H. Bagley, USN.

and the guy who relieved me was Tom Hayward.*

Q: What was the specific area that was set out for the Under Secretary?

Admiral Long: Well, that's a good question. It's not the same as today. The Under Secretary really was more the hands-on program guy in the Navy secretariat. He probably spent as much time looking at air programs as any, very much interested in those. He was also interested in what we call MilCon, military construction. The Naval Academy would be an example.

The Secretary, Paul Nitze, of course, was interested in those things, too, but he spent a lot of his time looking at conceptual studies--what will the DDG umpty-ump look like?** What's going on in the Vietnam War. Of course, the Vietnam War consumed an awful lot of interest, and it was driven a great deal by the demands or the requirements of the Secretary of Defense. McNamara had all sorts of ways of measuring effectiveness and so on.

I had been over there for just a few months, and Bob Baldwin decided he wanted to take a trip to Vietnam, and so we went. That was a real eye-opener for me.

---
*Captain Thomas B. Hayward, USN, CNO from 1978 to 1982.
**DDG--guided missile destroyer.

Q: Please tell me about it.

Admiral Long: When we went, Bob Baldwin had authorized some media people to travel with us part of the time. One of them was Helen Bentley, who at that time was a reporter for the <u>Baltimore Sun</u>. Then there was a fellow named Bernard Fall, who had written several books on Vietnam, not all supportive of the effort. He started back with the French. He later died, and I remember we went to that funeral.

When we arrived, we went to Danang, where the Marines were. I never will forget feeling some disillusionment. We were being shown sort of a pacification project they had. We were walking down this dirt road with the governor of that particular province. He happened to be a civilian, a graduate of the University of Michigan. We were going to this village, and in my rather naive way I said, "Governor, I just don't understand why these people are Communists, looking at all of the things that Communism stands for."

He looked at me like I had been dropped from the moon, and he said, "Captain, these people don't give a damn about Communism or democracy or socialism or any of that stuff. All they want is to be left alone and be able to grow what they need to eat."

Q: Whoever will provide them those things will win their

hearts and minds.

Admiral Long: Well, his point was that for us to go in there thinking that we were going to turn them all into Jeffersonian Democrats was very naive. I think that that's probably very true today, some of the things. Most of these people in developing countries are so terribly poor, they really don't care very much about the political ideology. What they want is something to eat and to be left alone.

So we then went on to other parts of Vietnam. I just remember how unreal it seemed to me. We were sitting out there in this one Army command post, and there was firing. Shells were going off all around us, and we were sitting down here to this beautiful luncheon with tablecloths and silver on the table and wine. I thought, "What the hell's going on here?" I mean, it was just very unreal to me. You know, I was pretty naive. But that was a very educational visit. Of course, subsequent to that, when I went back as a task force commander in the Seventh Fleet, I had command of all of the support ships in country, so I had many occasions then to go back and get even better educated.

Q: What were your impressions of that?

Admiral Long: Well, here again, you go down these beautiful boulevards and see lovely homes. We stayed, I guess, with MACV in a beautiful house.* It was just unreal. Then you go a little bit out of town, and here you've got all of this combat going on.

Q: Did you have a sense that the command structure was out of touch with the fighting element?

Admiral Long: No. I just had the question--and, of course, this was reinforced later--of what we were trying to accomplish and did we really know how to get there? Something that I have believed even more strongly later on, and that is that you put military forces into play when you want to achieve a certain political objective. You have to have a very good idea as to how you're going to achieve those political objectives. I don't think we had a real good idea of the political objectives, nor did we have any good strategy for achieving those objectives.

Q: One of the complaints has been about McNamara's fetish with numbers, that everything can be quantified, that the more enemy you kill, the more likely you are to be successful.

---
*MACV--Military Assistance Command Vietnam.

Admiral Long: Yes, but, of course, the fundamental flaw was that we didn't have realistic political objectives.

Q: What was the purpose of the trip?

Admiral Long: Just orientation for the Under Secretary so he could learn what was going on. And I don't say that in a pejorative way. I think it's valid that he have some idea of how the forces were doing over there and what they needed.

Q: Especially with that war consuming so much of the Navy's effort and resources.

Admiral Long: You bet. You bet. So it was worthwhile. We didn't spend an awful lot of time sitting in the lap of luxury. It was plodding around.

Q: Did you get out on board ships?

Admiral Long: No, not really. We flew into Vietnam and flew out. That's what we really were interested in.

Then also during this time was my first introduction to Ross Perot.* We had in the office a Marine aide, Bill

---

*H. Ross Perot, a 1953 Naval Academy graduate, became a highly successful businessman and later ran for President in 1992.

Leftwich, and as I described Zumwalt earlier, he was just like an all-American boy.* I mean, he was a superb athlete, writer, professional Marine, just great. Later, he left us, went to Vietnam, and was killed.** I was really impressed by Ross Perot, whom I hadn't known before that. Boy, Ross Perot did all sorts of things to honor this guy, who was a classmate of his.

Q: Including what?

Admiral Long: Well, setting up memorials for him down here at the Naval Academy. My understanding was that he was very helpful to Bill's family. I guess the Leftwich Room is still over here in Dahlgren Hall. The Marine who replaced him in the Under Secretary's office also went to Vietnam and was killed.

Q: What kinds of projects did you undertake personally on behalf of the Under Secretary?

Admiral Long: The executive assistant to Bob Baldwin was really a chief of staff. He was the one that ran that secretariat. The Under Secretary, with Paul Nitze as the Secretary, was a hands-on guy--I mean, very active in the

---
*Lieutenant Colonel William G. Leftwich, Jr., USMC.
**Leftwich was killed in action in Vietnam 19 November 1970.

program. So I was, I guess, personally involved in everything that the Under Secretary did. I was the guy who collected the arguments, the briefs. For example, we had a special assistant for the merchant marine. We had a special assistant for Marine Corps matters. We had special assistants for other things. I remember one thing that Bob Baldwin wanted to do, and that was to set up a special group on computers, and so I set that up. That's where we brought in Grace Hopper.*

Q: What was her status at the time?

Admiral Long: I think she was maybe a commander. But she was down in here somewhere. I saw very little of her. There were other people above.

I also tried to coordinate the activities of the assistant secretaries--Bannerman was I&L; Frosch was R&D; Baird was financial management. I had a very demanding job. My recollection was that the day started about 7:00 o'clock in the morning and ended about 7:00 to 9:00 at night. Sara was not all that particularly happy with the hours.

Q: It's like being at sea.

---
*Commander Grace M. Hopper, USNR, made enormous contributions to the Navy's use of computers.

Admiral Long: But the reason for that was that the Secretary of Defense kept those hours. When the boss man is there, I think the rest of the people feel that they're almost constrained to stay. The classic example was when Arleigh Burke was the CNO and someone said that these people were all sticking around because he didn't go home until 7:30 or 8:00. He said, "They don't need to stay as long as I stay. If I'm not gone, they don't need to stay beyond 6:00 at night." [Laughter]

Q: Was this when you picked up the squash again to relieve the stress?

Admiral Long: Yes. Bob Baldwin and I played squash. Here again, that was very helpful to me to do that.

Q: That could be a real health factor if you work that kind of pace all the time, unrelenting.

Admiral Long: That's right. That's right. So you need to get out.

Q: It says something for your administrative ability to keep all these balls in the air at the same time. How did you know what to work on at a given time?

Robert L. J. Long #2 - 247

Admiral Long: I think sort of the press of the moment drives you.

Q: The squeaky wheel syndrome?

Admiral Long: Yes. I can't say that I'm a great detail guy. As I indicated earlier, I don't have a lot of patience. But you're right, there were a lot of balls in the air.

Q: Any other specifics that you remember from that job?

Admiral Long: No, I think we pretty well covered it. While I was there, I was picked up for rear admiral, lower half.

Q: Please tell me about learning the news and the reaction to it.

Admiral Long: I wasn't selected the first year I was in what you might call the deep zone. A couple of classmates of mine were selected earlier, but the second time around I was selected. And I'll have to say, Paul, that although I hoped to be selected for rear admiral, every additional star I received after that was always a surprise to me. I never sought any particular job. I know some people do, but I never did.

Q: You certainly didn't seek out that job as EA to Secretary Baldwin.

Admiral Long: No, I did not. I tried to avoid it. [Laughter] But in hindsight, that job as EA was very broadening for me. It gave me a perspective at the political level that was invaluable for me later on.

Q: You had been in submarines almost continuously for 15, 20 years.

Admiral Long: Right. And even in OpNav, I was almost totally immersed in submarine matters. Bob Baldwin was right on when he said, "Wouldn't you like to learn a little something more than submarines?" [Laughter] As I say, he keeps reminding me of that.

Q: What was the reaction, personally and at home, to the news?

Admiral Long: Well, one of great joy. I think we received a card at that time that said, "Behind every successful man is a surprised wife." [Laughter] So we received this news, and I received my orders shortly thereafter. I was assigned by the flag detailer, who was Mickey Weisner.* He sent me to relieve Bub Ward as the commander of Service Group Three, home-ported in Sasebo, Japan.** I was to be frocked when we left the continental U.S.***

We flew out to California, and flying with us was my oldest son, Charles, who had entered the Army at this point. My number-two son was at the Naval Academy, and we also had with us our youngster Rob, the third one. The oldest son had been valedictorian of his high school and captain of his swimming team. He had been selected and admitted to go to Brown University in the mid-Sixties. Here was this straight-A student, and his grades just went down, down, down, down. This was during that Sixties culture. I remember one night in the kitchen, one of these famous midnight talks. I told him, "Charlie, I just don't understand you. Look at you. You're sort of dirty. You're failing in school. I think you're wasting my money and your time."

He said, "Dad, don't worry. I'll be okay. You've given me better values than that."

Well, anyway, he dropped out of college and, of

---
*Rear Admiral Maurice F. Weisner, USN.
**Rear Admiral Norvell G. Ward, USN. As a captain, he had been Commander Submarine Squadron 14 when Long was commanding officer of the <u>Patrick Henry</u>.
***Frocking meant putting on the uniform insignia of a rear admiral, even though he would continue to draw captain's pay until a vacancy occurred on the Navy's list.

Robert L. J. Long #2 - 250

course, the draft got him. He went down to Fort Bragg and went through the airborne school. He went to the Army NCO school down in Mississippi.* He stood number one in this noncommissioned officers school, and he came out as an E-6 staff sergeant.

Q: Pretty good deal.

Admiral Long: Yes. As a matter of fact, he used to tell me about going into the noncom club. These old sergeants would be sitting around, and they'd say, "Hey, Sarge, how long have you been in the Army?" and he'd say, "Six months." [Laughter]

Anyway, he was assigned to the Ninth Infantry Division as a platoon sergeant, and it just so happened that he was sent to Vietnam about the same time that we went to Japan. So we flew across country together, and he went on to Vietnam and we went on to Sasebo. Several months later, he was wounded; he stepped on a land mine and almost lost his foot. I would go to Vietnam at least once a month, because I had under my command all of the major support ships that were in country. Bud Zumwalt was there, and I normally stayed with Bud.** Bud would call down to the Ninth

───────────
*NCO—noncommissioned officer.
**Vice Admiral Elmo R. Zumwalt, Jr., USN, served as Commander U.S. Naval Forces Vietnam from September 1968 to May 1970. Zumwalt's headquarters were in Saigon, South Vietnam.

Infantry Division and ask Charlie to come on up in Saigon when I was there, but Charlie never would do it. He said, "My place is with my platoon."

I did get him one time when we went down to the southern coast to see a support ship. I took him on down, and I never will forget what I saw when we went swimming. He took off his boots, and his feet were just literally raw from this jungle rot that set in. So he finished up his tour in Vietnam. After he stepped on that land mine, the Army sent him back to the hospital in Sasebo, Japan, for rehab. As I say, he damn near lost his foot, but they saved it. He finished up in Camp Zama, went back to Brown, graduated, got himself married to a gal at Pembroke, Brown's girls' school. To show you how ideas change, he called me up one night and said, "You know, there's some of these radical students up here that want to shut down this school because they're anti-Vietnam." He said, "I'll take the bastards to court." So his ideas changed a little bit.

Q: Far more mature than when you had that midnight discussion.

Admiral Long: Yes, that's right. But anyway, we moved into Sasebo, and I relieved Bub Ward.

Q: His son had been killed in Vietnam.*

Admiral Long: Yes, that's right. We spent just about a year there, and I guess I spent about 50% of my time outside of Sasebo. We had a flagship, the Ajax, and we'd move from Sasebo to Subic to Kaohsiung in Taiwan or to Vietnam. I certainly tried to get out and visit the unrep ships, and in Service Group Three, I guess I had more ships than anybody else.** I had all the oilers, the ammunition ships, the hospital ships, the stores ships, the spy ships, the communication ships, as well as the ships that were support ships in Vietnam.

So it was a fascinating experience for me, getting away from submarines with all their handpicked crews, getting over here to these service force ships, where the quality of the people wasn't all that great, but they did a great job out there.

Q: Admiral Shear was practically rhapsodic in singing the praises of the Sacramento.

Admiral Long: Yes. He had command of the Sacramento, that's right. Fantastic ships.

Periodically, we'd have Seventh Fleet conferences.

---

*Admiral Ward discussed this in his own Naval Insittute oral history.
**Unrep--underway replenishment.

Bush Bringle was the Commander Seventh Fleet, and Ralph Cousins was the commander of the carrier force, so I would see them quite a bit.* I also had command of the salvage forces, and I never will forget I received a message from Bush Bringle, saying that the Seventh Fleet flagship had gone aground off Vietnam. It was a personal message to me. I looked at that message and I said, "I think he's telling me this privately, but he doesn't want this to go public."

Well, here again, I was so dumb. I'd been told, "Look, if you've got a salvage job, get the stuff moving as quickly as you can."

So anyway, I went public with it, and later on he said, "I didn't expect you to do that, but I'm glad you did."

Q: Well, what did he expect? [Laughter]

Admiral Long: [Laughter] I don't know. I think he just felt the need to tell somebody.

Q: Was it bad enough that he needed help?

Admiral Long: No, the ship finally got off. I remember one case where a destroyer, and I forget the name of it,

---

*Vice Admiral William F. Bringle, USN, commanded the Seventh Fleet from November 1967 to March 1970. Rear Admiral Ralph W. Cousins, USN, was Commander Task Force 77.

was aground just a short distance off Viet Cong territory. We went in there and, at some risk, pulled that off.

But here again, visiting Vietnam, I was struck with our unwillingness to put together a real strategy to achieve those ends that we announced. I think that all of us who reached senior positions and were privy to that period of time, we all have pretty strong views about the commitment of military force, when and how. Of course, this was also reinforced with me again in the Beirut bombing of the Marines in 1983. Later we went through this again with the Gulf War as to how to do it and how not to do it. Those are terribly important lessons, and we may be forgetting them again--not so much in Somalia, but Yugoslavia.

Q: Please tell me how you went about scheduling these unreps, not only picking up the products, but then delivering them in timely fashion to the combatant forces.

Admiral Long: Well, that was a very orderly process, and I was not all that personally involved. I had a task group commander, CTG 73.1. His name was Ray Wilhite, and he was the one that actually rode with the ships at sea.* His wife was the daughter of Admiral Struble.** She just

_____
*Captain D. R. Wilhite, USN.
**Vice Admiral Arthur D. Struble, USN, was Commander Seventh Fleet during the Korean War.

recently died of cancer. But Ray was the one that really kept this thing going. Also, I had a very strong logistic group, and one of my junior officers on the CTF 73 staff at that time was a young man, Lieutenant David Gergen.*

Q: What do you remember of him from that period?

Admiral Long: I'll have to say, candidly, I don't remember a lot, other than he was just a charming young man. I don't recall having that much to do with him.

Q: Beyond charm, I have been impressed, watching on television, by his analysis and how much on target it is.

Admiral Long: Yes. He's very sharp, a very sharp guy.

That tour of duty was also our exposure to the Japanese. We lived in Sasebo. Of course, Sara was there most of the time, although she did avail herself of a lot of travel around. She was particularly fortunate in joining a group of ladies who would get together weekly. Nancy Wilhite was one of the ladies who organized this group. Also included were several Japanese ladies. Ostensibly their purpose was to teach English, but it was also a great opportunity for these Japanese ladies to take

---

*Lieutenant (junior grade) David R. Gergen, USNR. In recent years Gergen has been prominent as a journalist and also a presidential adviser.

the Americans around and let them see parts of Japan that would have been impossible. So Sara really benefited from that. Sara also took advantage of being able to travel to Hong Kong and Thailand. It was a real educational experience for both of us.

This also gave me an insight into the Japanese. Maybe southern Japanese are not all that typical, but I think they probably are pretty well. They're very slow to be friends, but when they finally decide you are a friend, they remember you.

Q: Both generous and gracious.

Admiral Long: Yes, yes.

Q: Were you entertained in the homes of the Japanese?

Admiral Long: Yes, and that's very unusual. There were two brothers, both doctors, that we used to see. Their wives were part of this group that Sara was in. Normally the Japanese will entertain you in a hotel or a restaurant. Rarely will they invite you into their home, or at least that was the situation 25 years ago. But occasionally we would be invited into their homes.

The mayor was Mayor Tsuji. He had lost his voice box, but he spoke. He would speak for a half an hour or so, so he would swallow air and it would come up. His wife was a very accomplished artist in calligraphy.

Q: The kanji characters.

Admiral Long: Yes, yes, and we still have some of her art. But we were accepted, and we really enjoyed living that year in Japan.

Q: One thing I remember from Japan in those years were the ritual protests. It seemed that people were almost hired for the job of going out and protesting.

Admiral Long: They had a bridge there in Sasebo, and the protesters would come running across the bridge. Then they'd stop, and then the police would then rush at them and they would all fall back. Then they would come up again, crossing the bridge, and then the police would rush them all back. It was just like a ballet.

Q: It was choreographed.

Admiral Long: That's right. That's right.

Q: What was the purpose of all that? Did you get an idea?

Admiral Long: Well, I guess we resumed some visits by nuclear-powered ships when Bub Ward was there. Sasebo was where they had a major confrontation when the Enterprise had been in there earlier. Then we started bringing submarines back in. Nuclear aircraft carriers did not come in, but we had a couple of visits of conventional aircraft carriers while I was there. Howie Greer came in, and he had command of an aircraft carrier.*

Of course, I was a frocked rear admiral. I had not made my number yet. I remember we always tried to throw a cocktail party or dinner whenever these ships would come in. Howie was there, and as he was drinking a cocktail he said to me, "Gee, it must be great to get all this money to entertain your friends."

I said, "Well, Howie, a little correction. One, admirals don't get money to entertain their friends; and second, that booze you're drinking is captain's booze."

It also gave me an opportunity to see some of the areas that later would become increasingly important, like the Philippines. Of course, at each one of these places we had Service Group Three contingent reps that would take care of the work requests of the ships coming into the shipyard or the ship repair facility there at Subic or the ship repair facility in Guam. Guam was also in my area of responsibility. All of the chaplains reported to Service

---
*Captain Howard E. Greer, USN, commanded the USS Hancock (CVA-19) from 1967 to 1969.

Group Three. We had a chaplain pool.

Q: That's interesting.

Admiral Long: It was really a very, very busy job at that time, of course, with all of the ammunition supply, the food supply, the hospitals. And, of course, every time I'd go to Vietnam, I'd always try to stop in to the hospital ships, the Repose and the Sanctuary. That was always a very sobering experience when you'd go aboard those hospital ships. Of course, whenever I went aboard, I was asked to pin Purple Hearts on people and so on, and I will always remember that Marine lying there, bare-chested, all sorts of bandages all over him. I was a little bit embarrassed. I said, "I have this Purple Heart for you. Where would you like to have me put it?"

He said, "Admiral, pin it on my chest. I'm a Marine." [Laughter]

So here again, that was a broadening experience for me and it's one that I really enjoyed.

Q: It was an amazingly diverse command, with all these things you've described.

Admiral Long: Oh, absolutely.

Q: The ship repair facilities were under you also?

Admiral Long: Yes, the control of them, the workload of them.

Q: So you were the one who scheduled overhauls or voyage repairs?

Admiral Long: Refits, yes. Upkeep periods.

Q: And in some cases, battle damage. I remember a sister of our LST got mined and went into Yokosuka, and I was amazed to see the size of the hole in her.

Admiral Long: Yokosuka was probably the top-quality yard.

Q: That was certainly our impression. We preferred going there rather than to Subic.

Admiral Long: Yes, but Subic wasn't all that bad. Of course, there was also an SRF at Guam; I always looked upon that as an insurance policy.* As a matter of fact, later on, when we first started talking about the possibility of leaving the Philippines, I urged at that time that we

---
*SRF--ship repair facility.

Robert L. J. Long #2 - 261

continue to support and upgrade the facilities in the Marianas, because operating from there is better than operating from the Hawaiian Islands.

Q: And now, of all places, we're into Singapore.

Admiral Long: That's right. Of course, I helped break that ground in Singapore a few years ago.

Q: Did you make your number as a rear admiral while you were there?

Admiral Long: I don't really remember. Maybe at the end. As a matter of fact, while I was Service Group Three, our Under Secretary of the Navy, John Warner, came through. We had lunch together at Subic, and he said, "Bob, I want you to know that we're going to send you to NavShips, Naval Ship Systems Command."

I said, "What have I done wrong?"

He said, "No, we're really making a conscious effort to upgrade the unrestricted line officers there, and we're sending some of our best people."

I thought to myself, "Boy, that's a line of baloney." But I went there.

I relieved Roho Adamson, a classmate of mine, who had been there for a short period of time.* He stood number
———
*Rear Admiral Robert E. Adamson, Jr., USN.

six in the class—a very sharp surface guy. Rear Admiral Sonenshein was the commander of NavShips and Bob Gooding was the vice commander.* I became the Deputy Commander NavShips for Fleet Support and was there for three years. Under me I had all of the type desks, the shipalts, and some parts of NavSEC.** We had an awful lot to do with the procurement of things and special programs like converting the entire fleet from Navy special fuel oil to diesel fuel. The habitability program was under me. I was fortunate, for some of those programs, such as the conversion of the fleet to diesel fuel, were no small programs.

Q: Especially when you've got leaky piping that was used for that thick stuff.

Admiral Long: Yes. I was fortunate to have an outstanding officer, Captain Max Duncan, in charge of those special programs.*** Max Duncan had been commanding officer of the Naval Support Activity Saigon when I was CTF 73, and, as such, I was his reporting senior. He had since been transferred back to the Joint Staff, conducted a study on his operation, and recommended that his billet be

---
*Rear Admiral Nathan Sonenshein, USN.
**Shipalt—ship alteration; NavSEC—Naval Ship Engineering Center.
***Captain Max C. Duncan, USN.

disestablished. So called me up and said, "You got a job over there?"

I said, "You betcha." He was a real self-starter. As a matter of fact, he lives right up the street here.

So there I was, surrounded by these engineers again. I had a great rapport with Sonenshein and Gooding. Of course, I had known Gooding from my days in SP.

I would say that this three-year tour, as much as anything, Paul, prepared me for being the DCNO for Submarine Warfare and the Vice Chief. That helped me as much as any job, because it clearly educated me as to how the Material Command worked, and so I therefore knew where the skeletons were buried, and that was helpful.

Q: What were some of the skeletons that you discovered?

Admiral Long: Well, sort of how overhauls are run. First let me say that many of us, when we look back over our lives, we don't see many footprints. I submit that if you can see two or three footprints, you're lucky. Unfortunately, so many times when people look back, they don't see anything. I mean, it's just like looking out on that snow; there's nothing. We just sort of took care of the incoming mail and put it in the outgoing box.

But there were a couple of things that I really take

great pride in that occurred during that time I was the Deputy NavShips. For instance, complex overhauls were something that I set up, where essentially I would personally monitor the ship's preparations for overhaul. These were normally carriers.

Q: What differentiates a complex overhaul from a regular overhaul?

Admiral Long: For a regular overhaul, you just drive into the shipyard, have an arrival conference, and you tell the shipyard commander and his production people, "These are the things I'd like to have done." With a complex overhaul, that process starts maybe six months before the ship ever arrives. You bring up the ship's commanding officer and whomever he wants, the type commander's representative, the shipyard commander or his reps, and you sit down and you say, "Now, these are the various things that we want to do. What do you need to do in order to be able to facilitate that?"

Then I had an organization in there that would track to see how the shipyard was making preparations to handle that ship. When it was a carrier being overhauled, it would cost several hundred millions dollars. During the course of that overhaul, we would then go through and have the leverage on the shipyard commander to make sure that

that ship got out on time with the right product. So it was a much more orderly way of executing these very expensive, very complex overhauls. So that was one thing.

Another one of the footprints was a program that's called SMMS--that's Submarine Material Maintenance System. Its objective was to extend the operating cycle for SSBNs from five years to ten years. In other words, you eliminate that unnecessary overhaul. What that required was setting up special support activities at Holy Loch or in Rota. We'd go through discipline maintenance procedures, switching pumps, replacing pumps, and doing maintenance on things that we would normally not do. We set up special categories of replacement equipment.

The result of that was that the submarines were really in better materiel condition under this plan than they were under the old system, when they had the overhaul every few years at 100 million bucks a pop.

Q: Was this because it was being done as you went along rather than saving up for discrepancies?

Admiral Long: Right. And we had tiger teams that would come out from Electric Boat and go over there and do sort of a super upkeep period. Just last year, they had a reunion of the SMMS team, and they presented me a big plaque and it was labeled, "Father of SMMS."

Robert L. J. Long #2 - 266

Q: That's a footprint engraved in silver.

Admiral Long: It was gold! And, of course, another one of those footprints was the conversion of the fleet to distillate fuel.

Q: What was the driving force behind that conversion?

Admiral Long: I'd say partly environmental and partly the better availability of fuel. Distillate fuel, interestingly, is more readily available than the old Navy fuel. It's cleaner, and it requires less maintenance. With the old Navy fuel you had to heat it before burning it in the boilers. That isn't necessary with the distillate.

Q: How did the cost compare with the black oil?

Admiral Long: My recollection is that it was about a wash.

Q: One of the items of concern during that period was the 1,200-pound steam plants. Do you remember addressing that issue?

Admiral Long: Yes. The 1,200-pound steam plant, if you remember, was a major item of concern for the operating forces. They had trouble maintaining it, they had trouble

Robert L. J. Long #2 - 267

operating it, and there was some question as to whether we should have even had 1,200-pound steam at that time.

Q: Do you remember any outcomes on that? It stayed in the fleet, obviously.

Admiral Long: Yes, so we beefed up the training and the instruction manuals that were not the best, according to my recollection.

Q: I guess that was a thing that was helped, in part, by the PEBs, that they codified that training and instruction and inspections and so forth so they could be operated safely.*

Admiral Long: Yes.

Q: What do you remember about the advent of gas turbine power during that era?

Admiral Long: Gas turbines were just really coming in at that time. My recollection was that gas turbines were available, they were flexible, and they were liked very much by the operating forces. Of course, since that time we have seen a major shift to gas turbines as main

---

*PEBs--Propulsion Examining Boards.

propulsion in the fleet.

Q: You've mentioned some of the other leaders you worked for. I wonder if you could provide brief character sketches of Sonenshein and Gooding, please.

Admiral Long: Well, I've already discussed Bob Gooding. He was a very sharp guy. He had more leadership ability than some of the other EDOs that I know. Some of them are rather academic. He's fair, square, sometimes rather arbitrary in his actions. I always enjoyed working with him. Sonenshein was a very nice guy. He gave NavShips leadership. I think at that time what it needed was stability. Nobody really got along all that well with Rickover, but he at least maintained a rapport with Rickover. He also was a strong proponent and was fairly effective in ensuring the health and stability of the EDO corps.

Of course, since that time we have seen a deterioration of a strong EDO corps. In my judgment, the material professional has not been a good substitute. We still need strong EDs if we are to have good analysis of design, construction, and operation of these technical plants.

Q: Do you think that the material professional has

undercut the self-esteem and morale of the EDO community?

Admiral Long: I believe that it has to some degree. Unfortunately, there is a view that many people hold today, and that is that you become a material professional if you're on the second team of the unrestricted line. I think that's a bad image to have. Now, whether it's true or not, that's debatable, but my perception is that is the view.

Q: What was the relationship between NavShips and Naval Material Command during that era?

Admiral Long: If you remember, I indicated that I was in the Navy secretariat when the Chief of Naval Material really was established in the chain of command.

Q: And the bureaus went out of business as reporting independently to the Secretary.

Admiral Long: That's correct. During this time I was there, the Chief of Naval Material was, in fact, in the chain of command. We had a very active, forceful Chief of Naval Material--Ike Kidd.* There were certain functions that the Chief of Naval Material performed. Those were
_____
*Admiral Isaac C. Kidd, Jr., USN, served as Chief of Naval Material from 1 December 1971 to 18 April 1975.

Robert L. J. Long #2 - 270

common contracting policies, procurement policies. Someone had set up standards for the various "ilities"--habitability, those kind of things.

But in my judgment, the Chief of Naval Material was always looking for a role to play. When I was the DCNO for submarines and the Vice Chief, I tried very hard to make the Chief of Naval Material a productive, useful level of command. But rather than being a pump or an amplifier, my observation was the Chief of Naval Material was always a filter. The position did not add to the efficiency of procurement or to the responsiveness of the Material Command to the requirements people.

Q: Presumably that was Secretary Lehman's argument in doing away with that level.

Admiral Long: Yes.

Q: What do you remember about Kidd personally and his impact?

Admiral Long: Well, I'm very fond of Ike Kidd today. We've known each other for a good number of years. I remember one incident where, having the various type desks under me, and specifically the submarine type desk, it came to my attention that some unsafe saltwater systems were at sea on some of the submarines. I put out a message to the submarine type commanders which, in effect, limited the operating depth of those submarines to 700 feet.

Ike got hold of this message, came storming over to Sonenshein's office, and demanded to see me. He was absolutely incensed that I would, in effect, tell the submarine type commanders how to run their ships. Of course, my position was that I, as the technical manager of those systems, had an obligation to tell the type commanders that they were unsafe. I remember he said, "Bob, I was going to fire you, but I found out that you have a lot of friends in high places." [Laughter] So Ike didn't fire me. But he was a very dynamic guy, and I think if anybody could have made it work, he would have.

Q: I know of very few people that loved the Navy more than Admiral Kidd. It's in his blood.

Admiral Long: Well, he's probably one of the finest speakers I've ever heard. He can take a rather mundane subject and turn it into a very stirring speech. So I've had the opportunity to be with him many times since then, and, of course, he was CinCLantFlt when I was the Vice Chief.* He was also a senior fellow at the Capstone

---
*Kidd was Commander in Chief Atlantic Fleet from 1975 to 1978.

course, and he and I used to meet there. So I have a great respect for him and his wonderful wife.

Q: You mentioned habitability. What was the emphasis there?

Admiral Long: There was a general program to improve the habitability of ships--the lighting, the air-conditioning, the amount of space per person, all of that. That was not as dynamic as the conversion of the fleet to distillate fuel. But this was particularly executed in ships' overhauls, and there were specific packages for those ships.

Q: Also, it's a thing that you look to in new ship designs, where you can really have more of an impact.

Admiral Long: Of course, my area of responsibility was not for a new ship design. I was in the type desk, which supported those ships that were in the fleet.

Q: Were you viewed as kind of a friend in court or an advocate for people in the fleet that had demands or wishes from the front office?

Admiral Long: I hope so, but you'll have to ask someone else on that.

Q: Did you get requests from the fleet for certain considerations?

Admiral Long: Oh, yes. Of course, this was particularly important insofar as shipalts and complex ship overhauls. Those would come in.

Q: I guess you wouldn't have gotten into aviation except as it interacted with the ships.

Admiral Long: That's right, not in the aircraft end.

Q: Did domestic political considerations play any part in overhaul scheduling allocation? For instance, did congressmen try to get more business for shipyards in their districts?

Admiral Long: Paul, I think that a principal consideration that we tried to follow at this time was to overhaul ships as near as possible to their home ports. I do not recall any specific instance where I was pressured to put Ship A into Shipyard B because the congressman was putting pressure. I don't recall a single instance of that.

Q: That's good.

Admiral Long: Yes, that is good. That might not be true today.

Q: Was the maintenance and upkeep of the mothball fleet a consideration at all?

Admiral Long: Yes, that also reported to me, and I'll have to say it did not take a lot of my time. I did visit those fleets a few times while I was Ships-04. A classmate of mine, Roy Cowdrey, had command of one of them.* They really didn't require an awful lot of attention, and I really inspected primarily to see that safety considerations were there and they were actually following the procedures. They were all in good shape. Frankly, that particular part of my job was not very demanding.

Q: It's kind of an eerie feeling to go visit those ghost ships.

Admiral Long: Yes.

Q: Did you get involved at all in the business of disposals, when ships would be taken out of mothballs and

_____
*Captain Roy B. Cowdrey, USN.

expended as targets or scrap or what have you?

Admiral Long: No, I don't recall a single case where we had ships taken out, Paul. I can't remember a single case.

Q: Anything else from that job?

Admiral Long: No. As I said, it was very useful for me, and particularly later on when I became SubLant, the DCNO for submarines, and the Vice Chief.

Q: Then, like an addict, you went back to your submarines. [Laughter]

Admiral Long: That's right.

Q: And delighted to get a third star, I'm sure.

Admiral Long: Yes. Admiral Zumwalt at this time was now the CNO. Mickey Weisner was the Vice Chief.* So I received orders to go and relieve Dennis Wilkinson and did in the summer of '72. We had a change of command aboard the Benjamin Franklin tied up at the submarine/destroyer piers in Norfolk.** John Warner, the Secretary of the

---
*Admiral Maurice F. Weisner, USN, served as Vice Chief of Naval Operations from 1 September 1972 to 1 September 1973.
**USS Benjamin Franklin (SSBN-640) was one of the Polaris/Poseidon ballistic missile submarines.

Navy, was the speaker.*

Q: You're smiling.

Admiral Long: The ceremony was, I would say, a near-disaster. The first crack out of the box was that a Navy jet flew over, just taking off from the naval air station in Norfolk. It flew very low and very loud and blew all the mikes. We finally got some communication back. Then the tender started up its huge blowers over there, so no one else could hear. We finally got that shut down. Then it started to rain. The Secretary of the Navy had written out his speech with a pen, and the rain caused all the ink to run. So it was a real disaster.

Q: Kind of an ominous beginning.

Admiral Long: It rained so much that the runways were flooded and no one could get out. Later, we had a big reception over at the officers' club at the Naval Base Norfolk. We had a grand time at the party, but no one could leave town. So that was the beginning. I thought it was a big joke. Dennis Wilkinson didn't think it was all that funny. But every time Senator Warner talks where I'm present, he always mentions that ceremony with great glee.

---
*John W. Warner served as Secretary of the Navy from 4 May 1972 to 8 April 1974.

SubLant, of course, that was sort of the pinnacle of success within the submarine force. Sixty percent of the submarines are in the Atlantic, 40% in the Pacific.

Q: Why that specific loading?

Admiral Long: That was the split from looking at the threat of Soviet submarines. Later on, when I was the DCNO for submarines, I did another study which confirmed that, but I made a major shift in the types of submarine that were in each fleet. Before, the 40% in the Pacific were really the oldest, least modern of the submarines. I insisted that there should be a split of modern submarines in both fleets. Fortunately, that was a good decision, because later on when I went to be CinCPac, I appreciated that. [Laughter]

Q: What does the force commander do?

Admiral Long: The force commander in the Atlantic, ComSubLant, is one of the two operational commanders reporting to CinCLantFlt, the other one being Commander Second Fleet. Operational control of submarines can sometimes be exercised by Second Fleet, or they can be exercised in other situations by someone else. But normally the submarine operating command is ComSubLant. Submarines that are out on special operations and so on report directly to him. So operational control is a major function of SubLant, and, as such, he's called the submarine operating authority.

Other functions of SubLant include the logistic support, maintenance of submarines, and extensive materiel support. Training is also a major function of the type commander, and so is personnel administration. SubLant maintains training courses that are specifically for prospective commanding officers. And the administration of discipline comes up through the type commander. SubLant is in the administrative chain of command of the Navy, and that's from the Secretary of the Navy to the CNO to the fleet commanders in chief, and down to the type commanders. SubLant is also in the operational chain of command, which means it goes from the President to the Secretary of Defense to the theater CinC and then down to CinCLantFlt and the operational commands. SubLant is unique in that regard, being both in the operational as well as the administrative chain of command.

He's also a major funds/budget recipient, since he controls the money going to the various shipyards. He also has a function in developing tactics and doctrine, developed primarily through the Submarine Development Group in New London. So those are the principal functions of the submarine type commander.

Q: Is that Submarine Development Group an outgrowth of Roy Benson's old outfit?

Admiral Long: Yes. It's now a Submarine Development Squadron, but it's the old Dev Group.

Q: I wonder what specific incidents you remember under each of these various headings you've enumerated. What happened during your period on watch?

Admiral Long: Oh, well, certainly I'd say the special operations were always very interesting, also when we had various crises in Sixth Fleet or so.

Q: The Yom Kippur War occurred during that time.* Was there involvement in that?

Admiral Long: This was a case where there was an increase in deployment. The Navy wanted the maximum number of submarines and the submarine force responded, my recollection is, within 48 hours. Within 48 hours, we had over half of the submarines ready to deploy.

---
*This Israeli-Egyptian war took place in October 1973.

Q: That's impressive.

Admiral Long: Very impressive. Very impressive. It was interesting at that time that the communication link went directly from the Joint Staff J-3 to ComSubLant.* If I had been CinCLant at that time, I would have lopped J-3's head off, but I wasn't that sophisticated then.

Q: What do you remember about the logistic support of this large, far-flung force?

Admiral Long: I think the operational expertise of SubLant and the materiel support of SubLant were really the two highlights. The SubLant staff was very strong in materiel support. Some of the best officers were assigned there, to N-4. These were the people who were not only interested in overhauls but also the performance of tenders and very much the monitoring of nuclear plants. It was also just before this when each fleet instituted an ORSE Board. This was the Operational Reactor Safeguards Examination, and it belonged to the fleet commander in chief. That board normally had topnotch officers, people who were in the top 10%.

But the materiel performance of SubLant was particularly outstanding to keep the ships up in the

---

*J-3 is the operations section of the Joint Staff.

highest state of readiness, I think, of any type command in the Atlantic Fleet. We were very much interested in making sure that there was formality in the operation of those plants. So, as I say, materiel and operations were at the top of the list.

The thing that was not at the top of the list, and it should be increasingly so, was the whole command, control, communications intelligence architecture. We had reliable communications, but, as you know, they were essentially one-way VLF communications.* Submarines have not been great supporters of two-way communications, but looking to the future we must develop improved C^3I architecture if we're really going to be part of, say, Navy carrier battle groups and things like that.

Q: Were you involved in the initiatives to set up a new ELF system?**

Admiral Long: Well, I've been involved in ELF off and on over the years from the time it was a testbed down, I think, in West Virginia. Then, of course, we went through the trials and tribulations of ELF as to whether it was detrimental to your health, whether it caused interference with your TV and your telephones.

---
*VLF--very low frequency.
**ELF--extremely low frequency.

Q: Sterilized cows.

Admiral Long: Sterilized cows. Since then, they have built the ELF station up in Wisconsin and Michigan, I think it is. But I was not involved in those active ELF days.

Q: In the Med, I would presume that you would try to keep dependence on foreign support to a minimum.

Admiral Long: Of course, in the Mediterranean what we did was shift operational control of submarines to CinCEur and, of course, to CinCUSNavEur and to the submarine group commander in Naples.* SubLant still exercised a lot of materiel control. It was during this time that we deployed a submarine tender to La Maddalena, Italy, and set up the base there. Before that, we did not have a tender permanently stationed over in the Med. Submarines operated out of Naples. So this was a major improvement in the capability of the submarines in the Mediterranean.

Q: Did you have a dry docking capability over there?

Admiral Long: Not initially, but I believe later on we put one there, and I think there is one there today.

---

*CinCEur--Commander in Chief Europe; CinUSNavEur--Commander in Chief U.S. Naval Forces Europe.

Q: What do you remember about people programs in the submarine force?

Admiral Long: This was at the time when my friend Bud Zumwalt was going through some of his T sessions, and we had some major arguments with the Bureau of Naval Personnel and Dave Bagley on these.* We did go through some of the interracial meetings and so on, but I drew the line on some of the extreme things that he was doing.

One of the things I did was threaten them with Admiral Rickover if we got too far involved in some of those programs. I'd say, "I'm going to have to tell Admiral Rickover about this, and I can assure you he's going to go to the Congress."

I'll have to say, Paul, that the submarine force did not play fully, during the Zumwalt days, with some of his initiatives. In looking back, I'm glad we didn't.

Q: Are there any specific examples that you remember?

Admiral Long: Well, in my opinion Bud went too far in some of the ombudsmen programs. It was almost a destruction of the chain of command, where junior people were encouraged to bypass the chain of command and put their leading petty

---
*Vice Admiral David W. Bagley, USN, was Chief of Naval Personnel.

officers on report. Some of it, I think, was necessary. I think the racial integration was all right. But I thought that he really did an awful lot to harm the chain of command, and it took us several years to recover from that.

Q: One perception was that it was well intentioned and poorly implemented.

Admiral Long: Well, I couldn't disagree with that. But we were pretty well shielded from most of that nonsense.

Q: Just with the Rickover threat?

Admiral Long: Well, that and my role as the uncooperative type commander.

Q: So you were the shield.

Admiral Long: That's right.

Q: Is it something that you discussed with Admiral Zumwalt personally?

Admiral Long: No, I don't think I ever did. I discussed it with Dave Bagley, who is a very close friend of mine.

Q: Very close to Zumwalt also.

Admiral Long: Yes, that's right.

Q: Any complaints from him, or did he accept that you were doing what you were doing?

Admiral Long: I never had any complaints from Bud. Dave and I talked freely, and I had a lot of respect for Dave, and I'd say we got along okay. Frankly, there was not the same problem in the submarine force. The submarine force was not buffeted by those big social waves. We were somewhat removed from all of that.

Q: And part of what Admiral Zumwalt was doing would appeal to the disaffected, which you probably did not have a lot of.

Admiral Long: That's right. So we were not really the target for much of that. Primarily the surface Navy and the aviation Navy.

Q: And some things just wouldn't apply, such as greater opportunities for women.

Robert L. J. Long #2 - 286

Admiral Long: Yes. We didn't have any of those.

Q: What do you remember about the business of inspecting to see how well ships were performing, both operationally and administratively?

Admiral Long: Of course, inspection is a major part of any command, and I'd say particularly in the submarine force there's almost a hands-on attitude by division commanders, squadron commanders, and even the force commander. I routinely would ride one or two ships a quarter. I'd go out for a few days and make my own observations, and those were very useful to me. One of the things that I found was that there was almost too much Rickover influence. Rickover was a great pusher for formal discipline in communications.

I remember riding one submarine. We were coming into Norfolk, Thimble Shoal Channel. I was on the bridge with the commanding officer, and I think he was trying to impress me with his formality of communication. So he turned to the officer of the deck and said, "What's the range and bearing to buoy two?"

The officer of the deck said, "Range and bearing to buoy two, aye, sir."

So he gets on the MC and he said, "Navigator, officer of the deck, what's the range and bearing to buoy two?"

The navigator said, "Range and bearing to buoy two, navigator, aye."

A little while later the navigator came back and says, "Officer of the deck, navigator, the range and bearing to buoy two is range 3,000 yards, bearing such and such."

The officer of the deck repeated that, even though the captain was standing right there. The officer of the deck then turned to the captain and repeated the same thing, whereupon three minutes later we hit the buoy. [Laughter]

Q: Major chagrin. [Laughter]

Admiral Long: So, you know, even with Rickover's discipline and his procedures, there comes a time for common sense. So that skipper didn't do very well.

Q: I can imagine it would have been a source of great pride for you to go on board those submarines and see the young men performing well, operating equipment that you'd never dreamed of when you first went into submarines.

Admiral Long: I agree completely. They were very, very impressive. Overall, the quality of the crews was truly outstanding. This was an exception. I would give you his name, but we got rid of him.

Q: What sort of relationship did you have with Admiral Rickover during that period?

Admiral Long: We had a very close relationship, sometimes very stormy. As I've said before, he was the kind of guy who would walk over you if he could. He was the kind of guy that when he got into your own area of responsibility, if you didn't come back at him and hit him hard, he would keep coming into it. So I was always very sensitive to respecting his area of responsibility, but at the same time, I absolutely reacted violently when he came into my area.

He was a tough guy to handle, and there were times when we had shouting matches over the phone and a lot of profanity and hanging up and "sons of bitches" and all the rest of that. But that's the only way I could deal with him. Sometimes I'd be exhausted after talking to him, but I learned over time that if I let him move into my area, he would do it and he'd be ruthless.

Q: Would he try to move into the operational areas?

Admiral Long: Oh, yes. I remember one classic example. As I said, he'd normally ride these submarines on their sea trials. At night submarines do what is called rig for red. That is, in the operating spaces, in the conning tower and control room where people are up and down to the bridge and so on, they have only red lights on. Rickover didn't like that. He wanted white lights on because people could see better. There's no question, you can see better. He wanted to get the submarine under way before sunrise, and he wanted the ship rigged for white. I said, "No. If you want that ship to get under way before sunrise, it will be rigged for red. If you want it rigged for white, I'll get it under way after sunrise."

"Are you telling me how to conduct sea trials?"

I said, "No, but I'm telling you how I'm going to operate that submarine."

"Well, goddamn it, I'll take it to the CNO."

I said, "You fucking well right take it to the CNO. Go right ahead." So I mean, that was the kind of dialogue that we would have.

Q: But that's so petty.

Admiral Long: It is! But it was the typical Rickover. Of course, he never did anything about it.

Q: It was a bluff.

Admiral Long: It was a bluff. But, as I said earlier, his people were real professionals. I didn't have that sort of baloney with his people. They were very fine. Bob Panoff, Bill Wegener, real solid people. But you had to deal with Rickover, though, and a lot of people never learned how, which was too bad.

Q: What do you remember about the training facility at New London? It's a marvelous asset in that area.

Admiral Long: Yes, I agree.

Q: How closely did you monitor that training?

Admiral Long: I don't think that I personally monitored it that closely. That was a function that we relied primarily on squadron commanders and division commanders. The division commander's principal function is really one of a training officer. A few years later, they changed that organization in the squadron and actually they called those people training officers. So that was really the primary function of the division commander--to see that that submarine is trained.

Q: With the establishment of the Strategic Command last year, did that rob SubLant of some of that operational control on the boomers?

Admiral Long: I'm not completely cognizant of just how that works, but my understanding is that SubLant and SubPac actually are double-hatted. They wear one hat to CinCLantFlt/CinCPacFlt, but they wear another hat as a component commander to StratCom.

Q: So they were still intimately involved.

Admiral Long: Yes. Now, I think that's the way it is, but I'm not real sure. That's my understanding.

Q: Anything else to mention on that before you go to OP-02?

Admiral Long: No, I think that was it. I might point out that my departure change of command was more felicitous than the first one.

Q: It would have had to be. [Laughter]

Admiral Long: [Laughter] So I went on up and relieved Dennis Wilkinson again as OP-02. As you know, there are three platform sponsors--submarine, surface, and air. They are called platform barons. Certainly in the past, they were the people who actually controlled or sponsored most of the budget, because the Navy was very much oriented to platforms. We now have a new organization that is looking more and more at roles and missions. Submarines, air, surface are still represented, but they are represented as part of the naval warfare group or the OP-N8 organization run by Vice Admiral Bill Owens.*

Having been a platform sponsor, platform baron, I applaud this new organization. In the past, when we were very much platform oriented, that resulted in duplication, not pursuing the best approach for doing certain roles and missions. I don't know how this new organization is going to work out, but it clearly has the possibility of being superior to what we had in the past, where each of the platform sponsors had a certain share of the budget and there was very little give and take.

As I mentioned earlier, OP-02, the DCNO for submarine warfare, really grew out of this OP-311 that I was with before. That, in turn, became OP-31, and then finally it was decided to set up a separate DCNO for submarines. OP-02 became the real sponsor of the budget for submarines, and all those programs came in to him and he then presented his budget to the CNO and VCNO. Unfortunately, he was normally given only a certain amount of money, and if he wanted something else, then he had to give up something.

---

*At the time of the interview Vice Admiral William A. Owens, USN, was Deputy CNO, Resources, Warfare Requirements, and Assessments, N8, Office of the Chief of Naval Operations. He has since been promoted to four-star admiral and become Deputy Chairman of the JCS.

When he wanted something else, in the past it was never judged versus all other programs, and that was the great weakness in the thing. So I'm hopeful that this is going to be a better arrangement than what we've had in the past.

Q: So it should set up an impartial arbiter to decide where the real requirements are?

Admiral Long: Yes. That's the challenge. Whether Bill Owens is able to do that or not, we're going to have to just wait and see.

Q: One opinion I've heard expressed is that he probably can, but very few other people would be capable of that.

Admiral Long: Well, I think that's not unreal. He's a very talented, very smart guy, and I think if anybody could do it, I think Bill Owens can do it. I just hope that he doesn't get discouraged and say the hell with it and leave.

Q: Or he could get promoted out of the job and leave.

Admiral Long: I think that's a possibility too.

Q: Do you think this new setup will help diminish parochialism?

Admiral Long: I think we'll always have some parochialism, and, Paul, I think a certain amount of parochialism is good. As a four-star officer, I am proud to have been a submarine officer. I think as a naval aviator, as a four-star, I'm proud to have been a naval aviator. And hopefully as a destroyer guy, I'm proud to have been that. I think the same thing is true whether you're an infantryman or an artilleryman.

That was one of the things that I always emphasized when I was CinCPac. A new officer would report aboard and I would say, "You wear Air Force wings. You are a bomber pilot. I don't want you to take those wings off. You're here because you give me expertise in Air Force bombers, and I want you to be parochial. I want you to tell me why bombers can do the job or why they can't do the job. And after I make the decision, I don't want you to fight me, but I want your opinions early on." So parochialism is good, and I disagreed with Bud Zumwalt when he, in effect, said everybody needed to take off his dolphins off or take off his wings.

Q: It sounds as if part of your role was as OP-02 was to be the Pope or the "big daddy" or whatever of submarine warfare.

Admiral Long: Yes. OP-02 was really the one who spoke for submarine requirements. Of course, that's one of the things that's confusing right now, and that is, who does speak for submarine requirements? The papers say that requirements are generated by ComSubLant. Well, if you look where ComSubLant lives and if you look to his access to the Material Command, to technical things, R&D, you sort of say, "How is he staffed in order to generate those new requirements?" And the answer is, he's not. So there's going to have to be some adjustment to these concepts. It's not going to work that easily.

Q: Since you did the planning and programming before in SP, then that would have been a comfortable function for you as OP-02.

Admiral Long: Yes.

Q: Do you remember specifics along those lines?

Admiral Long: Well, I remember being frustrated because I didn't have any real flexibility. If I wanted something, I really had to give something else up, and that, in effect, said, "My new requirement is no higher priority than anyone else's lowest requirement." And so it just didn't make sense. But there was not a lot of flexibility. But we did all right. Of course, this was a time of a certain amount of building. This was from '74 to '76.

Q: The Los Angeles class was coming along.*

Admiral Long: Yes, that's right. At this time, Jim Holloway was the CNO, and Hal Shear was the Vice Chief.** Jim Holloway did an awful lot to bring stability and order back into the Navy. Bud Zumwalt had sort of thrown everything up in the air, and there was a lot of instability and unhappiness with the chain of command. Jim Holloway, I think, did a tremendous job in settling everything down.

We also still had Levering over in SP. I pushed very hard for him to get three stars on retirement, and we finally did.*** We got that for him. Bob Wertheim came in. And we had at that time Joe Williams as SubLant, who relieved me, and Chuck Griffiths was SubPac.**** I was sort of the father figure to both of them, so I didn't have any problem being the Pope. Two great guys, and we all got along. We periodically would have meetings where we would

---

*The Los Angeles (SSN-688)-class submarines have been the heart of the attack submarine force since the mid-1970s.
**Admiral James L. Holloway III, USN, served as CNO from 29 June 1974 to 1 July 1978. Admiral Harold E. Shear, USN, served as VCNO from 30 June 1975 to 5 July 1977.
***Rear Admiral Levering Smith officially retired in April 1972 upon reaching the statutory age limit. He remained on active duty until November 1977.
****Vice Admiral Joe Williams, Jr., USN; Rear Admiral Charles H. Griffiths, USN.

get together and discuss where we were going.

We were now beginning to discuss submarines in direct support of battle groups. We were still a long way from getting consensus on this, but this was the beginning of this idea that, "Hey, maybe we ought to operate more directly in support of the carrier battle group." So there began some exercises and concepts doctrine to develop that.

Q: Would the Naval War College and CNA get involved in things like that?*

Admiral Long: No, I don't think so. This primarily would be the development group getting to do that. But there wasn't any great enthusiasm by the surface people or the aviation people. It's sometimes difficult to get these new concepts and new ideas going. You have to have people receptive to the idea, as well as have people who are willing to develop it. But we were beginning to make an impact on this.

Q: So you tried this out during exercises?

Admiral Long: Yes.

Q: Well, the best way to settle it is to show how this can

---

*CNA--Center for Naval Analyses.

help make the force stronger and better protect it.

Admiral Long: But here again, those exercises always showed that the submarines were deficient in command and control, and a lot of the battle group commanders just said, "The hell with it. It's too hard. It ain't worth it." But today I think we're beginning to make some real progress, and people are beginning to understand that you are going to have to do better in the command and control to do that.

Q: What about under-ice operations? Do you remember anything in that area?

Admiral Long: Yes, that's one of the things that I supported. We had a very strong Arctic program. Dr. Waldo Lyon, was really one of our early scientists in Arctic ops, and so we routinely would conduct periodic Arctic under-ice operations.* Of course, that was, here again, oriented principally against the Soviets, but that was a capability that we needed, and we still should continue it, in my opinion.

Q: An argument that comes up from time to time is on the usefulness of diesel submarines as lower cost alternatives,

_____
*Lyon's oral history is in the Naval Institute collection.

as choke point operators and what have you. Did you address that during your period?

Admiral Long: Oh, I'm sure we did several times. That comes up many times in the Congress, "Why don't we just build diesel submarines?" Of course, it is somewhat subjective in the answer, but the answer is fundamentally that diesel submarines make a lot of sense for some countries where you're interested in your own territorial waters. But the United States' strategic concepts require the deployment of force, and we need to travel long distances to be able to get there, and diesel submarines can't do that submerged. Nuclear submarines are best for us, but we don't object to the Brits or the French or the Norwegians or the Dutch or the Germans, any of those building diesel submarines. They make sense for them, but not for us.

This argument will, I'm sure, surface again, and there is an argument right now that if we want to keep the submarine industrial base alive, what we should do is build submarines for export, and there might be some argument to that. But this has been shot down in the past because there has been this perceived idea that this will transfer a lot of technology that is very sensitive to the United States. There's some truth to that, but, in my opinion, the argument's overdrawn.

Q: Was Trident emerging as an issue during your time on watch?

Admiral Long: Yes, just in the beginning stage. I think that Bud Zumwalt was a great supporter of the Trident concept. Of course, it's turning out that if and when we draw down all the nuclear weapons, I'm confident that we'll see that the bulk of the nuclear weapons will end up in the Trident submarines. That makes a lot of sense.

Q: What advantages does Trident offer over Poseidon?

Admiral Long: Principally, range. It's a more powerful missile. You also have an advantage, as well as a disadvantage, and that is that you have 24 missiles in this submarine as opposed to 16. Now, you could make the argument, "Why don't we build a submarine that will have 500?" But that's the argument of trying to put all your eggs in one basket. We probably would be better off today if we had more platforms and fewer missiles, but we're not going to go that way. But there is an argument as to how far down you draw the number of submarines. In looking at the future of nuclear weapons, several of us, including the latest Defense Policy Board Task Force, have recommended strongly to the Secretary of Defense that the number of Trident submarines should not be reduced below 18. And we certainly should not disestablish either of the Trident bases. Hurricane Andrew clearly demonstrated that that would be a foolish thing to do.

Q: Were the bases at Bangor, Washington, and Kings Bay, Georgia, in progress when you were OP-02?

Admiral Long: Yes. We embarked on Bangor first, and that was in progress when I was OP-02. If you've never been to Bangor, you should go, because that's a base that out-SACs SAC.* It's absolutely magnificent. The care that they use in protecting the environment is great. An example is that they built the piers out far enough so they would not interfere with the salmon going to spawn. The trees were protected. It's a beautiful, environmentally sound base. I visited Bangor when it was first opening when I was CinCPac.

Kings Bay was an Army ammunition depot, and I negotiated with the Army in order to transfer that over to the Navy. That also is a very impressive base. When I was a member of the Kirkpatrick Advisory Committee just last year, we made a trip down there to look at the Trident facilities, and I can assure you they are really impressive

---

*SAC--Strategic Air Command.

Robert L. J. Long #2 - 302

down there. So those are two bases that the Navy can be very proud of.

Q: How much interaction did you have in that job with the other platform "popes," or whatever term we might use?

Admiral Long: Of course, we had many, many meetings, CNO executive boards. Essentially all of the DCNOs would get together and comment on various programs to the CNO. All major programs come before that. So we had those formal meetings, but we also had a continuing number of informal meetings. I carpooled with the DCNO (Air), Bill Houser, so we had many conversations in the morning and in the afternoon and established a good rapport.*

Q: Anything else from that tour you remember?

Admiral Long: During the time I was the DCNO for Submarine Warfare, we then really became very, very serious about SSBN security. I formed a group that acted as a board of directors for SSBN security, and that consisted of the Special Projects office; it consisted of the Naval Sea Systems Command; it included Rickover's people; it included the operational commander from the operational side; and was chaired by OP-02. We essentially looked at technical

_____
*Vice Admiral William D. Houser, USN.

problems that could contribute to threats to the SSBN, or operational practices that could be bad, or some other thing from the Sea Systems Command that could give a greater vulnerability for the SSBN and all of those. It was a synergistic type of thing.

As an example, we found out that a water sensor in the tubes emitted signals that were highly detectable by an enemy submarine. So, of course, that was corrected.

Q: How would you find out something like that?

Admiral Long: By conducting tests and monitoring it. I should have mentioned that the intelligence community was a major player in this SSBN security. At that time, Bobby Inman was the Director of Naval Intelligence, and he was a member of this group that I established.* His action officer was Rich Haver.** Rich Haver is now special assistant to the Director of Central Intelligence.

We, at that time, had intelligence that the Soviets had some special detection gear, and we brought in experts from the Scripps Laboratory, and we pursued that. These were called the Jasons, and they were some of the leading scientists in the United States. So there were some very, very important changes that were made in operational

---

*Rear Admiral Bobby R. Inman, USN, later deputy director of the Central Intelligence Agency.
**Richard Haver is a civilian.

Robert L. J. Long #2 - 304

procedures as well as in technical requirements in order to ensure that the SSBNs were not vulnerable.

Q: After that you stayed in the Pentagon and received your fourth star. How did that come about?

Admiral Long: I was OP-02 for three years. Then in 1977 Jim Holloway called me up and asked if I would be the next Vice Chief. I was a little bit surprised and pleased. He said, "Bob, you're a submariner and I'm a naval aviator, and you and I have to bend over backwards so that we do not appear to be parochial."

I said, "Jim, I'm going to be just as non-parochial as you are." He laughed. [Laughter] We had a great one year together, and then, of course, Tom Hayward came in as the new CNO.*

The Vice Chief is really the one that runs it all. He's the one that has to keep peace in the family, and he's the one who has to lay down the law every now and then. Here again, I was blessed by having some outstanding executive assistants.

Q: Who were they?

Admiral Long: Jim Service was really my first one.** He

---
*Admiral Thomas B. Hayward, USN, was Chief of Naval Operations from 1978 to 1982.
**Captain James E. Service, USN.

went on to be NavAirPac.* Jim Flatley, who was the famous Admiral Flatley's son, was my next one.** We also had some younger assistant executive assistants. Vernon Clark is now a rear admiral; Jerry Smith was a commander and he's a two-star now.*** I also had a young man by the name of Commander Paul David Miller, who was sort of the administrative assistant, and, of course, he now is four stars. So those are the kind of people that you surround yourself with, and if you screw it up, you're pretty dumb. Wonderful talent.

Q: What are some of the events and issues you remember from that job?

Admiral Long: Well, We had a whole series of meetings on programs, Paul. This was '77 to '79, and, if you remember, this was the time of the Carter Administration.**** This is the time when we lost money for personnel, we lost money for maintenance, and during this period, the readiness of the Navy and all of the armed forces went downhill. As a matter of fact, when I went to the job of CinCPac in '79, 25% of the Pacific Fleet ships were in the readiness

---

*NavAirPac--Naval Air Force Pacific Fleet.
**Captain James H. Flatley III, USN.
***Lieutenant Commander Vernon E. Clark, USN; Commander Jerome F. Smith, Jr., USN.
****Jimmy Carter was President of the United States from January 1977 to January 1981.

category C-4. That means that they were not capable of carrying out their mission, and that was a low point. So we really struggled at that time.

Harold Brown was the Secretary of Defense. Harold Brown is a very, very bright guy. I'd say he was probably more interested in technical and programmatic aspects than in operational matters. The Secretary of the Navy was a wonderful guy, Graham Claytor, and Jim Woolsey was the Under Secretary.* Good rapport with them, but we had lousy budgets, we had lousy readiness, people were leaving, retention rate was poor.

There was also another experience that I had that shaped my thinking for the future. There were times when I was the acting Chief of Naval Operations, and as a member of the Joint Chiefs of Staff, we'd meet on issues going to the President and the Secretary of Defense. I never will forget that in those meetings sometimes someone would say, "Let's give the President only our military advice. Let's not give him that political stuff. Let's just keep it pure military advice."

Of course, on reflection, that advice wasn't worth the paper it was written on, because you cannot separate out, really, military factors from political factors from economic factors when you're dealing with national

---
*W. Graham Claytor, Jr., was Secretary of the Navy; R. James Woolsey, Jr., was Under Secretary.

security. So that is something that impressed me at the time, and certainly when I became CinCPac, I realized it in spades. When you're dealing with an area the size of half the world, you can't deal only with the military considerations in national security out there. There never was a major economic or political issue that did not impact the security of the United States. So I'd say that if I learned nothing else as the Vice Chief, that was a very important thing to learn.

Q: How ironic that this should happen under the only President who was a Naval Academy graduate.

Admiral Long: Strange fellow. We used to have receptions at the White House, and I never had the feeling that there was any warmth there.

Q: What impressions did you have of Secretary Claytor?

Admiral Long: Very warm person, very interested in the Navy and the Marines.

Q: And he had served at sea.

Admiral Long: Oh, yes. He had been a DE skipper.

Q: He rescued survivors from the Indianapolis.*

Admiral Long: That's correct. That's correct. And very easy to talk to. I remember he came in with the idea that we ought to get rid of this medical support business, which he thought was nonsense. He said, "At Southern Railroad, we just issue everybody a card and they can go down to the doctor and get themselves treated. Why don't we do the same thing with the military?" We went through that drill for a while and finally came to realize that those doctors out there are not just to treat dependents and people in peacetime; they're actually there to support us in wartime. So he was very supportive, but he was unsuccessful in some cases. Of course, he went on down to be the Deputy SecDef in latter stages.

But I communicated very well with my counterpart, who was the Under Secretary. Jim Woolsey was very imaginative; he had lots of ideas. He and I could sit and discuss something and arrive at a solution fairly well.

One of the examples that I remember was that we had some very sophisticated undersea monitoring equipment--I mean, stuff that went down really deep, really deep. Nicholas Boratinsky was a Russian who had lived here almost all of his life, a very well-to-do, very personable guy.

---

*As a lieutenant commander, Claytor was commanding officer of the USS Cecil J. Doyle (DE-368), the first rescue ship on the scene after the cruiser Indianapolis (CA-35) was torpedoed and sunk by the Japanese in July 1945.

His company, called Techtratech, had developed this technology, and he had received permission from somebody in the government to sell one of these systems to the Japanese so that they could put it aboard a Russian cabler. Well, there are a lot of things down at the bottom of the ocean that we would prefer that the Russians did not get. Finally it came to my attention, and I called in Nick and I said, "You can't do this."

He said, "I thought we had permission to do it."

I said, "Well, we can't do that."

He said, "Okay."

So I went to see Jim Woolsey and what we did was form up a team of people. We sent them to Japan, where they broke into the warehouse and took off the sensitive gear. They put on the other gear, with the 2,000-foot capability on it, and left. [Laughter]

Q: Some of that pragmatism you inherited from your father.

Admiral Long: Nick Boratinsky has since passed on. He was a very fine entrepreneur.

Q: Speaking of deep-diving things, what do you remember about that <u>Glomar Explorer</u> operation and the Soviet submarine that sank out in the Pacific?*

---
*The Central Intelligence Agency tried in the 1970s to recover a Soviet submarine from the bottom of the Pacific.

Robert L. J. Long #2 - 310

Admiral Long: Well, we had a lot of that when I was over in NavShips, and I was very much involved in that. The guy who was my deputy was the action officer for that in NavShips. That was really quite a remarkable technical feat, and I was absolutely amazed every time I reviewed it. Even though they didn't get a damn thing, it was a major technical accomplishment.

Q: Now it appears maybe all we'd have to do is just buy Soviet submarines. [Laughter]

Admiral Long: I'm sure that they're for sale if we want one.

Q: What do you remember about the administrative part of the job? You say you were running the internal Navy in many aspects while the CNO was concentrating on JCS business. What all came under your span of control?

Admiral Long: Well, I think it was anything that the Navy was doing. At that time, a major difference from today, was that we couldn't spell "joint" very well, and I probably was one of the worst spellers there was. I remember there were times when the director of the Joint

Staff would come to me and say, "You know, you're not sending us very good people." That was the truth. So I cut a deal with him. I said, "You give me your top spots that you want filled with quality, and I will undertake to see that they're filled with quality."

He also came and said, "We'd like to review the Navy budget."

I said, "You can review it after we submit it to the Secretary of Defense." But that was sort of the attitude that I think that the Navy had toward jointness.

I saw this in spades when I got to be CinCPac, and it didn't play very well there. The Navy, understandably, has always been rather independent. They operate alone. They don't need the Army, they don't need the Air Force. That was true in the past. That is no longer true. I cannot conceive of any significant operation that does not have joint implications, and I don't mean I'm going to get some Army and get some Air Force just because it's PC.* But if you just look at the command and control implications, there's no way the Navy can mount an operation without using the support of other services.

Q: There have been examples of jointness for the sake of jointness, and one that comes to mind is the Libya raid,

---

*PC--politically correct.

where Air Force planes flew all the way from England and through the Strait of Gibraltar.

Admiral Long: Yes, and I think that's irresponsible. But there are others. Of course, the Gulf War is a classic example.

Q: We're near the end of the tape. Maybe we can save the rest of the story for the next time.

Admiral Long: All right.

Interview Number 3 with Admiral Robert L. J. Long,
U.S. Navy (Retired)

Place: Admiral Long's home, Annapolis, Maryland

Date: Friday, 5 March 1993

Interviewer: Paul Stillwell

Q: Admiral Long, last time we talked briefly about your time as VCNO. You mentioned that Admiral Holloway provided some stability as CNO following the Zumwalt years. What more can you say about your relationship with Admiral Holloway? How did you divide things up?

Admiral Long: Of course, Admiral Holloway had been the Vice Chief prior to his being confirmed as the Chief of Naval Operations. He was very familiar with what was going on at that time. I became the Vice Chief in the latter part of his tour. I relieved Admiral Harold Shear. It was a normal split in the functioning of the CNO's office. Admiral Holloway, of course, spent a considerable amount of his time acting as one of the Joint Chiefs, and I spent quite a bit of my time reviewing programs that would eventually end up in the budget.

We also had a CNO Executive Board that was composed of all of the Deputy Chiefs of Naval Operations and the other senior naval officers that were on the OpNav staff. That would meet maybe once or twice a week, where we would sit and review major programs--major air programs, surface programs, submarine programs.

So I would say that most of my time was really in acting as the chief of staff for Admiral Holloway and actually reviewing and sorting out those things that were of prime importance to the Navy at that time. Of course, when Admiral Holloway was out of town, or his successor, Admiral Hayward, then I would also serve as the acting chief in the Joint Chiefs of Staff.

Q: What do you remember about the times that you were acting chief? What kinds of issues got discussed?

Admiral Long: Those were clearly things that were major budget issues. One of the times I was acting chief was when we were negotiating with Panama for return of sovereignty of the Panama Canal to Panama. It just worked out that I ended up being the acting chief of the Navy at the time when the Secretary of Defense testified before the Senate. I went along as a member of the Joint Chiefs to support that treaty. The testimony was televised, and I received a call from my brother that evening. My brother was a farmer in Missouri, and he asked, "What in the world were you doing supporting that treaty where we're going to give that canal back to Panama?"

So I went into some detail, explaining that in the view of the chiefs, our security was better protected this way than continuing on the way we were. I pointed out that the greatest threat to the use of the canal was internal security rather than external security. So I went through this ten minutes or so. At the end of it, his comment was, "Yes, but goddamn it, we own it." And that was a rather common reaction, I think, with the American public.

Q: The people said, "Yes, we stole it fair and square back in 1903." [Laughter]

Admiral Long: We still have to see how that treaty is going to turn out.

Q: Why did you believe it was better for U.S. interests to go along with the treaty?

Admiral Long: The greatest threat to the canal was the possibility of internal threats. Of course, if you've ever been to the Panama Canal, you know that there are many places where if you would disable one ship, you could put the canal out of business.

Q: So sabotage was a concern.

Admiral Long: Sabotage was a principal concern that we had at that time, and I think that that is still true today. If you had an unfriendly indigenous population, you could find that there could be some serious threats to the use of the canal.

Q: Fueled by resentment of the United States, presumably.

Admiral Long: Yes, yes. Of course, the truth, as I had said before, is that if you're looking at a major national security issue, you cannot look at it only from the standpoint of the military aspect. National security really involves, normally, military considerations, political considerations, economic considerations, and very much cultural considerations. Of course, I learned that was quite true later when I became CinCPac.

Q: Panama is a perfect example. If military were the only consideration, you'd say keep it.

Admiral Long: That's right. But there are other considerations. Now, when I say political considerations, I'm not talking about Republican versus Democrat.

Q: One thing, perhaps, that could come out of a treaty would be more political stability in Panama.

Robert L. J. Long #3 - 317

Admiral Long: That's right. And of course, that was one of the considerations at that time.

Q: How much was the Navy position formulated by OP-06 on issues like that?

Admiral Long: I think OP-06 was quite instrumental in developing the Navy's position. Admiral Joe Moorer was OP-06 at that time.* He was quite influential with the Vice Chief and the CNO.

Q: Both you and Admiral Holloway were extremely busy. Did you and he have time to talk these issues through on occasion?

Admiral Long: Normally, at least once a day. In the morning or in the afternoon, in the evening, we would have some time, just the two of us. I remember one time I had spent a considerable amount of time during the day reviewing a Saudi Arabia military assistance program. I think it was called SNEP, Saudi Navy Expansion Program.

Q: They were getting some gunboats, I remember.

---
*Vice Admiral Joseph P. Moorer, USN.

Robert L. J. Long #3 - 318

Admiral Long: That's right. Jim and I met late in the afternoon and he said, "Well, what did you do today?"

I said, "Well, I'll tell you. I reviewed probably the worst program I've ever reviewed. That was the SNEP program, and it was not well managed, it was very fuzzy. There were no real clear objectives. With a new program manager, hopefully we can turn that program around."

Q: What was his reaction? Did he just say, "Make it so"?

Admiral Long: He just concurred, and away we went. We had a very good working relationship.

Q: I would think part of your job would be to decide what things you can handle yourself and which ones to buck up to him.

Admiral Long: Yes, that's true. But I also was quite conscientious in keeping him informed of what I was doing. He was the one ultimately responsible for the running of the Navy, and I felt that it was terribly important that I take action, but also make sure that he was informed on those that were significant actions.

Q: Since he had confidence in you, it makes his job easier if you would just give him solutions instead of more problems. What do you remember about his working style and personality?

Admiral Long: Jim was a very conscientious person. He was not a hip-shooter. He many times kept his own counsel. As I said earlier, I thought that he did a lot of healing within the Navy. Because as much as I admire my good friend Admiral Zumwalt, he left some scars, primarily in the chain of command and in the attitude from juniors to seniors. My sense is that Jim Holloway did a masterful job in healing those and bringing the Navy back into a more cohesive force.

Q: Admiral Holloway has a number of the qualities that one associates with a politician or a statesman--very smooth, very polished, good speaker, able to bring people together.

Admiral Long: Yes, yes, and has some very good fundamental values about leadership and discipline and the culture of the Navy. Of course, his father was a senior naval officer, and I'm sure that Jim acquired some of those traits directly from his dad.*

Q: His dad was a very inspiring man. He lived the Navy.

---
*His father was James L. Holloway, Jr., who served on active duty from the time he was sworn in as a midshipman in 1915 until he retired as a four-star admiral in 1960.

Admiral Long: Yes, yes.

Q: What do you remember about the drug problem and its ramifications in those years?

Admiral Long: I think this was the time when we really saw the policy of the Navy on zero tolerance put this problem to bed. So the drug problem was not all that dominant at that time. The principal problem that we had was the readiness of the Navy. If you remember back, this was at the time of the Carter Administration. The pay was low, the retention of our people was low, and inflation at one time or another was over 15%. So, frankly, some of our officers and enlisted people just couldn't make ends meet, particularly those with families.

Q: I think the readiness probably really hit bottom during Admiral Hayward's watch, didn't it, and then he started to turn it around.

Admiral Long: Yes.

Q: Did the situation change any when Admiral Hayward came in as CNO? Did you have the same sort of relationship with him, or was it different?

Admiral Long: I was the Vice Chief when Admiral Hayward was the CNO for about a year. Our relationship was amicable, and no great change to that.

Q: What do you remember of his personality? He strikes me as a very glib individual, very good in public situations.

Admiral Long: He was much more of an extrovert than Jim Holloway, but fairly effective, and I think he also was more of a hands-on kind of a chief.

Q: Any examples in that regard?

Admiral Long: The title of the chief of the Navy is the Chief of Naval Operations, and, of course, the military head of the Navy is not the operational head of the Navy. Sometimes there were a few cases where the chief didn't quite realize that he was not really the operational commander.

Q: Do you remember examples of that?

Admiral Long: I remember examples of when I became CinCPac when I had to go ahead and remind the chief of the Navy that he was not really the operational commander.

Q: Do you want to mention any of those?

Admiral Long: Well, we can later when we get into that particular billet.

Q: He had struck me as a workaholic. Perhaps that goes with the job, but that's the impression I had.

Admiral Long: Yes, I'd say that Tom Hayward probably was a very hard worker, very aggressive in some of the things that he did.

Q: What do you remember about the developing Iranian situation during the late Seventies, first the attempt to build up the Iranian Navy, working with the Shah, and then the overthrow and the Ayatollah?

Admiral Long: The Iranian Government had a special mission in the United States to facilitate training and transfer of various equipment, submarines, destroyers, so on. One of the things that was involved was building some destroyer types by Litton in Pascagoula, Mississippi.* The officer who was in charge of the mission was Vice Admiral Dariusd

---

*After the overthrow of the Shah in 1979, Litton completed these four ships for the U.S. Navy. They are now in service as the Kidd (DDG-993) class.

Farzaneh. He still lives in the United States. He and I became friends, and we are still friends today. He's a dedicated sailor, has been active in the support of the Naval Academy sailing, maintains a home here in Annapolis and also, as far as I know, still maintains a residence at the Watergate Apartments in Washington.

There were several very important programs that were going on at that time. Of course, one was the transfer of submarines and the training of the submarine crews. We worked with the Iranian Embassy out on Massachusetts Avenue. Mr. Zahedi, the ambassador at that time, was a very personable man.* The relationship between the Iranian Navy and the United States Navy at that time was very healthy, very positive. Then the Shah was overthrown in 1979, near the end of my time as the Vice Chief and shortly before I went to CinCPac. Of course, we all remember that that was the time when The Iranians took the hostages.**

Q: One of the suggestions was that the Shah had overly ambitious schemes for his country and that the populace wasn't really in the position to support this large and sophisticated a navy. What was the perception in our Navy on that point?

---
*Ambassador Ardeshir Zahedi.
**The hostages were seized by Iranian militants on 4 November 1979 and held until the day President Ronald Reagan was inaugurated, 20 January 1981.

Admiral Long: Certainly I was not sensitive to that particular aspect. My impression was that the Shah was pushing his country into democratic ideals, a capitalist free-market economy. I guess if I had one criticism, that would be that the Shah was pushing too far too fast. It's the old philosophy, and that is, when you get a revolution under way, it's pretty hard to stop it and control it. Of course, there was at that time, and still is today a very strong fundamentalist sect to the Islamic religion.

Q: That's what the Ayatollah tapped into.

Admiral Long: The Ayatollah was at that time living in France, and he was just waiting for the opportunity to return. Of course, he finally did return, and that set in train a whole series of events that finally resulted in the overthrow of the Shah and, of course, the taking of the American hostages.

Q: Which became a preoccupation, or even an obsession, with our government after that.

Admiral Long: Right.

Q: That period in the late Seventies was probably the height for the Soviet Navy in terms of new ships and deployment schedules and what have you. What concern was that in Washington during your time as VCNO?

Admiral Long: Looking back on that time, the late Seventies, I believe we can show that this was the time when really the Soviets made their greatest expansion. This was the time when there were major improvements.

Q: They brought out their new V/STOL carriers and the new cruisers, submarines.*

Admiral Long: Major improvements in aircraft carriers, submarines. My recollection is that they were turning out some eight to ten submarines a year versus our one or two. This was also a time when there was also not just military expansion, but there was also a time when there was great political expansion, political influence by the Soviets. And, of course, this was the time when there was great concern on the part of some of our so-called friends and allies as to whether the United States was able to stand up to this expansion.

The Soviets had a growing influence in the Pacific. They were building up the Soviet Navy and the Air Force at

---
*V/STOL--vertical and short takeoff and landing aircraft.

that time. The ground forces that they had at that time in the eastern Soviet Union, my recollection was that there were some 50 divisions at that time. The Soviet Pacific Fleet was their largest fleet, and there was great consternation within our allies at that time as to whether the United States would be able to maintain a stable area.

Shortly after I took over as the U.S. commander in chief of the Pacific theater, we had a meeting of chiefs of mission. We had this in Singapore. The Secretary of State's representative was Richard Holbrooke, and we had a separate special meeting that consisted of Dick Holbrooke and myself.* We had Mike Mansfield, who was our ambassador in Japan, and we had our ambassador to China, Leonard Woodcock.** Woodcock he was a fine fellow; he had been a labor leader.

That group met at night with the President of Singapore, Lee Kuan Yew. When we walked in, he turned to me, and the first thing that he said was, "Admiral, how are you going to protect the straits?" That represented some of the concern that countries out there had with the United States's resolution.

I gave him not a very good answer. Then I asked, "What would you suggest?"

He said, "I think you should position another carrier

---
*Richard C. A. Holbrooke was Assistant Secretary of State for East Asian and Pacific Affairs.
**Michael J. Mansfield, who previously had been a U.S. senator from Montana.

battle group out here."

I said, "Do you have any suggestion as to where we could position it? Could we position it in Singapore?"

He said, "I wouldn't rule that out."

That was the beginning of a dialogue that even continues today, which clearly reveals the Singapore Government being willing to have United States military forces stationed there in Singapore.

Q: And useful to us after being closed out of the Philippines.

Admiral Long: Yes. I did look at the possibility of home-porting a carrier at Singapore, but at that time we still had very strong ties with the Philippines, and we also had the Midway home-ported in Yokosuka, Japan. At the time it did not appear to be an attractive proposition to position another carrier in Singapore, primarily because of the distance from training areas, the distance from other forces, the distance from logistic support. Although the naval base at Singapore was a magnificent base, it was not readily available. With a deep-draft carrier, there would have had to have been some significant dredging, because the naval base is on the north side, the landward side of Singapore.

Q: Did they have adequate dry docking facilities?

Admiral Long: Yes, they did. It was a magnificent old Royal Navy base.

Q: So distance was the main consideration.

Admiral Long: Distance, cost, and need, per se. As I say, the Philippines was an excellent base. Not only did it have the ship repair facilities, but it also had the logistic depots, ammunition, supply depots. And also very important, it also had the training ranges where United States military forces could exercise with live ammunition.

Q: How much of a sense of frustration was there in OpNav that you had this growing Soviet threat on the one hand, and then the Carter Administration not seeming to want to build up to meet it?

Admiral Long: I think it was a quiet frustration. This goes to a point that I made earlier and one that I would make again later on when I conducted a study for the Chairman of the Joint Chiefs of Staff on the education of senior officers. Senior military officers clearly are subject to civilian control, but military officers also have an obligation to tell their civilian bosses their views not only on the military implications of a national security issue, but the political, economic, and, as I say, cultural aspects. Looking back at that time, I don't think that the senior military in the Pentagon was as forceful and articulate as we should have been to really put forth the concerns that we had.

When I took over as CinCPac, 25% of the ships of the Pacific Fleet were considered not available or not ready for combat. It was what we would call C-4, which is a readiness condition, C-1 being fully ready and then on down, C-4 not being able to carry out its primary mission. The principal reason why not just naval ships but Army and Marine units were not able to carry out their assigned missions was because so many of them had lost the necessary personnel talent. The Air Force was not in as bad a shape as the Navy, Army, or Marine Corps at that time.

Q: That was partly tied to pay rates, as I remember.

Admiral Long: Very much tied to pay rate. As I said earlier, these military people were having difficulty in making ends meet.

Q: What do you remember about the issue of sealift shortage while you were in the VCNO job? Later, a remedy came along around 1980 by putting prepositioned forces overseas.

Admiral Long: Before discussing that, I think it's important that I try to paint a bigger picture of the military strategic view. This was at the time when we had what was called the swing strategy. This was at the time when we went into programs called POMCUS, which is prepositioned material overseas for use in wartime. What this national military strategy really envisioned was that if we went to war with the Soviets, then the United States would elect to fight that war in Europe. The swing strategy required that most of the forces that were assigned in the Pacific would be swung to the Atlantic.

Insofar as the services were concerned, most of the chiefs really did not see any need for military forces in the Pacific other than if there was a Korean contingency. I remember discussing this with the Chief of Staff of the Air Force at the time, and he remarked, "Bob, as far as I'm concerned, the only reason that we provide air forces for the Pacific is for a Korean contingency." To me, that was completely unrealistic--the very idea that we would go ahead and engage the Soviets in Europe and in the Atlantic and essentially wave to them as we go by in the Pacific.

There were some strong supporters of this. The Secretary of Defense at that time was Harold Brown, a very sharp guy. But I'd have to say, candidly, that Dr. Brown was primarily interested in the programmatic aspects of defense rather than the strategic aspects.

Q: He came from a technology and an R&D background.*

Admiral Long: Yes, great technologist, and during his time some great technology programs were initiated, one of those being, of course, the stealth aircraft programs.

So one of the first things that I did when I went to the Pacific was to review the strategic plans of the theater. I found that the planning really envisioned moving most of the force out of the Pacific. I then set about to change that.

Q: But that's not something you can change unilaterally.

Admiral Long: No. No. Fortunately we had a change of administration shortly thereafter. The Reagan administration came in, and Mr. Weinberger then became the Secretary of Defense.** However, even at the end of the Carter Administration, there were already expressions of doubt as to whether the swing strategy made a lot of sense. Even in my discussions with Harold Brown, there was some

---
*R&D--research and development.
**Caspar W. Weinberger served as Secretary of Defense from 1981 to 1987.

indication that the swing strategy might be more political than it was an actual military strategy.

Q: Do you have anything else to mention specifically about your tenure as Vice Chief of Naval Operations?

Admiral Long: Yes. There was also another significant deficiency in the organization that I observed at that time, and that was the relationship between the Department of Defense and the intelligence community. Of course, the Secretary of Defense was Dr. Harold Brown, and the Director of Central Intelligence at that time was Admiral Stansfield Turner.* There were some initiatives on Admiral Turner's part to do net assessments of certain situations which would involve having access to United States military information. These never got off the ground, and there was almost a Chinese wall that existed between the Pentagon and the Director of Central Intelligence, primarily CIA.

That's something that did not work to the advantage of the United States nor to the advantage of the military. It's something that we now have seen some major improvements in that relationship under Bob Gates and now, of course, under Jim Woolsey.**

---
*Admiral Stansfield Turner, USN, was a 1947 Naval Academy classmate of President Jimmy Carter.
**Robert M. Gates, Director of Central Intelligence, 1991-93.

Q: Was this because of jealousy over separate fiefdoms, or what caused the problem?

Admiral Long: Well, I wouldn't categorize it that shallow. I think that there were some genuine concern as to sharing some of this sensitive information with the intelligence community, and I'm sure that there were personalities involved between Turner and Brown. This was not a healthy situation.

Q: Of course, that's always one of the classic dilemmas on intelligence. If you tell too many people, it's not a secret anymore, but if you don't tell enough, it's of no value. It's not being used.

Admiral Long: Yes. Well, we still don't have a perfect relationship. I remember when I was on the Science and Technology Advisory Panel to the Director of Central Intelligence, and we were trying to figure out what the Soviets were doing in stealth. Bill Casey was the Director of Central Intelligence.* So we formed a little group to look into what the organization was, and our first conclusion was that the intelligence community wasn't really looking for the right things. In other words, the

---

*William J. Casey, Director of Central Intelligence from 1981 to 1987.

collection requirements were not correct. And second, even if they collected the right stuff, they didn't have the talent to analyze it. Of course, to get that talent, you have to have some appreciation of what the United States is doing. It's an iterative kind of a process.

Now, obviously you don't want to reveal everything. As you say, it's no longer a secret. But somewhere there needs to be a policy which, in effect, will facilitate not only the collection of critical intelligence, but the analysis of that intelligence for the benefit of both the intelligence people and the customers who are policy-level people.

Q: One of the other technological things coming along in that period was Aegis. How much did you keep track on that?

Admiral Long: Of course, we looked at Aegis from time to time, and my assessment was that Aegis was being very well run. There was a rather aggressive young admiral over there, Wayne Meyer, that was the program manager.* I think that's one of the programs that the Navy can be very proud of.

Q: You can draw a parallel between that and Admiral
------
*Rear Admiral Wayne E. Meyer, USN, Project Manager, Aegis Shipbuilding Project.

Rickover in having a longtime czar of a particular development program.

Admiral Long: That's right. That's right. Wayne Meyer would probably never win a popularity contest, but he was an extremely effective program manager.

Q: And a great salesman for it too.

Admiral Long: Yes.

Q: Anything more to say before we move you out to Honolulu?

Admiral Long: No, I think that's it.

Q: I can imagine that there was a great satisfaction being an operational commander after working in the Pentagon for those years.

Admiral Long: Yes. I spent what at that time was a rather long period for someone to be assigned to the Pentagon--five years--but I'll have to say, Paul, that it was a very broadening experience for me at that time. Of course, the Navy was going through some very troubling times during the late Seventies, so when I did arrive in Honolulu to relieve Admiral Weisner, not only was the climate refreshing, but the whole command was refreshing.* I relieved in the fall, and, as I've said earlier, the materiel condition, the readiness condition of the command was really quite low.

In looking at the ability of the command to fight, I found such things that we had about a week's supply of sophisticated air-to-air munitions, I found that we had less than a week's supply of aviation fuel in Korea. I found that there were similar deficiencies in ammunition and critical stores throughout the theater.

Q: Probably training readiness, as well.

Admiral Long: So those were things that we set about to try to correct. As I say, the thing that facilitated the change, of course, was the new administration and Mr. Weinberger coming on as the Secretary of Defense.

I think also it's important to note that up to that point, the role of the theater commander was not all that well defined, and in some cases the service chiefs almost ignored the theater commander. The theater commanders technically reported to the Secretary of Defense through

---

*Admiral Maurice F. Weisner, USN, served as Commander in Chief Pacific and Commander in Chief U.S. Pacific Fleet from 30 August 1976 to 31 October 1979.

the Joint Chiefs of Staff. When I first took over, it was normal procedure that the CinC would write a quarterly letter to the Secretary of Defense. What he did with it, I don't know. That gradually turned around when Weinberger came in so that there was a much closer tie between the Secretary of Defense and the CinC.

I want to remind you that there are two chains of command. One is what we would call the operational chain of command, and that goes from the President to the Secretary of Defense through the Joint Chiefs of Staff to the unified and specified commanders. The other is what we might call the administrative chain of command, or as the Army would call it, the line command. That goes from the President to the Secretary of Defense, to the service secretaries, to the chief of service, then out to the various commands underneath him, specifically CinCPacFlt, CinCLantFlt, CinCUSNavEur. That chain of command deals with such things as personnel and discipline and logistics and training, those kind of things, but clearly not the operational chain of command.

Mr. Weinberger started putting greater emphasis on the operational chain of command and greater emphasis and greater visibility on the unified and specified commands. Of course, that process continued on until it finally culminated in the Goldwater-Nichols Act.* As a result, I think it's recognized now that the theater commanders have a tremendous amount of clout, and I think their position is very well established.

Q: How was Weinberger's sense of emphasis manifested? In what ways were you getting more attention?

Admiral Long: There was a greater personal communication between the Secretary of Defense and the CinCs. For the first time that I'm aware of, the Secretary of Defense started bringing the CinCs back to Washington for the critical budget and program meetings, and they were asked to present their requirements. At that time, we set up procedures whereby the services were required to receive these requirements and to do something about them.

I'll have to say, in those first meetings, the CinCs didn't do a very good job because, that was a brand-new chore for them, and also they hadn't quite set up the architecture as to how they developed those requirements on their own staffs.

Q: So there was probably a sense of awkwardness, as well.

---

*The Goldwater-Nichols Defense Reorganization Act became law of 1 October 1986. For more information, see James K. Gruetner and William Caldwell, "Defense Reorganization," U.S. Naval Institute Proceedings, May 1987, pages 136-145.

Admiral Long: That's right. Of course, in order to develop those requirements for the theater, you had to have a good rapport with the component commanders: Navy, Air, Army, Marines.

Q: Had CinCPac staff had a program planning shop up till then?

Admiral Long: No, I wouldn't categorize it that way. It was something that was developed over time. I think it's important also, and that is that when you talk about requirements, clearly a theater commander is not competent to say what the characteristics of a new aircraft or a ship or a tank would be. The requirements that theater commanders properly should be concerned with are capabilities, force levels, logistic support, command, control, communication intelligence architecture. As I say, those years in the early 1980s were really sort of the beginning, I think, of effective architectures in order to set forth requirements.

Q: What are your assessments of Secretary Weinberger? He had not really had a defense background prior to then. Was he a quick study?

Admiral Long: The Secretary of Defense, to oversimplify, really has two jobs. One is that he's the head of one of the largest businesses in the country, and that's the business of procurement, contracting, requirements, all of that. Of course, the other one is that he is the principal adviser to the President insofar as the development of national security, strategy, military strategy, military operations.

Mr. Weinberger, who is a lawyer, had several years of previous government experience and was close to the President. One of the things that he did on the first one of those tasks, running the business of defense, was to delegate a tremendous amount of authority to the service secretaries. One of the service secretaries, of course, was John Lehman, and John Lehman picked up that delegation of authority and ran with it. The services were almost independent. That would not be my way of running that particular aspect of defense, but that's the way Mr. Weinberger did it. We had an expanding budget, and it worked pretty well.

In the other function of the Secretary of Defense, as the principal adviser to the President on national security affairs, he was my direct boss in the operational chain of command. I thought that he did a superb job in that. Whereas Harold Brown, I'd say, was more interested in the programmatic and technical aspects of the job, Caspar

Weinberger, I thought, had a balance. He had a good rapport with the CinCs, he had a good rapport with the chiefs, and I thought his judgment was really quite good on operational matters.

Q: Do you have examples from your dealing with him in operational matters?

Admiral Long: Well, before, when Harold Brown was the Secretary of Defense, General Jones was the Chairman of the Joint Chiefs of Staff, we had one operational event that demonstrated clearly the wrong way to do it.* That was Desert One.** Desert One, just to remind you, was the operation that was designed to rescue the hostages in Iran. The planning was done primarily in Washington, very tightly held, did not bring in necessary expertise in weaponry, platforms, command, control, communications intelligence. Unfortunately, that operation was not successful. That was done in the Persian Gulf. Since it was not in my theater, my principal role in that was to provide a platform from which these helicopters could take off.

---

*General David C. Jones, USAF, served as Chairman of the Joint Chiefs of Staff from 21 June 1978 to 18 June 1982.
**On 24 April 1980, after diplomatic initiatives had failed to resolve the crisis in Iran, U.S. military forces tried to rescue the American hostages held there. Because of equipment failures, the rescue was called off. During the pullout, two aircraft collided in darkness. Eight Americans were killed and five injured.

One operation that was done later on was mounted in response to hostile actions by North Korea where they attempted to shoot down a SR-71 reconnaissance aircraft. I formed a joint task force directly on scene rather than the cumbersome system that many had tried before. I formed a strong joint group at my headquarters to advise me, and, of course, we also had direct links with the Secretary of Defense back in Washington. That's an example of the kind of improvements that we had made in operational matters.

Q: What do you remember of your face-to-face dealings with Secretary Weinberger?

Admiral Long: He's a gentleman. Mr. Weinberger is a gentleman. He has a great sense of humor, he's very easy to talk to, he has very high standards. He visited the theater, so he had hands-on experience out with the troops, with the ships. I always felt very comfortable in dealing with him. I wouldn't hesitate picking up the telephone and talking to him personally. I always knew, and he wanted it that way, that he was my immediate boss. Now, I was conscientious in keeping the Chairman of the Joint Chiefs of Staff informed, because the Chairman of the Joint Chiefs of Staff and the other chiefs at that time were military advisers to the Secretary of Defense and to the President.

Robert L. J. Long #3 - 343

There was always a little question as to where the chiefs stood in this chain of command. In his testimony before Senator Nunn and Senator Goldwater, General Jones wanted the Chairman of the Joint Chiefs of Staff, or the Joint Chiefs of Staff, placed in the chain of command.*

I testified against that, because when I go to Washington for authority or advice, I don't need military advice. I have plenty of that with my own component commanders. What I need from Washington is political advice, and the Joint Chiefs of Staff cannot give me that. I have to get that from the Secretary of Defense and the President. Fortunately, I believe that the Goldwater-Nichols bill agreed with that. So that even today, the Joint Chiefs of Staff, and specifically the chairman, are not in the chain of command. They're in the channel of command, and that's the way it should be.

Q: You mentioned there were a couple of cases in which you had to talk to Admiral Hayward, the CNO, about that role. Do you want to put those on the record?

Admiral Long: Well, it was not only Admiral Hayward, but there were a couple of instances where in one way or another I had intercepted messages from the chiefs, from CNO or from the Chief of Staff of the Air Force, where they

---
*Senator Sam Nunn--Democraft, Georgia; Senator Barry Goldwater--Republican, Arizona.

were actually directing forces under my command to do things. So it was necessary for me to pick up the phone and remind those people that they were not in that operational chain of command. That was not only necessary with Admiral Hayward, but it was even necessary with my good friend Admiral Watkins, when he later became the Chief of Naval Operations.* In all fairness, I'd say that those messages from "the CNO" were probably messages that were released by officers beneath the actual CNO.

Q: Did you go along with the directions or countermand them? What was the outcome?

Admiral Long: I don't recall in each case. But there was a principle involved, and the principle was that CinCPac—not the service chiefs—ought to exercise operational command of all of those forces.

Q: I can almost see a parallel here to your dealings with Admiral Rickover. If you don't assert yourself, you'll be preempted.

Admiral Long: I think you're absolutely right, and I think that that probably was why I might have been more sensitive

---

*Admiral James D. Watkins, USN, served as Chief of Naval Operations from 1982 to 1986.

Robert L. J. Long #3 - 345

than others so as to protect my turf.

Q: Speaking of your turf and your component commanders, I wonder if you could run through the individual services and the relations you had out in Hawaii, please.

Admiral Long: Well, that's a very important point. There have been situations in the past where the theater CinC didn't have very good rapport with his component commanders, and in the Pacific we saw some confusion and a lack of good rapport with some of the senior officers involved in the Vietnam War. Admittedly, at that time there was some real confusion in the command structure, where you have General Westmoreland in Vietnam, who was a very prominent person in the press and politically, and then you have Admiral Sharp, who was CinCPac, and you had the Seventh Fleet, who was directly supporting Westmoreland, and there was some confusion as to who worked for whom.*

Even beyond that, there was some lack of harmony because of personalities involved in the past and there were also some poor relations because, as I've said earlier, the position of the CinC was not all that firmly established. Many of the component commanders had their

---
*General William C. Westmoreland, USA, Commander U.S. Military Assistance Commander Vietnam, 1964-68; Admiral U.S. Grant Sharp, USN, Commander in Chief Pacific, 1964-68.

allegiance primarily to the service chief, and, "Well, you know, the CinC doesn't control my career. If I'm going to go anyplace else, the chief of service is going to have the principal say." So those things sort of added to some of this lack of harmony.

Q: What was the situation when you took over?

Admiral Long: When I took over, I thought that Mickey Weisner had done a magnificent job in improving the rapport between the CinC and the component commanders. When he took over, it wasn't all that good. But what he passed on to me was, I thought, a healthy situation, and hopefully I built on that.

Q: What kind of techniques did you use to promote this kind of harmony?

Admiral Long: Well, there are a couple of things. One is, you need to get those people together periodically and make sure that they understand what you want, and then you also get a feedback so you can understand their problems. And so we did that. We'd routinely get together weekly or so for a meeting.

I think also they have to understand that you're there to help them when they have a problem. Problems could vary widely. But they need to understand that you're there not only to tell them what to do, but when they have a problem, you can help them. And I think, last, and fortunately we didn't have to exercise that, is that when they don't do the proper thing, you let them know.

One of the instances I remember dealt with Commander U.S. Forces Korea. Both he and Commander U.S. Forces Japan report to CinCPac. We had a coup in Korea about that time. General Wickham was the U.S. commander.* One of the things that I did was that I maintained him in residence with me until things sort of settled down. He was the one that really set up the special reconnaissance flights for me, and that was also a very healthy experience.

The Army had previously allowed the job of Commander in Chief of U.S. Army Pacific to deteriorate so that it was two-star and it was actually called USWestCom. General Forrester and I had excellent rapport, and we eventually turned that around and it became U.S. Army Pacific, and that's doing well.** I had a U.S. Air Force Pacific, good rapport there. When I arrived, the Pacific Fleet Commander in Chief was a classmate of mine, Donald Davis, otherwise known as "Red Dog," and he and I were close friends.*** He had been the program and budget officer on the CNO staff

---
*General John A. Wickham, Jr., commanding general of the Eighth U.S. Army, headquarters in South Korea.
**Major General Eugene P. Forrester, USA.
***Admiral Donald C. Davis, USN, served as Commander in Chief Pacific Fleet, 9 May 1978 to 31 July 1981.

when I was the Vice Chief, and so there was absolutely no question that he was a good, strong, loyal supporter. He was then eventually replaced by Admiral Watkins, who was an old-time friend, and then finally Admiral Foley, so I went through three of them.* At the end of the tour, it was pretty well recognized that CinCPac was in charge.

Q: Any specific memories of those three Navy commanders you've mentioned?

Admiral Long: Well, they were all different. Of course, Admiral Davis was a naval aviator, Admiral Watkins was a submariner, and Admiral Foley was a naval aviator. Admiral Davis and Admiral Watkins were both very, very zealous in making sure that I was never surprised. They kept me fully informed. Admiral Foley was also very careful, but initially he didn't have the same rapport with me, and I guess maybe difference in age was beginning to show up a little bit.

Q: But you didn't have the previous ties with him, either.

Admiral Long: That's right, and it took Admiral Foley a little while to develop, I'd say, being comfortable with

---

*Admiral James D. Watkins, USN, served as Commander in Chief Pacific Fleet from July 1981 to May 1982. Admiral Sylvester R. Foley, Jr., USN, was in the billet from May 1982 to September 1985.

me. Of course, since then there has been a significant change in the support that CinCPac provides those component commanders. Here recently we have established what we call a Joint Intelligence Center, a JIC. They established that first at CinCPac, and it has now become a model for intelligence centers around the world. That is a more efficient, effective way of handling intelligence and distributing all of this.

Q: It's sort of interesting, because there was a JICPac when Admiral Nimitz was commander in chief.* [Laughter]

Admiral Long: [Laughter] We sort of relearn these lessons. Right.

PacCom, the Pacific Command, is truly a very interesting, unique place. PacCom is over half the earth's surface. Whereas in NATO you have a very tight alliance of some 10 to 15 countries, in the Pacific you have a series of alliances.** Normally, they are bilateral.

But here again, as the Pacific commander, you really are impressed with the importance not only of military relations, but political and economic relations. There never was a significant political or economic event that did not impact on the security of the United States.

---
*Fleet Admiral Chester W. Nimitz, USN, was CinCPac during World War II.
**NATO--North Atlantic Treaty Organization.

That's a major message for anyone that is looking at national military strategy.

Q: Did you have advisers in those areas, political and economic?

Admiral Long: Yes. There was a political adviser, who was a Foreign Service officer. Mike Connors was a younger political adviser, and he went on from CinCPac to become the deputy chief of mission in Malaysia and then the deputy chief of mission in Indonesia with Paul Wolfowitz, who was the ambassador at that time and a tremendous help.*

I tried to keep the political adviser fully apprised of what was going on. Every morning I'd have a meeting of my senior advisers, and the political adviser, the PolAd, would always be part of that. As a result, when he gave advice, he gave that advice in the context of knowing all of the background of the problem. We also had a political adviser from the National Security Agency. Here again, sort of recognizing that Chinese wall that had been built up between the Director of Central Intelligence and the Secretary of Defense, we needed, but did not have, a DCI representative. We are now seeing that.

Q: How large a staff did you have to deal with this vast

---

*Paul D. Wolfowitz, U.S. ambassador to Indonesia, 1986-89.

Robert L. J. Long #3 - 351

Admiral Long: My recollection, Paul, was about 500. I quickly point out that seems like a lot of people, but it was probably one of the smallest of the unified commander staffs.

Q: How deeply can you get involved? You certainly can't deal with 500 people on a daily basis.

Admiral Long: Well, of course, you are very dependent on your senior advisers, but you also have the option of being in as deeply as you want in any one thing.

Q: Do you remember any things that you dug particularly deeply on?

Admiral Long: Well, for certain operations. I mentioned the SR-71. Another time I remember, we had indications that there were live Caucasians that were in a camp in Cambodia. Obviously, we were thinking that these were prisoners of war from the Vietnam era. What I did was to form a joint task force that had naval forces, air forces, and special operations forces from the Army. Something like that you get pretty deeply involved in it, knowing what they can and cannot do, what the command, control, communications intelligence requirements are, making sure that it all fits together, pulling together a senior advisory staff right at CinCPac headquarters, and sitting in there watching this thing unfold.

One of the things that I did was to completely revamp the command center. As part of that, rather than keeping the intelligence watch behind locked doors, what we called the "green door," we then brought the intelligence watch officer and put him right directly with the operations duty officer. Then there was no longer any of this nonsense about, "Well, you're not cleared for this or that."

Q: How much did you travel around the theater in the course of that job?

Admiral Long: The theater, as I said, is about half the earth's surface and 30-some countries. We also had an increased number of congressional testimony appearances and meetings in the Pentagon. So I would estimate that during the four years that I was there, I traveled over half a million miles. I estimate that I was gone on travel 25 to 30% of the time. Those countries where we do have bilateral arrangements--Japan, Korea, ANZUS, others, Philippines--all want to meet at least once a year.* I tried never to be gone for more than two weeks at a time. The reason for that is sort of keeping in mind that "when the cat's away the mice will play." I just thought that if

---
*ANZUS--Australia, New Zealand, United States.

the boss wasn't around, the staff would have a tendency to drop into sort of a mañana attitude. So two weeks was about the max.

Q: Did you ever see any evidence that the mice had been playing in your absence?

Admiral Long: No, I don't think so. I don't think so.

Q: What sort of creature comforts went with all this responsibility you had?

Admiral Long: Oh, there was very nice living. We had a beautiful home there at Pearl Harbor, which, incidentally, was about one block from where I reported to my first duty station in the Pacific, the <u>Colorado</u>. The aircraft provided was a 707, which we called Beauty, manned by the Air Force. It was a converted tanker, so it had very, very long legs, and you needed long legs, because almost anywhere you went out there was at least eight hours. So we didn't lack for creature comforts.

We also had an entertainment allowance. As I said earlier, admirals don't get entertainment allowances to entertain their friends. We had a steady stream of foreign visitors, as well as some VIPs from the United States--congressmen, senators, so on. Being the senior U.S.

Robert L. J. Long #3 - 354

representative there, you always have the task of arranging to meet those people and, as appropriate, brief them, feed them, and so on. We had adequate facilities to do that and adequate resources to do that. But I will just note that during the four years that I was CinCPac, we ran in the red every year on a personal finance basis. So you can't do all of that and expect to save a lot of money.

Q: Some of that must have been irritating, especially if you've perceived the travelers were on a boondoggle.

Admiral Long: Well, I guess there were a few of those.

Q: I interviewed Admiral Persons, an old submariner who was Com 14, and I think he had those quarters and then Admiral McCain took them over.*

Admiral Long: You're correct. Admiral McCain decided that he wanted to live at Pearl Harbor rather than up at Makalapa.

Q: Admiral Persons felt a sense of loss. He said those were splendid quarters. [Laughter]

---

*Rear Admiral Henry Persons, USN, Commandant of the 14th Naval District; Admiral John S. McCain, Jr., USN, CinCPac, 1968-72.

Robert L. J. Long #3 - 355

Admiral Long: [Laughter] They are. They are. It's a great place to live.

Q: How much did you get involved with the community?

Admiral Long: That was one of the real pleasures of the job. Sara and I set out to be members of the community, and, as a result, even today we have many friends in the community, some of them retired military, others are civilians. Some of my predecessors had not established the same level of relationship with the community, but it was a great source of personal pleasure, as well as, I think, getting the attitude of the community very supportive of the military.

When I first arrived, there were some ugly incidents between the military and the civilian population, and we took steps to improve that. I had a good relationship, of course, with the governor. That was George Ariyoshi, and the mayor was Eileen Anderson.* As I say, we were host to almost every dignitary that would come through-- presidents of countries, foreign ministers, ministers of defense. We saw President Marcos several times, and when he would come through, he would sometimes ask if we could just have dinner somewhere private.** So I would take him to the Oahu Country Club or eat at the quarters.

----
*Governor George R. Ariyoshi, Democrat.
**Ferdinand Marcos, President of the Philippines.

I remember one time it was a memorable visit, and that was the Minister of Defense from China, which was one of the first times that a senior official came through. His name was Geng Biao. For that dinner, we had the Honolulu Boy Choir, which is a unique thing there, and he was so taken when they sang the Chinese national anthem.

Q: In Chinese, I take it.

Admiral Long: Yes. During that visit, he extended a formal invitation for me to visit China, which is the first time that a senior active-duty military had been invited. I was authorized to accept the invitation, but not say when I would go. I finally did go a few years after I had retired from the Navy.

Q: So you weren't authorized to go while on active duty, was that essentially it?

Admiral Long: Not authorized to go at that time, when there were still some political issues that needed to be resolved. Of course, today, and shortly after I retired, active-duty military could go, but not at that time. Shortly after I retired, I received another invitation, and so I did visit China. I think it was 1987.

Q: What are your impressions of Marcos and what sorts of things did you discuss?

Admiral Long: I knew Marcos well. Every time I would go to the Philippines, I would always go and see him and we'd have dinner or lunch. I liked him. I guess the first time I met him was at Baguio at the Philippine Military Academy, and that was also the first time I had met Mrs. Marcos. She asked me what was the first time I'd ever visited the Philippines, and I told her October 1944, when I was at the Battle of Leyte Gulf.

My impression of Marcos was that he was a good person at one time. He came into a situation where there was almost anarchy, and brought stability to the Philippines. But if people stay in power too long, then they set up sort of a dry rot, and he stayed in power too long. He was a strong supporter of the United States. He had some people around him that I thought did not serve him well.

I guess most of the time that I was CinCPac, Juan Enrile was the Minister of Defense.* He had a senior general there who was almost out of a movie. I mean, he was almost a Svengali. But also at that time, as the head of the constabulary, was General Eddie Ramos, who is now the President. And I always admired General Ramos. He was

---
*Juan Ponce Enrile.

a West Point graduate. He seemed to have integrity. He also had a very lovely wife who was a teacher. He didn't seem to be of that group that were heavily involved in graft and corruption. But you have to keep in mind that in many countries in that part of the world, graft and corruption is a way of life. Marcos and I played a lot of golf. As I say, I liked him personally.

Q: What do you remember of your dealings with the Japanese?

Admiral Long: Of course, we had lived in Japan, so I had some understanding of the Japanese. I'm convinced that an American can live in Japan all of his adult life and still not really understand the Japanese, they are so different from us. We had good rapport. One of the significant things that we developed was with the Japanese. When I first became CinCPac, we had no joint military operations at all. We then got the Japanese involved in a multinational exercise that was called RimPac. We then developed some other joint air operations. As I was leaving, we were then conducting joint ground operations. So we had brought Japan all to that point.

During that time, the Japanese significantly increased its investment in the military, still being capped at 1%, but 1% of their GNP still made them within the top ten free-world countries.* The Japanese are always interesting to deal with. And I thought at the time that we were very fortunate to have as our ambassador to Japan Mike Mansfield. When I would go and visit Japan, I'd always have close consultation with our ambassador there. Mike Mansfield, years ago, I'd say, was somewhat anti-military, but while he was the ambassador during the entire period that I was CinCPac, he was a very strong supporter of the U.S. military, particularly the Seventh Fleet.

Q: What do you recall of him personally?

Admiral Long: A real gentleman.

Q: And literally a scholar. He'd been a professor out in Montana earlier.

Admiral Long: Yes. I could almost give his speeches because I've heard them so many times. They always had the same points. Very strong supporter of U.S.-Japanese relations, and one of his favorite expressions was that the U.S.-Japanese relationship was the most important relationship in the world, bar none. As he would always say, bar none.

So I visited Japan many times. Of course, we had

---

*GNP--Gross national product.

meetings. The heads of the military there were wonderful people.

I remember one time I'd been asked to come to Japan to brief the Prime Minister prior to his trip to the United States to meet with the President.* The day before I was scheduled to arrive, the USS George Washington, an SSBN, struck a Japanese merchant, the Nissho Maru, and sank it.** Not only did the U.S. submarine not go back and look for survivors, but the George Washington did not report this until hours later. So when I arrived in Tokyo, the press was very hostile, and I'd have to say that my briefing of the Prime Minister was not on substantive issues within the theater. It really dealt with the incident.

Q: What sorts of things were you able to tell him about the incident?

Admiral Long: Not very much at that time. Of course, it was a huge political issue in Japan, where the Nissho Maru had been sunk with loss of life. I apologized publicly.

---

*The Japanese Premier was Zenko Suzuki.
**The collision took place on 9 April 1981 in the East China Sea, about 110 miles off the southern tip of Japan. It was between the ballistic missile submarine George Washington (SSBN-598) and the 2,350-ton freighter Nissho Maru, bound for Shanghai. The Japanese ship sank within 15 minutes, with the master and first mate lost at sea. The rest of the 15-man crew spent 18 hours in life rafts before being rescued by a Japanese destroyer.

But to give another insight into the Japanese, from there Sara and I had planned to visit Sasebo, where we had lived years before. The mayor of Sasebo, Mayor Tsuji, had set up this large banquet to honor us. And I remember Mayor Tsuji saying, "You have had a very difficult time in Tokyo. You are now home. You are a Sasebo boy." Which is, "You are one of us. You are one of us."

Q: That's a very warm kind of a greeting to get.

Admiral Long: Yes, yes. And the Japanese don't make friends all that quickly, but when they once decide you're a friend, you stay a friend. We still see our wonderful friends even today. When they come to this country, we will normally have dinner with them. So they're all different out there.

Q: Did you have to make amends for the submarine and what she should have done but didn't?

Admiral Long: Apologized, oh, yes, absolutely, and also fired the skipper of the submarine. I have rather strong views about commanding officers of ships, submarines particularly. That is, I will try to protect the skipper who is aggressive and has bad luck, but I have no absolutely no sympathy for a skipper who shows very poor

Robert L. J. Long #3 - 362

judgment. And this skipper, in my judgment, was abysmal in judgment.

Q: In two ways--not going for survivors and not notifying.

Admiral Long: Yes, poor judgment.

Q: You mentioned these joint U.S.-Japanese military operations. In what ways did those benefit the United States?

Admiral Long: We have consistently urged the Japanese to invest more in their own defense. We have not urged them to invest in such things as aircraft carriers or nuclear weapons or bombers. We have urged them to invest in defense, and these operations, whether they were naval operations in RimPac or air defense or ground operations, have improved the readiness and capabilities of the Japanese military forces. In my view, that is in our best interest to do that.

Q: And to that extent it makes them less dependent on the United States.

Admiral Long: That's right. Now, having said that, I think it's terribly important that we recognize that the

United States military provides stability in that part of the world. I never will forget, years later when Sara and I were attending the Olympics in Seoul.* An old friend who had been the Minister of Foreign Affairs when I first became CinCPac and then later became the Prime Minister--he was no longer in office--at lunch one day he said, "Please take back to Washington a message that the United States needs to maintain a presence here."

I said, "What are you worried about? Are you worried about the Soviets?"

He said, "No, no, no. We're worried about the Japanese."

So United States military presence is accepted there, but they still remember World War II quite clearly, particularly the older people, not just in Korea but the Philippines also. So U.S. military presence does add to stability out there. That's not just stability in military operations, but stability in economic affairs as well as political affairs.

Q: And the Korean War resulted from a perceived power vacuum in which the United States was not committing that many forces to the area.

Admiral Long: That's right. That's right. So those

---

*The Olympics were held in Seoul, South Korea, in 1988.

countries are fascinating and they're all a little different.

Q: During the Carter years, there had been some talk of reducing the commitment of troops, and General Singlaub came out publicly.* Did you still see some backlash from that when you were commander in chief?

Admiral Long: There sometimes is some confusion, I think, on the part of particularly Americans as to why do we have all those troops in Korea. Some people would say, "Well, they're there to deter the North Koreans from coming south." I would prefer to say they're there to deter the North Koreans from coming south, but they're also there to provide stability in that part of the world in Northeast Asia. And I think that is true today, and that's why I would oppose removing those troops from Korea. Now, some day we may, but I'd say that as of now, the U.S. military forces there provide that stability.

Q: Any issues involving the Soviets to discuss from that period?

Admiral Long: At that time we didn't have much rapport with the Soviets. [Laughter]

---

*In April 1978 Major General John K. Singlaub, USA, publicly denounced the idea of reducing the U.S. commitment to South Korea. He resigned shortly thereafter.

Q: That's true.

Admiral Long: We watched them carefully. Every day I would receive briefings as to the location of their major units, major forces. The Soviets became increasingly the major arms supplier and supporter of the North Koreans and less and less the Chinese. The Soviets established a major base at Cam Ranh Bay, and I guess also at this time the Soviets were also threatening in the Indian Ocean.* So during this time there were some very interesting things that occurred. Not only did we have the Iranian hostages, but we had the Afghanistan problem. We also had the situation in Southeast Asia in Cambodia and Laos, and we also had the coup going on in Korea. So there was a lot of activity that went on.

Q: Afghanistan for the Soviets has been compared to Vietnam for the United States. It was a big drain with not much apparent success out of it.

Admiral Long: Yes, and we watched that very carefully, because airfields in Afghanistan were within fighter range of the northern Arabian Sea. So it was a great concern and

---

*The United States had used the base at Cam Ranh Bay, South Vietnam, during the war there.

that is that they were going to essentially push on down to establish a foothold in that region.

Q: And then possibly take over Iran.

Admiral Long: That's right. That's right. Of course, at that time, my area of responsibility went all the way up to the Straits of Hormuz, up to the coast of Africa. One time I took a trip to the east coast of Africa. I went to Kenya and also to Somalia, where I met with the President, Siad Barré.* I don't think I've ever seen a country as poor as Somalia. Afghanistan is a close second. But those are terribly, terribly poor countries. At that time, the President of Somalia offered to station U.S. forces in his country. We did not do that, but certainly in Kenya we used Mombasa as a port of call for the ships that were over in that area.

Q: There not being a whole lot else available.

Admiral Long: No. And several times I visited Diego Garcia, and Diego Garcia is really a major strategic base. We got that from the British. But even as valuable as it is, when we were really looking at the possibility of using B-52s against Iran, I found out that that airfield there

---
*Major General Mohammed Siad Barré.

was unsuitable. You know, you could maybe land one, but the runway wasn't really strong enough, nor the width of it; the wings would drop over. So it was not suitable. I then set about to get permission to use the airfields in Thailand, which we did. There are not a lot of airfields in that part of the world where you can operate B-52s from.

Q: That's a long haul.

Admiral Long: You bet. You bet. But, you know, you talk about such a huge area, and this goes to a point that I think that sometimes we forget: it takes at least a year to understand the territory and, most important, the people that you're dealing with. So normal tour lengths of two years are just completely unrealistic, and it was not until after my second year that I really had a feeling of confidence that I understood all of these countries, and some of them not very well. So for a theater commander, I would urge that we try to make the tours at least three years and preferably four for something like this large.

Q: Too bad there can't be an experience transfusion as part of the change of command. [Laughter]

Admiral Long: That's right. [Laughter]

Q: You've alluded earlier several times to the swing strategy that you inherited. How did you go about changing that?

Admiral Long: Well, I think one of the things that I used that was very effective was that I set up an independent advisory board that was funded by the Defense Nuclear Agency. The group was headed by Ambassador Seymour Weiss. He's a guy that had been in defense consulting for years, an old friend of mine. He was a member of the CNO Executive Panel, the Defense Policy Board. So he went out and got some of these people who were knowledgeable of the whole national security arena, and they used to meet with me and give ideas as to things that maybe we should change. I found that extremely helpful to me.

After we went ahead and laid out these plans and we developed the necessary requirements and strategies for the Pacific, then we embedded these in strategic plans and sent them on back to the Joint Chiefs of Staff. With the new administration, we turned it around. But it was completely unrealistic to think that we could go ahead and move essentially the bulk of our forces out of the Pacific and allow that part of the world, the northwest Pacific and Northeast Asia, just to drop into the Soviets' lap. It just didn't make sense, so we finally turned that around.

Q: One other thing you inherited was that low level of readiness. What happened on that front?

Admiral Long: Well, we brought some more ammunition out, sophisticated weapons. We beefed up the POL supplies.* We eventually turned that on around so that we could have sufficient supplies to be able to fight for an extended period of time.

Q: What about in the area of people and training?

Admiral Long: After we adjusted the pay and so on, then the readiness of the units came up. Not immediately, but I guess '81, '82, we saw some marked improvement then.

Q: That was an area that you couldn't control as much as, say, ammunition and POL.

Admiral Long: That's right.

Q: Among other things in this beefing-up of the fleet was the program to reactivate the battleships. What impact, if any, did that have in the theater?

---

*POL--petroleum, oil, and lubricants.

Robert L. J. Long #3 - 370

Admiral Long: Well, that came a little bit later. I was not a great proponent of reactivating the battleships. The Marines liked them because they're tremendous fire support units. Politically it added ships to move toward the 600-ship Navy, but I thought we could have spent the money better on some other things.

Q: Such as?

Admiral Long: Well, I mean, other types of ships and improving the readiness, improving the strategic sealift. Even today, we still have a deficiency in strategic sealift. One thing that I'll have to say that was a good idea, and that was prepositioning these ships at Diego Garcia and elsewhere around the world. These ships support the Marines and, of course, they also support other forces. Those ships really showed their value in the Gulf War.

Q: From thousands of miles away, what perception did you have of Secretary Lehman and his initiatives, which included these battleships?

Admiral Long: John Lehman and I were good friends, and I thought that he was a breath of fresh air in the Navy. Unfortunately, as he stayed on and on, there were certain issues where he and I disagreed, and this was after I had retired. One of those areas where we disagreed had to do with what I perceived to be his improper manipulation of selection boards. I was sorry he did that, and I tried to counsel him not to, but it didn't work out. But overall, I thought initially he was very, very good. He had some good plans, good programs. A very, very sharp guy. He's like a lot of us and that is that even though he is very, very sharp, he needs some good strong people that will tell him from time to time, "That's a dumb idea." But I still have a great respect for him.

Q: Your mention of selection boards reminds me that's something we didn't really talk about from your Washington years. Any memories of those experiences?

Admiral Long: You know, there's no such thing as a perfect system, but I believe that the selection process that the Navy has followed in the past has been about as good as you can make it. I've been on several selection boards and continuation boards. It's very easy to recognize this top group, but then you normally end up with too many. It's also very easy to put a guy in what we call the pack. In other words, he's a guy that has sort of average performance and not very challenging jobs. So that's easy. The problem is, and that is when you have this large group of really outstanding people and how do you select out those that are the best. Probably as important as anything and that is the job that they are doing.

There has been a bias in the Navy against people that, unless they're actually in operating units, are not in Washington. Because Washington is perceived in peacetime as where the future of the Navy is decided. So for a guy to be an attaché someplace is not considered to be as demanding as a guy who is on duty in OpNav, and that sometimes is not in the best interest of the Navy. As an example, being an instructor in the Naval Academy, we should send good people here, but sometimes it's very difficult to get the Navy to send good people to these places. It was also very difficult, certainly not too long ago, to get the Navy to send good people to joint jobs.

When I became CinCPac, I noticed that the promotion rate for the people on my staff was less than the service average--Army, Air Force, Navy, and the Marines. So, here again, you pick up the telephone and you call the chief of the service, and say, "Hey, you're not doing right by me." That situation has solved itself now with the Goldwater-Nichols bill, and that is where officers, particularly senior officers, being promoted have to have joint duty.

Q: It makes it that much more attractive.

Admiral Long: Yes. And also the joint commanders have

sufficient clout that they can go ahead and reject people that are not good. But it has been a difficult thing to get quality for the joint jobs. As I say, that's not a problem today.

Q: And part of the problem is that everybody wants the best people, understandably.

Admiral Long: Well, you know, if you're the chief of service, the chances are you're going to be able to get the best people for your own staff.

Q: What do you remember about the internal procedures as a selection board deliberates and discusses people? Is there horse trading and what have you?

Admiral Long: Oh, I think so. I think most of these people come in there sort of representing platforms--submarines, aviation--and I think there also used to be a little bit of horse trading insofar as, "Well, now, you guys in aviation, you can't have all of the billets here. We've got to sort of split them up." So I think in the past there has been some allocation so that submariners get this number, the aviators get that, and the surface people get that. But overall, I think it's probably a pretty good process.

Q: Any specifics--incidents or what have you--from these selection boards that you remember?

Admiral Long: Paul, I don't think so. As I said, I think that my recollections of selection boards have been all pretty positive. I don't recall any real skullduggery on these.

Q: I imagine as you get down very close to the quota, the line is thin between who makes it and who doesn't, and that's got to be tough.

Admiral Long: Yes. And I think a lot depends really on the president of the board, who has to be a very skillful negotiator.

Q: In what ways? What sort of negotiation is required?

Admiral Long: Well, make sure these various factions don't get too rigid in their positions.

Q: I would think that it would be even tougher to be on a plucking board, because you are ending a person's career with that.

Admiral Long: That's right. I remember on one plucking board--and here I think you probably get even more pressure when you're dealing with flag officers--we had this one senior flag officer who really was putting the pressure on the board to keep this one flag officer. It got to be a little bit embarrassing. I guess I was the head of that board. So finally we said, "Okay. How about this guy? Do you want to keep him or not?"

One guy, whom I greatly respect, spoke up and said, "Look. I've been told that this guy won't come to Washington unless we make him three stars. If the son of a bitch doesn't want to come back here and count altimeters along with the rest of us, to hell with him." So we didn't continue him.

Of course, when you're dealing with a continuation board, most of these people are personally known to the members of the board.

Q: That would make it even harder.

Admiral Long: Oh, that's absolutely right. But as I say, I don't know of a better way to do it.

Q: Back to the Pacific. This period we've been talking about was the time when there were those long, long deployments of battle groups to the North Arabian Sea.

What do you remember about that and the difficulty in both personnel and logistics?

Admiral Long: Well, this was the time when we had long deployments coming out of the West Coast. Six months is long enough. I was just reading this article in The New York Times here saying that five carrier battle groups is enough. You can't operate the fleet and keep the people away from the home port forever. You must permit people to get back to live with their families, take care of their families. I think the worst thing that could happen would be to start driving the fleet without regard to the people, and that's something that the senior naval officers must protect.

There is a tendency on the part of some senior military people, and that is they always want to be responsive. The truth is that the Navy is normally the force of choice when there is a political or military crisis. As Kissinger used to say, "Where are the carriers?"* So there were, and there are today, long deployments, but I submit that that's one area where the chiefs of service, the commanders in chief, must stand up and say, "Hey, you can't drive this force into the ground. You can do it for a short period of time, but you must give the people an opportunity to be home for a period of time."

---
*Henry Kissinger, Secretary of State, 1973-77.

What we have as a standard is 50%, but that has been violated in the past in several instances. You can do it for a short period, but you cannot do it over the long haul.

Q: What do you remember about the logistical aspects of that operation?

Admiral Long: During that time I think we had sufficient underway replenishment ships, service force ships, and that is a great strength that the United States Navy has-- oilers, ammunition ships, these huge composite logistic support ships like the Sacramento and the Camden. Those things truly make that task force independent. That's something else that we need to protect. It gives the Navy the ability to operate for long periods of time without having to put into port, and thereby you get away from the political considerations if you would have to operate in and out of a foreign port.

Q: On Diego Garcia, it was a great asset in that support.

Admiral Long: Yes, that's right.

Q: In addition to the swing strategy, there must have been a host of contingency plans for all sorts of eventualities.

What kind of condition were they in when you started?

Admiral Long: The principal contingency was Korea, and my recollection was that we didn't have too many other contingencies other than that. Now, as we went on, we did have contingencies dealing with situations in the Indian Ocean, we did have contingencies dealing with possible incidents in the Gulf, and, of course, there were contingencies like SR-71, like the possible prisoners of war in Southeast Asia. They all needed to be beefed up and brought up to date.

Q: One of your predecessors of CinCPac, Admiral Gayler became rather vocal on the subject of nuclear weapons.* How much of a consideration were nuclear weapons during your tour?

Admiral Long: CinCPac is one of the so-called nuclear CinCs, and we would exercise periodically on release of nuclear weapons and have exercises that were called Night Blues, where there would be conferences with the CinCs, the Secretary of Defense, and occasionally the President. We also maintained nuclear weapons at various places throughout the theater. These were so-called theater

---

*Admiral Noel A. M. Gayler, USN, served as Commander in Chief Pacific and Commander in Chief U.S. Pacific Fleet from 1 September 1972 to 30 August 1976. His oral history is in the Naval Institute collection.

Robert L. J. Long #3 - 379

nuclear weapons, tactical nuclear weapons. Of course, we had them in carriers. We had nuclear depth bombs, I guess, at Adak, Alaska. We were always very careful that we didn't confirm or deny their presence in foreign places such as the Philippines or Korea.

Q: Especially any ships going into Japan, you wouldn't mention that.

Admiral Long: That was the policy, and so far as I know, that's still the policy, although I don't think we have any nuclear weapons on ships other than SSBNs. But we would neither confirm or deny their presence.

I was not a great supporter of so-called theater nuclear weapons. I did believe, and do believe today, that they can provide a very useful deterrent purpose. I had trouble believing that we could go ahead and throw these theater nuclear weapons around and not trigger the entire nuclear exchange. That debate continues today. I believe so long as there's a possibility of having nuclear weapons in the world, we're going to have to continue to have nuclear weapons, and that includes not only strategic nuclear weapons, but it also includes some limited number or capability of theater nuclear weapons. That doesn't mean that you have to have theater nuclear weapons on aircraft carriers or on other ships continually, but you have to have the ability to put them on when it suits the national security interest.

Q: Were you concerned about proliferation to countries other than superpowers?

Admiral Long: No, I don't think we were as much concerned about proliferation then. Of course, we knew that China had nuclear weapons. We were concerned with Japan in that she would not be tempted to break with the United States and develop nuclear weapons on her own. That was always a fundamental rationale or underpinning of United States policy toward Japan. In other words, "Go ahead and increase your expenditures for defense, but don't get into the business of nuclear weapons or any weapons of mass destruction or long-range offensive weapons."

Q: Given their traditional abhorrence, I didn't realize that was a concern with the Japanese.

Admiral Long: Well, I'll tell you, when you look at the Japanese factions, even back then there were groups who wanted to return to their old independent ways. I'd say that there are very militaristic groups that existed then and exist today. So the thing is that we must be very careful that we don't encourage those groups to get into a dominant position.

Q: What did you do to relax from this demanding job? You had played squash in Washington.

Admiral Long: I played golf normally once or twice a week and played with some of my friends in the civilian community as well as in the military. Talking about relations with this community, they were very generous to me. They gave me an honorary membership in two of the best golf courses in town, Waialai Country Club as well as Oahu Country Club, and also one of the city's main dining clubs, the Pacific Club. So those were very, very nice things to have for relaxation.

Q: I remember having dinner once at that Pacific Club as the sun was setting in the ocean, and it's a memorable experience.

Admiral Long: Yes. I think they also gave me a membership in the Outrigger, which is right on the beach and also a very fascinating club. So, all in all, it was a great experience.

Q: You were certainly one of the most senior officers in

the Navy at that time. Did you have any kind of a father figure or a statesman status? I mean, did people look to you for guidance within the profession?

Admiral Long: Oh, Paul, I think that at that point if you're lucky, people will always come to you for advice, but I don't recall that I had a special status at all.

Q: Did it come as a sense of regret when you finally took off the uniform?

Admiral Long: Well, I think it was not so much regret as complete bewilderment as to what this new life consisted of. I should tell you that I was privileged to remain four years as CinCPac, and at that time the tour length was two years with one-year extensions. So I was extended twice. The normal retirement age was 62, and I was kept on by the President until I was 63.

Q: Did that take a special waiver or something?

Admiral Long: It took a waiver from the President, because by law, military officers are required to retire at 62. One of the things that was interesting was that in 1982 Mr. Weinberger queried me as to whether I would be willing to be the Chief of Naval Operations. I said no, and I still think that was a good decision. I don't think you need a CNO who is 62 to 66. Then, when I was getting ready to retire, Mr. Weinberger said that he wanted to submit my name to be the chairman, and that was along with Jack Vessey.* So he and I had a very good relationship. I admired him then, and I admire him today.

Q: Did you say no to the idea of the chairmanship?

Admiral Long: No, I didn't, but I must say that I'm delighted that I did not get the chairmanship.

Q: Why do you say that?

Admiral Long: Well, I guess from a purely selfish point of view, I decided that I needed to get out and make a little money. As I said, during the four years I was CinCPac, we ran a deficit every year. So I needed to get out and make a little money so Sara could not be too dependent on Social Security or the children. So that's what we did.

Q: Might you have taken the CNO post if it had been offered earlier?

---

*General John W. Vessey, Jr., USA, served as Chairman of the Joint Chiefs of Staff, 18 June 1982 to 30 September 1985.

Robert L. J. Long #3 - 384

Admiral Long: Yes. I would have been delighted being the CNO if it, say, had been offered during my Vice Chief's tour, but it was not. I personally believe that the job of CinCPac is the finest job in the military. So many interesting things going on.

Q: Would that be in any way because of the CNO not being in the operational chain of things? Did that diminish it in your view?

Admiral Long: About this time, I think the nature of the jobs changed. Of course, power is finite, and if you enhance the power of one part of this net, you're going to decrease the power of other parts of the net. So today we see a very powerful Chairman of the Joint Chiefs of Staff, we also see very powerful unified and specified CinCs. And, of course, the ones who have given up some of that power are the chiefs of service.

Q: So you were where the power was?

Admiral Long: Well, at that time.

Q: I presume you had some grand going-away bash out at Pearl Harbor.

Admiral Long: Well, I guess we had sort of the traditional change-of-command ceremony that was very, very nice. And right afterwards Sara and I got aboard Beauty and came to Annapolis, where we had built a home some eight years before. At that time, I thought that I had more than my share of jobs in the Navy, and so we had planned to retire and come here to Annapolis and settle down. We've never regretted moving here.

Q: Admiral Moorer said in his oral history it was kind of a shock after all those years in the Navy to go out and find out what the price of a haircut was and a loaf of bread and what have you.* Did you have any withdrawal symptoms?

Admiral Long: I think that we had a few after having had people in the house that would help us and people who would drive cars for us and write letters and make telephone calls. It takes a little while to adjust, but it doesn't take very long. I think the most embarrassed that I became was shortly after retirement, when I was asked to come and visit this company in Washington. They had a huge underground parking lot. I drove the car in, got out, went up to meet these people, came back, and I said, "Where in

---
*Admiral Thomas H. Moorer, USN, retired in 1974 after serving as Chairman of the Joint Chiefs of Staff. These observations about his retirement are in his Naval Institute oral history.

the world did I park my car?" I spent about half an hour looking for that car. I mean, that gives you a sense of reality very, very quickly.

Q: I've had that experience. It's frustrating. [Laughter] Had you had any contact with the job market before retiring?

Admiral Long: None, and I very purposefully did not want any contact. A couple of companies had come to me and said, "Would you be interested in doing some consulting for us?" I said, "I can't talk to you now, but if you're still interested after I retire, I'll be happy to talk to you." So things picked up very quickly after I retired. I was asked to consult for a variety of companies, some of whom I still consult for today.

But that free enterprise time stopped very quickly in October when I was called in by Mr. Weinberger, the Secretary of Defense, and asked to chair a commission looking at the bombing at Beirut.*

Q: Did he ask you because he knew you so well?

---

*On the morning of 23 October 1983, a suicide terrorist drove a truck filled with explosives equivalent to 12,000 pounds of TNT into the U.S. Marines' compound at Beirut, Lebanon. The blast killed 241 Marines.

Admiral Long: I suspect that was part of it, Paul. I told him at the time, "Gee, you know, I just retired. I've got all of these things I need to do. I'm just starting out on a new career."

He said, "I'm sorry, Bob, but I need you." So we then started the Long Commission.

Q: That's not the sort of job that one volunteers for and embraces eagerly.

Admiral Long: Absolutely not. It's not a very pleasant experience. But I set out to form the commission. He had named no other members to the commission, but I decided that we needed a representative from each of the services.

Q: Are there any standing ground rules for these kinds of commissions, or do you make up your own?

Admiral Long: Well, there were a few things that I thought were important. One thing I did was talk to Admiral Holloway.

Q: He, of course, had had a similar role after the Desert One experience.

Admiral Long: Right. He gave me some very good advice,

Robert L. J. Long #3 - 388

and that was, "Write your own terms of reference." He said, "Don't allow some bureaucrat to hand these terms to you."

So one of the first things that I did was to get myself a good lawyer, and I found this in the lawyer who had been my JAG officer on CinCPac staff, Captain Jack Grunawalt.* As a matter of fact, he was still attached at CinCPac. I also asked for, and received, a public relations person, and that was Colonel Al Lynn, who was also attached to CinCPac.** After I had come up with a list of names as members of the commission, I submitted the list to Secretary Weinberger. Those included an Army officer, who was Lieutenant General Palastra; a retired Air Force officer; and a Marine retired officer.***

I presented these to Mr. Weinberger, and he said, "Don't you think you need a civilian?" I responded that I didn't really see any need for one, since this was pretty much of a military situation. He said, "Well, I think you might be well advised to take a civilian." So, somewhat reluctantly, I gave him the name of Bob Murray, who had been the Under Secretary of the Navy when I was the Vice Chief.**** He was then at Harvard. That was probably one of the smartest things that I did, because he gave a

---
*Captain Richard Jack Grunawalt, JAGC, USN.
**Colonel Alfred Lynn, USAF (Ret.).
***Lieutenant General Joseph Palastra, USA.
****Robert J. Murray, Under Secretary of the Navy during the Carter Administration.

perspective that we never would have had without him.

Q: In a sense, this was following your own advice that there's more than just a military aspect to a situation.

Admiral Long: You're absolutely right. You're absolutely right. Anyway, we formed this team, and we then formed the rest of the staff, in addition to my lawyer, Jack Grunawalt.

Q: Did you have a wordsmith as part of this team, someone able to draft a narrative of conclusions?

Admiral Long: We assembled the rest of the staff and received an executive assistant. For the executive assistant, I wanted an Air Force officer, and Admiral Bobby Inman had recommended Colonel Mike Christy.[*] I also wanted someone who would be the editor, and this was a Colonel Ralph Cosa, U.S. Air Force, who had also worked with me at CinCPac. We then had specialists in medicine, we had doctors, we had special forces. We had a complete team that were Army, Navy, Air Force, and Marines.

Q: How large was the whole collection?

---
[*]Admiral Bobby R. Inman, USN, had been Deputy Director of Central Intelligence until his retirement in July 1982.

Robert L. J. Long #3 - 390

Admiral Long: I'd say not more than 30 people. We then set forth some ground rules as to how we would proceed, and we decided that we didn't want one final draft. We wanted to develop this thing on an iterative basis as we went along. We decided that we would not have any conclusions; we called them issues. Instead, the commission would meet and say, "Well, we think this is an issue." We then turned that over to the staff. The staff would then work on that, come back to us with something that was written, and that's the way we proceeded. Of course, we interviewed lots of people in Washington.

Q: Did you do this in a court of inquiry type of format?

Admiral Long: No, we didn't do it insofar as sworn testimony or anything like that. We did it sitting as a group, and we would invite people in and we would just question them.

Q: Could they be represented by counsel?

Admiral Long: They could have been, but I don't recall any of them who did.

Q: I was thinking, for example, somebody like Colonel

Geraghty might want to be represented.*

Admiral Long: No, I don't recall anyone who was represented by counsel. Of course, we talked to the people in the Pentagon, including the chiefs, the Chairman, who at that time was General Vessey. We also talked to terrorist experts from around the country. We talked to the FBI, who has had a very impressive forensic laboratory. We went and talked to the State Department. We never did talk to Secretary of State Shultz, but we talked to the Under Secretary and, of course, at that time we also talked to the Assistant Secretary for Political Military Affairs--that was Jonathan Howe.** In the White House, we talked to the national security adviser and that was Judge Clark.*** Then we went out into the field, visiting Bernie Rogers, who was CinCEur, and Admiral Small, who was CinCUSNavEur.**** The commander of the Sixth Fleet was Vice Admiral Ed Martin.***** We went on down the line until we actually visited Beirut and talked to Colonel Geraghty and

---
*Colonel Timothy J. Geraghty, USMC, commander 24th Marine Amphibious Unit.
**George P. Shultz, Secretary of State, 1982-89; Rear Admiral Jonathan T. Howe, USN, Director, Politico-Military Affairs, Department of State.
***William P. Clark, national security adviser to the President.
****General Bernard W. Rogers, USA, Commander in Chief Allied Forces Europe; Admiral William N. Small, USN, Commander in Chief Allied Forces Southern Europe and Commander in Chief U.S. Naval Forces Europe.
*****Vice Admiral Edward H. Martin, USN, Commander Sixth Fleet.

Robert L. J. Long #3 - 392

the rest of the people there.

Q: Did you go through the bombing site?

Admiral Long: Yes, we visited the bombing site.

Q: What are your impressions from that?

Admiral Long: One of the things that I think impressed us was the size of the explosion that destroyed that place. According to the FBI forensic laboratory, that bomb was somewhere over 12,000 pounds equivalent TNT.

Q: In that range you're talking nuclear weapon yield, aren't you?

Admiral Long: My recollection is that we had nuclear weapons that had a lesser yield than the size of the bomb. But it's important to understand that the bomb was not only just explosive, it was what we call a gas-enhanced explosive. That is where you take an explosive and you surround it with gas bottles such as you would use in welding, and that gives it a tremendous increase in pressure. Not only does it increase in pressure, but more important to that, as the pressure goes up, it sustains that pressure, which gives you then a massively more destructive force than just a pressure blip.

So we went and interviewed all those people, took all of the testimony. One of the individuals that I remember was interviewing General Rogers, who was CinCEur. The mission of the Marines over there had not been changed from the beginning, so we asked, "Why did you not change the mission? Why had you not given them adequate rules of engagement? Why had you not given them increased intelligence support? Why had you not given them increased security and so forth?"

His response was, I thought, indicative of some command philosophy: "Bob, I wouldn't think of telling the Marines how to do their job."

So we spent about a month doing the investigation and then finally gave the report to the Secretary of Defense, highly classified. He then directed that an unclassified version be prepared, which was done, and it was remarkably true to the classified version. Then, after it had gone to the White House for okay, it was finally released.

Before it was actually released, someone leaked the information. This was receiving a lot of attention in the press at this time. I remember it was Saturday night, and one person at the White House called me and he had, in effect, accused me of leaking it, which made me a little bit mad. I pointed out that nothing had been leaked until it got to the White House.

So, anyway, it was finally released, and it received a lot of press. The report made several significant points. We talked about alternate means of achieving U.S. objectives in Lebanon. It was interesting that there were some comments made by people in the State Department and elsewhere, that they thought that this was improper, that this defense commission should really get into the business of criticizing the civilian political leadership of the country. Another comment was made about the rules of engagement, and we were critical of the fact that there was not a comprehensive, realistic set of rules of engagement.

We also criticized the people in the chain of command and pointed out that they had not really done an appropriate job of monitoring and supervising the security and the procedures that were used. We also found that the intelligence support at all levels was unsatisfactory, and we observed that human intelligence was almost nonexistent. We observed that this was not just because of recent decisions by the United States to rely more heavily on overhead sensors, but this really had been deteriorating for a good number of years.

There also had been criticisms by the Israelis that the United States, and specifically Mr. Weinberger, had not utilized appropriately the medical facilities of Israel, and we found that that charge was without merit. We also recognized that the security of the Marines there continued to be inadequate, and we urged that steps be taken to correct that. One of the significant points was that we recommended that the Secretary of Defense direct the Joint Chiefs to develop a broad range of appropriate military responses to terrorism for review along with political and diplomatic actions by the National Security Council. Finally, we observed that the military was not prepared to defend against terrorism, and we recommended that the Secretary of Defense direct the development of doctrine planning, organization, force structure, education, and training necessary to defend against and counter terrorism.

It's interesting to note that Mr. Weinberger agreed with all of those observations, but probably the message I thought for the military more than any other point was the question of command responsibility. In the opening parts of the report, the commission made the statement, "The commission holds the view that military commanders are responsible for the performance of their subordinates. The commander can delegate some or all of his authority to his subordinates, but he cannot delegate his responsibility for the performance of the forces he commands. In that sense, the responsibility of military command is absolute. This view of command authority and responsibility guided the commission in its analysis of the effectiveness of the exercise of command authority and responsibility of the chain of command charged with the security and performance of the United States multinational force."

Q: What sort of reaction did you get after that came out?

Admiral Long: I thought the response was interesting. Overall, the press was very supportive. There were editorials in The Washington Post and The New York Times, some of which were labeled "No Whitewash Here." The Marines, interestingly, were also very supportive, and, I think, almost all of the military. There were a couple of places where the report was not well received. One of them was in Secretary of State's office. Mr. Shultz thought that it was too harsh. Another place where it was not well received was in General Rogers's office. After the report came out, he sent a personal message to the Secretary of Defense, which, in effect, demanded that the commission come to Europe and explain to him why he should be held accountable. Mr. Weinberger ignored the request. But I think overall the reaction was positive, and it's also interesting to note that even today that report is still a text at the various war colleges around the country.

Q: It sounds as if you were given complete independence in pursuing your charter, no directed conclusions.

Admiral Long: Mr. Weinberger made it very clear to me that

I had absolutely carte blanche authority to look at anything, ask anyone, and in no way did he direct that my conclusions and recommendations should be limited in any way. As a matter of fact, he put out directives within the department directing that full support should be given to the commission. So it was a very broad charter.

Q: Were you looking at the question of whether it was appropriate for the United States to have that sort of a military presence in Beirut?

Admiral Long: Well, that clearly was the thrust of that first conclusion and recommendation that I cited, and that was we should be looking at alternate ways to carry out the objectives of the United States. It's important to note that the mission of the Marines never changed: it was one of peace keeping. It was a very innocuous one when they first went in. Also the environment when the Marines went in was they were looked on as heroes. The Marines could play football on the beach. The children used to come and chat with them. They actually went in as almost an interpositional force between the Israelis on the south and the Lebanese and Syrians on the north. So they were very popular when they first came.

Then the United States began changing some of the things, such as providing support and eventually gunfire support, for the Lebanese armed forces against these other factions. Then popular opinion started turning against them, and Marines were then considered partisan. That's when sniper fire started, mortar fire started against the Marines, and a series of harassments. If you've ever looked at where the Marines were, they were essentially just like sitting in the parking lot outside of National Airport.

Q: It's not a spot you would pick for military advantage.

Admiral Long: No. The opposition had the high ground above them where fire could be directed on the Marines. So it was a very unmilitary place for them to be. And, as I said, nothing was ever changed insofar as their mission. So it was not a good way to conduct a military operation.

Q: What was the nature of the interrogations? Was it like a courtroom or was it more informal? How did it go?

Admiral Long: I never intended for it to be like a courtroom. It was just that we were there sort of saying, "Nothing but the facts, ma'am."

Q: Just listening to the questions that you mentioned that you asked General Rogers, I can see why he would feel

Robert L. J. Long #3 - 399

defensive.

Admiral Long: No, we really didn't try to make it into a courtroom. As I say, there was nothing under oath. We just took testimony.

Q: What do you remember of the morale around the Marine compound in that area when you visited?

Admiral Long: My recollection is that the morale was not the best. Of course, we did criticize the performance of Colonel Geraghty, who was the Marine commander there. But I'll have to add that I don't think I have ever seen a finer young man than Colonel Geraghty. Extremely conscientious. And although we criticized him for putting all of those people in the barracks at one time, in view of the other things that were going on--and we did criticize him for not trying to tighten up the rules of engagement-- we also observed that he was also operating under some extremely difficult circumstances that were beyond his control, and he had previously asked for some relief from those conditions. So it was unfortunate that Colonel Geraghty was in that position. He was reprimanded by the Secretary of the Navy. But before the rest of the reprimand or disciplinary actions were taken, the President came out and indicated that he would take full

Robert L. J. Long #3 - 400

responsibility and that he did not want anyone else disciplined for the incident. I thought he did a great disservice by doing that.

Q: Why do you say that?

Admiral Long: Well, he was quite correct in accepting the responsibility, because so much of this was being directed from the White House--Bud McFarlane--and the State Department.* But he should have allowed the system to work the rest of it.

Q: So that the people would literally have had their day in court.

Admiral Long: Yes. Yes. We came out with certain recommendations for discipline, and I thought it was commendable that he would accept the responsibility, but I still submit that he should have allowed the Secretary of Defense to take those actions within the Defense Department.

Q: Let me pose a hypothetical question. Would it be fair to say that sort of an incident was inevitable and it just happened that it caught Geraghty on his watch?

---

*On 17 October 1983 President Ronald Reagan named Robert C. McFarlane to become national security adviser, replacing William Clark, who became Secretary of the Interior.

Admiral Long: They rotated the Marine units there, and it clearly was possible that if it hadn't happened to Geraghty, it could have happened to someone else that was the commanding officer of a subsequent Marine detachment there.

Q: Did you see that he was in any way less vigilant than his predecessor, let's say, or not doing as well?

Admiral Long: Paul, we really didn't inspect or interrogate all of the units that were there, because clearly what we had was a situation that changed from one of being very friendly over a period of a year to one that was very hostile. So actually the whole environment changed, and during that time the location of the Marines was not changed, their mission was not changed, and very little was done on the rules of engagement. As a matter of fact, during the course of the investigation, there was controversy within the chain of command as to who had the authority to change the rules of engagement. So it was a very mushy situation.

Q: Wasn't there also some criticism that the chain of command was rather cumbersome?

Admiral Long: Yes. Remember we talked earlier about the

operational chain of command and CinCEur's role in setting this thing up. He still relied on the normal peacetime operational chain of command, and that is to go from the President to the Secretary of Defense, to CinCEur, to the deputy CinCEur, to Commander-in-Chief Naval Forces Europe, to the deputy CinCUSNavEur, to the Commander Sixth Fleet, to a task force commander within the Sixth Fleet, and then finally to Colonel Geraghty on the beach. You ask what did each one of those levels of command actually do to support that operation, and the answer is, "Not very much." So it was cumbersome, and that is a lesson that I think has been learned. I think you find that most operations that are conducted now are done using a joint task force.

Q: In early '84, the Marines began withdrawing. Was that in any way tied in with your report, or was that just a consequence of the action itself?

Admiral Long: I think that the bombing was one factor that caused the United States to withdraw those forces. If you remember, there was also an agreement with Congress as to how long they were going to be there. This was under the War Powers Act. I think that there was a growing unhappiness not only with the public, but the Congress, with troops over there. Of course, the bombing just added emphasis to that. So I think all together, it just said we

Robert L. J. Long #3 - 403

ought to get them out of there.

Q: General P. X. Kelley, the Marine commandant, was emotionally involved in this.* He testified before Congress. What was your interaction with him on the commission?

Admiral Long: Of course, we talked to him, and there was some action on the part of the Marines prior to all of this, and I think some attitude on the Marines that were over there that gave rise to the question in some quarters as to who was really calling the shots on this. Of course, when the bombing occurred, people then remembered which command really had the responsibility for the Marines in Beirut, and, of course, it wasn't the Commandant of the Marine Corps; it was that operational chain of command that I have spoken of. We made this point very clear in the report. I expect that P. X. Kelley welcomed that report to clarify his own responsibility.

Q: I got the impression, rightly or wrongly, though, that that incident attached some stigma to him as commandant.

Admiral Long: I don't think it helped him, but he clearly wasn't the one that was responsible. However, I'm sure as

---
*Generalk Paul X. Kelley, USMC.

Robert L. J. Long #3 - 404

the Commandant of the Marines, he did feel strongly some element of responsibility just for the training, for the doctrine. So from that point of view, he clearly shouldered some of the responsibility.

Q: What association or discussions did you have with Congress either during or after this process?

Admiral Long: After it was over, the Secretary of Defense authorized me to go up and brief congressional committees on this, which I did in closed-door sessions. Those went well. There was a lot of questioning. But the Congress was fully briefed on this.

Q: It was interesting that some of them who had made supportive statements before the bombing were very condemning afterward, as you might expect from Congress. Any larger lessons or conclusions you might draw from this and your own involvement in it?

Admiral Long: Paul, I cited one of the lessons that I think clearly should be remembered by all military people, and that is keep in mind that the commander is, in fact, responsible for the actions of his subordinates and responsible for the support of his subordinates. I think the other larger national lesson is that the United States needs to be very careful about committing military force. I think we see that lesson learned in the present situation in Somalia, Yugoslavia, the other places around the world. It's very easy to commit military force, but sometimes it's very difficult to disengage. There's an old rule that I think we need to remind ourselves of from time to time, and that is before you commit military forces, you should have a clear understanding of the political outcomes that you expect to achieve, and you should also have a clear understanding of the strategy with which you will achieve those outcomes. So here we committed military force, and I don't think we had a very clear understanding of what we intended to achieve, and we certainly did not have a clear strategic view of how to do it.

Q: I think one thing that's worth mentioning is that the withdrawal soon after that kept it from being another Vietnam. We did not make an open-ended commitment.

Admiral Long: Right.

Q: Anything else on that topic to mention?

Admiral Long: No, I think that wraps it up.

Q: One thing you said earlier in this series is that the

commission on the Beirut bombing brought you to a degree of public notice that led on to other things. What were some of those?

Admiral Long: Well, there was a lot of publicity given to that report, and I think this then opened the door into both government advisory boards and also commercial or civilian advisory boards.

I guess the next thing that came on the horizon was the movement to clarify the organization of the military, the role of CinCs, the question as to where was the Department of Defense going organization-wise, acquisition-wise. Two things occurred on that. One was that I was asked to chair a study for the CNO, looking at changes that should take place in organization. The second was much broader, and that was the testimony that led up to the enactment of the Goldwater-Nichols Bill.

Let me be perfectly candid and say that my support of jointness was not nearly as enthusiastic before I became CinCPac as after. After I became CinCPac, there certainly was no question in my mind that jointness was here to stay, that there were literally no significant operations that could be conducted by one service alone. If you just look at the C3I architecture, every operation would be dependent on that, and, of course, that C3I architecture is, in fact, joint.

So when I testified before the Senate Armed Services Committee, I strongly supported the idea that increased authority needed to be granted to the unified and specified commanders. I differed from some of the other witnesses in that I did not support the idea that the Chairman or the Joint Chiefs of Staff should be in the operational chain of command. As I have said before, a theater CinC, a unified CinC, really does not need military guidance from Washington as much as he needs political guidance, and you cannot get political guidance from the Joint Chiefs of Staff. This was in 1984. In '85 the Goldwater-Nichols bill was passed, and, in my judgment, it was a good law. There is a danger, though, like everything that's good, and that is if you carry it too far, you pick up some problems. This emphasis on jointness has now encouraged people to push jointness too far, and we see that in some of the road maps that have come out of the Congress, specifically out of the House Armed Services Committee.

In the past, there have been some proposals that would almost make an officer's career one of jointness and going to war college. Here again, we have to remind ourselves that the proficiency of the military, the actual war-fighting ability of the military, depends not only how well staffed we are at the top, but also how well prepared are we at the lower end of the base in order to be able to fight. This includes the ability to be a tank commander, the ability to operate submarines with great skill and effectiveness, the ability to be able to conduct air strikes with proficiency. When you go ahead and you try to push the jointness and the war colleges too far, inevitably you're going to push into the time that you have available to make effective warriors. Of course, we're not just staff people; the military should also be warriors.

Q: Plus you've got to operate the fleet even in peacetime, and you need people to do that.

Admiral Long: That's right. You need people to drive ships and fly airplanes and run submarines. So that was an important point, and I was pleased to be part of that Goldwater-Nichols debate.

Also in 1985, we finally were able to take our trip to China. As I said earlier, Gung Biao extended that invitation, but I was not authorized at that time because of the U.S.-Chinese relations to actually go. Then in 1985, I received reaffirmation of that earlier invitation from the Chinese ambassador to the United States. I was at that time then permitted to accept, and the ambassador said that I could go anywhere in China that I wanted after I had visited Beijing. He asked that I make a couple of speeches and call on several people.

Sara and I then went to China in the fall of '85 and

went to Beijing, where I spoke to the war college and called on the Minister of Defense and the Beijing Institute of International Studies. After that, we set out to visit about seven different cities.

Q: Did they have simultaneous translation on your speech? How did that work?

Admiral Long: The answer is yes. I certainly gave the speech in English. They then translated that to the students sitting out there.

Q: Did you get questions from the students?

Admiral Long: Yes.

Q: What sorts of things?

Admiral Long: Many of the questions centered around our support of Taiwan. Many of the questions wanted to know about our attitude toward China. One of the areas that I discussed there, as well as other places in China, of course, was U.S.-Sino relations. I think, overall, the people with whom I discussed U.S.-Sino relations believed that relations with the United States were developing quite satisfactorily, particularly over those three years just before arriving. That was '82 to '85. They specifically cited the top-level exchanges of people--presidents and vice presidents and ministerial-level officers. They also cited tremendous expansion in U.S.-Sino trade and economic relations and the increase in cultural relations. Military relations they saw were going very, very well. As they say, there were plenty of contacts in that area.

Of course, the problems that they would point out, having gone through all of this very positive assessment, Taiwan would come up first, but it never came up in a strong emotional way. It came up almost pro forma. It was also of interest that while I was there, a group of businessmen met with Deng Xiaoping, and Deng was asked, "What's the biggest problem that China has with the United States?"*

He immediately responded, "Technology transfer." That came out loud and clear. In my own assessment, that was their primary interest in the United States at that time. They wanted a positive relationship with the United States, principally because of technology transfer and U.S. capital investment. They would also say if the United States would just act in accordance with the three communiques that are on the books--those are the agreements that the United States had made with China--then our relations would be even better.

---

*Deng Xiaoping, Deputy Prime Minister.

But I guess Taiwan was still a problem. I think some of them thought that the United States really didn't see this problem, but they were concerned that we just didn't think the Taiwan question was very important.

Q: What were your impressions of that exotic land in the Orient?

Admiral Long: I've traveled an awful lot around the world, but that trip to China was the most interesting one that I have ever taken. First of all, let me say that our official host in China was the Beijing Institute of Strategic Studies, and it was headed by the former defense attaché in Washington, General Xu-Yimin. He was a very interesting guy. He joined the Communist guerrillas at the age of 15, and I estimated he was about 62 to 65 when I was with him. A few years later, he joined the Communist Army and was active against the Japanese occupation. After World War II, the Communist Army then started the intensive campaign against Chiang Kai-shek's forces.* At the time of the latter's overthrow, General Xu was a regimental commander, and he took great pride in pointing out the headquarters he established when his forces took Nanjing.

The only change that was made in the itinerary that I

---

*Generalissimo Chiang Kai-shek served as President of Nationalist China on the mainland from 1943 to 1949 and as President of the Republic of China on Taiwan from 1950 until his death in 1975.

gave to the Chinese defense attaché months earlier was to delete one town and substitute another. The reason for that was General Xu was a native of that area, and he specifically wanted to take us to his home. It was just like a homecoming for him. I mean, the people genuinely seemed to admire him and respect him.

So we started out. We had not only General Xu with us, but we also had a young army officer named Li Brolin. The Brolin was supposed to be Berlin. His father was a Foreign Service officer, and Li Brolin was born in Berlin. A very sharp young man. We would take the normal transportation. We would fly in commercial aircraft or get on the train and travel from city to city, or we'd have a car, but we didn't travel in anything special. We just traveled along with the rest of the public, but we traveled pretty well.

Every town we would go to, we would be met by the local governor, who then would assign us a guide who was a member of what they called the Foreign Service. The guides were universally very sharp and, I thought, rather outspoken and candid. Almost without exception, they would complain about the great revolution. They would complain about that period when Mao Tse-Tung was the great Communist dictator. They complained about the Mao policies.

There were a few things that stand out. One was, everywhere we went, we were always told of their desire to have American capital, American technology, come into China for business. Without exception, we were told that by the governor or the mayor or whatever official that we talked to. I guess another observation, I was truly impressed with the number of independent business operations that were going on. I guess a third observation was that at no time did we ever experience anything that would appear hostile to us. We would go to a town, and probably late in the afternoon Sara and I would take a walk all by ourselves through the town. At no time did we ever feel threatened. People were very hospitable, friendly. They'd come up and want to practice their English on us. So those were observations.

No, in addition to all of the very interesting things in Beijing, the Walled City at Xian, all of the varied figures that we saw, fascinating sights. We also went to Tsingtao, as they call it "Gingtao," and where we were on a submarine, which I must say was quite an old submarine, and it was so beautifully polished it looked like it was almost on exhibit for visitors.

Q: Perhaps it was.

Admiral Long: It could well have been. [Laughter] I did not ask, nor did they really take me to any other military bases. We saw lots of military people, and in Shanghai we were given tours up and down the river there. At no time were we told we couldn't take pictures. We took lots of snapshots. So it was a very relaxed, open visit. As a matter of fact, I still receive the Chinese-English paper that they send. So we spent a little less than two weeks, there in China.

There is a question as to how strongly we object to Tiananmen Square today.* I think it personally would be a big mistake on the part of the United States if we tied all of our future relations with China to only human rights. There is one school of thought by the so-called China experts that says with the progress that the Chinese are making in the free market economy, that inevitably political change will occur. There's another argument, too, from a more selfish point of view. That is, with an economy that's growing at a faster rate than any other economy in the world, about 9% last year, the United States needs to be very, very careful that they do not participate in that economy by severing relations because of the human rights. If we want to get on that train, we better get on it before it leaves the station. Otherwise, we're not going to find a seat because of the efforts of the Japanese, the Koreans, and other people that are busily

---
*Tianamen Square in Beijing was the site of pro-democracy, anti-government demonstrations in early 1989. The result was a government crackdown on Chinese dissidents.

working the market today.

Q: What degree of prosperity did you see in these various localities you visited?

Admiral Long: At our request, we concentrated our trip on what I would call old China. We didn't go into Manchuria. We didn't go into Tibet. It was Beijing, Tsingtao, down to Nanjing, Shanghai. Clearly, there were a lot of poor people. I don't recall seeing beggars on the street. I do recall seeing a vast amount of construction, buildings going up, apartments going up. Not many cars. Thousands of bicycles.

The accommodations were just one measure that at that time they were going through a dramatic change in the modernization of their tourist facilities. Some of the hotels that we stayed in in Beijing and Xian were the old Chinese hotels that were rather primitive, but then after that when we'd get into places like Nanjing and Shanghai, these were modern hotels that had just been opened up in the last few years. They were, in general, managed by foreign interests--Australians being one of the managers--and they were as good as you'd find anywhere in the West.

Q: Was Hong Kong an issue at all?

Admiral Long: For a long time Hong Kong has been extremely important to China, because it was really the front to the world. It was really the source where Chinese interest there provided lots of hard currency for China itself, for the PRC.* One of the other things that I think is worth noting, even at that time in 1985-'86, there was a tremendous amount of trade between the PRC and Taiwan. They didn't make a lot of noise about it, but the dollar value was significant.

Q: I didn't realize that. Well, now they just have to wait a few more years and Hong Kong drops into their laps.

Admiral Long: Well, that's right. We'll see how they do that.

Q: Did you have any specific messages to carry back? You mentioned these generalized messages from people who said they were looking for a closer association with the United States.

Admiral Long: I didn't bring back any specific personal messages. Of course, I gave a rather complete report of my trip to the appropriate people in the United States, the

---
*PRC--People's Republic of China.

State Department and others. After the trip, I went by and personally debriefed Mike Mansfield in Japan. I personally debriefed our ambassador in Seoul, Walker, and, of course, the intelligence community in Washington.*

Q: What other ventures have you been involved in during the post-Navy years?

Admiral Long: I think just a few other points that I would make, sort of going down the calendar. There are a few other commissions that I was on. The Stilwell Commission, which was the Security Review Commission, which really was focusing principally on the security reviews that are conducted for security clearances.** It encompassed such things as are polygraphs good ideas or not. I think the points that we really made to the Secretary of Defense on that were, one, we're doing an abysmal job on follow-on security investigations.

Q: Was this something that grew out of the Walker spy case?***

Admiral Long: Yes. Yes. In other words, we give initial

---
*Richard L. Walker, U.S. ambassador to the Republic of Korea.
**The chairman was General Richard G. Stilwell, USA (Ret.).
***In 1985 several members of the Walker family were arrested in connection with selling classified information, specifically cryptographic material, to the Soviet Union.

security investigations, but most people get into problems not initially but after they're out for five, ten years when they have marital problems, when they have financial problems, drinking problems, and so on. At that time, we were doing a very poor job of doing those follow-on investigations. So we strongly urged that that should be corrected.

Then there was a case about the value of polygraphs. We had testimony from former KGB people who made it very clear that you can train to foil the polygraph, but at the same time we supported the continued use of polygraphs. There are two parts of the polygraph. One is sort of the security side as, "Have you ever spied for the United States or any other country?" Then there's the other side and that's personal lifestyle. We strongly supported continuing to do the security polygraphs.

I guess the next thing other than my continuing consulting in business was in the spring of 1986, the President sent a commission to the Philippines to observe the elections. It was headed by Senator Lugar, and we had a few others.* I participated in that.

Q: Was this after the Aquino assassination?**

---
*Senator Richard G. Lugar, Republican-Indiana, of the Senate Foreign Relations Committee.
**Filipino opposition leader Benigno S. Aquino was shot and killed on 21 August 1983, minutes after arriving in Manila to challenge President Ferdinand E. Marcos. Aquino's widow, Corazon, later became President.

Admiral Long: Yes. This was about January-February of 1986, just prior to the time that Marcos then left the Philippines. We arrived in Manila and were briefed by the ambassador there. We then broke the team up into several different pieces. I was teamed with Senator Kerry from Massachusetts, and we were to go down to the island of Mindanao, all the way south.* We had a helicopter and we had no scheduled itinerary. We just looked at the map and decided where we were going to go, and we moved around from point to point. I'd say there and other places it became obvious that both sides were involved in fraud.

Interestingly, everywhere we went we were warmly welcomed, not as the enemy. There was one exception. We landed at one place and all at once, guys came out of the trees carrying guns. They fired a few shots, and we immediately took off. As a result of that, the commission met in Manila, and it was apparent to us that Marcos and his people probably were on pretty thin ice. There was a question as to whether the United States should really support Marcos continuing in office, and there was a great discussion with the members of the commission. I think really as a result of that, the United States withdrew that strong support from Marcos.

---
*Senator John F. Kerry, Democrat-Massachusetts.

Robert L. J. Long #3 - 420

Q: What were the symptoms you saw of this widespread fraud?

Admiral Long: "Well, what have you got in the bag?"

"Well, that's five pounds of sugar."

"Where did you get that?"

"I just got it for voting like this."

"How did they know you voted for him?"

"Well, I had to bring out this thing that's got the imprint of the ballot on it."

That was sort of on both sides. It wasn't just that. Sometimes they paid the people to vote the way they wanted them to.

Q: It sounds as if they were bidding for votes.

Admiral Long: Right.

Q: What do you remember of Kerry, another former Navy man?

Admiral Long: I liked him.

Q: He's very articulate and glib.

Admiral Long: I liked him personally. We'd sit and have

long discussions and eat together, and I would say, "John, that's a bunch of nonsense."

He'd say, "Yes, I know, I know, but I've got to say that." [Laughter]

Q: What might be an example of a bunch of nonsense?

Admiral Long: Oh, you know, talking about some of the things going on. He carried his newspaper reporter with him. I think he was with the Boston Globe. John was a very personable young man, had worked for an old friend of mine, Admiral Schlech.* Senator Kerry talked very, very well of him. He and I would not agree on some of the social issues, but a very charming kind of guy.

Q: Obviously a committed guy, because he was one of the veterans speaking out against the Vietnam War while it was still in progress.

Admiral Long: Yes.
Well, moving on, Paul, of course, I think we should mention the Defense Policy Board, which I joined in 1984, Just a couple of words about the Defense Policy Board. That was, I thought, a very worthwhile board for the Secretary of Defense. It did not have only, you might say,

---
*Rear Admiral Walter F. Schlech, Jr., USN.

right-wingers on there. There were other people, let's say were more Democrats than they were Republicans. Dr. Graham Allison, who is at Harvard, was a member. John Deutsch, who was the provost of MIT and who is now the Under Secretary of Defense for Acquisition, was a member. The board was chaired by a person I referred to before and that was Ambassador Seymour Weiss, who was a very effective chairman.

Just to give you an example of one of the recent products that we gave the Secretary of Defense was a report looking at the future of nuclear weapons. In that report we were looking at what happens when we draw down on the strategic weapons as well as the drawdown on the tactical nuclear weapons. Without going into any great detail, it emphasizes the need to maintain an adequate nuclear level just so that you don't encourage someone else to try to be the king of the mountain. It places primary emphasis on the need to maintain your strategic nuclear arsenal and your SSBNs. It also recommends that we maintain an adequate technical base in laboratories, design of nuclear weapons, as well as testing. We pointed out that this capability is not only important for developing and building new nuclear weapons that we may or may not want to do in the future, but is also very important to maintain this, to assist in the nonproliferation efforts of the United States. We also urged that we maintain a reconstitution capability for certain of the so-called theater tactical nuclear weapons.

The other effort that is worthwhile mentioning is the Advisory Committee on Command and Control of Nuclear Weapons, known as the Kirkpatrick Committee.* That encompasses not just communications, but it encompasses intelligence, it encompasses the security of nuclear weapons, it encompasses the safety, it encompasses the release procedures, it encompasses unauthorized watch, it encompasses risk reduction measures. So it was very, very broad. It was probably the most comprehensive look at the subject that we've ever had, and it should serve as a base from which to do upgrades in the years ahead.

I cannot get into all of the details on this because of the classification, but the Secretary of Defense received it well. It has been briefed in the Congress, and I think it will serve the interests of the United States well. It also gives, I think, a solid basis for discussion and negotiation with other countries who possess nuclear weapons. In other words, we can say, "This is what we're doing. What are you doing?" Hopefully we might be able to make the possibility of inadvertent nuclear use less likely in the future.

Q: Where do you view the establishment last year of the

---

*The chairman was Jeane D. Jordan Kirkpatrick, U.S. permanent representative to the United Nations, 1981-85.

Robert L. J. Long #3 - 424

Strategic Command in that whole framework?

Admiral Long: We have gone from an inventory of 30,000 or so nuclear weapons, and we're on our way down now to less than 5,000, which is still an awful lot. I think it made a lot of sense that we would go ahead and essentially try to consolidate the control of these, rather than having all the separate nuclear CinCs.

Q: It ties in with jointness too.

Admiral Long: That's right. A very important point that we tried to make to the Secretary is that with the reduction of nuclear weapons and with, you might say, the removal of the threat as we had known in the past with the Soviets, we anticipate there could be a reduction in the amount of emphasis, priority, that various commands place on nuclear weapons, a decreased emphasis on security and safety, knowledge.

So I think the Strategic Command can help maintain that sensitivity to the importance of dealing with nuclear weapons in a very responsible way. One of the things that we observed in the Kirkpatrick Committee hearings in the trips that we took was that some commands weren't all that knowledgeable as to the command and control of nuclear weapons. You don't need many of these things to go off really to get your attention. So I think that the strategic command can assist in maintaining the visibility of these terrible weapons.

Q: And the corporate memory too.

Admiral Long: That's right. That is right.

Q: What impressions do you have of Jeane Kirkpatrick?

Admiral Long: Ambassador Kirkpatrick is one of the most impressive people I have ever met. Very, very smart. Has a tremendous drive to get at the important message that she's looking at. She's not a technician, but she tries very hard to understand the technical aspects of the thing. She clearly has a great sensitivity to the political message of what we're looking at, and she would invariably bring us back to what was really the important political message that we were dealing with.

She also is a very warm human person. As an example, she's married to a political scientist who is quite ill, and she rarely will leave him overnight. If she's making a speech in New York, she will come back to spend the night with him. So she has a very warm human side to her. So she's a pretty impressive gal.

Q: You've mentioned your official government work. During all this time, how did you go about the process of earning a living following retirement?

Admiral Long: Well, I must admit, Paul, I've been very fortunate there. Over the years I've done a fair amount of consulting as an employee of Long & Associates, Inc., consulting for such outfits as General Dynamics, Applied Physics Laboratory, Johns Hopkins, Kaman Corporation, the Institute of Defense Analysis, TRW. I mean, it's a whole list. So I've not lacked that. I've also been asked to serve on corporate boards--Northrop Corporation, ConTel, GTE. And I've also been asked to serve as the trustee of some corporations that have been bought by foreign entities, and I've normally done this in concert with General Vessey. We essentially set up a separate corporation in order to protect United States classified information, and we, in effect, provide a Chinese wall to prevent that information from flowing to a foreign entity. So we have done several of those--Gould, Data Products, and so on. So it has been a very full life, a lot of pro bono work, but also an awful lot of activities that help pay the rent.

Q: I'm grateful to you, Admiral Long, for sharing that

full life with me and, through me, the Naval Institute and historians and researchers in the years to come. I appreciate very much what you've done for us.

Admiral Long: Thank you, Paul. I've enjoyed this oral history.

Q: Great. Thank you.

Index

to

The Reminiscences of

Admiral Robert L. J. Long,
United States Navy (Retired)

Acoustics
   The Navy initiated a wide-ranging program in the mid-1970s to protect ballistic missile submarines from detection, 302-304

Afghanistan
   Area of concern for the United States after the Soviet invasion in the late 1970s, 365-366

Ajax, USS (AR-6)
   Repair ship that served as flagship for Commander Service Group Three in the Western Pacific in the late 1960s, 252

Alcohol
   Drinking on board the battleship Colorado (BB-45) in the spring of 1945 to celebrate the birth of Ensign Tom Polk's first child, 66-67; in 1946 students at submarine school in New London had to curtail their drinking in order to pass the course, 89

Ammunition
   The battleship Colorado (BB-45) experienced a fire while loading 16-inch powder charges at Kerama-retto in the spring of 1945, 72-73

Antiair Warfare
   Gunnery against kamikazes off Okinawa in the spring of 1945, 67-68, 78

Antisubmarine Warfare
   Tactical work of Submarine Development Group Two in the late 1940s, using submarines against other submarines, 97-100; in the early 1950s U.S. ASW forces had difficulty coping with diesel submarines that had the GUPPY improvements, 125-126; work of Task Group Alfa in the mid-1950s, 140-146; the Navy initiated a wide-ranging program in the mid-1970s to protect ballistic missile submarines from detection, 302-304

Arco, Idaho
   Site of Navy nuclear power training around 1960, 183-184

Army, U.S.
   After being drafted in the 1960s, Long's son Charles quickly became a sergeant, later was wounded by a land mine in Vietnam, 249-251; relationship of Army component commander with CinCPac in the early 1980s, 347

B-52 Stratofortress
   Possibility of use against Iran in the late 1970s and early 1980s, 366-367

Backus, Commander Paul H., USN (USNA, 1941)
    Role in conceptual planning during the development of the Polaris program in the late 1950s, 171-173

Bagley, Vice Admiral David H., USN (USNA, 1944)
    As Chief of Naval Personnel in the early 1970s, discussed the Zumwalt personnel reforms with Long, 283-285

Baldwin, Robert H. B.
    Under Secretary of the Navy who in 1966 interviewed Long as a possible executive assistant, 225-226, 248; hands-on personality, 233-234, 244-245; had a civilian career in investment banking, 235; role as under secretary, 239; took a fact-finding trip to Vietnam, 239-243

Bangor, Washington, Submarine Base
    Beautiful facility built in the 1970s to accommodate Trident submarines, 301

Bayne, Commander Marmaduke G., USN
    Role in OpNav in coordinating North Pole submarine operations in the late 1950s, 176-177

Beirut, Lebanon
    Long headed the commission that investigated the October 1983 bombing of the U.S. Marine barracks at Beirut, 386-405

Benjamin Franklin, USS (SSBN-640)
    Site of a rain-drenched ComSubLant change of command ceremony in 1972, 275-276

Benson, Captain Roy S., USN (USNA, 1929)
    Energetic officer who commanded Submarine Development Group Two in the late 1940s, 97-98

Bledsoe, Chief Torpedoman's Mate Samuel H., USN
    Did a fine job as chief of the boat in the submarines Patrick Henry (SSBN-599) and Casimir Pulaski (SSBN-633) in the early 1960s, 209-211

Bowen, Captain Harold G., USN (USNA, 1933)
    Perceptive officer who served as chief of staff of ASW Task Group Alfa in the mid-1950s, 141, 143-144

Bowers, Captain William A., USN (USNA, 1923)
    Was difficult on subordinates as executive officer of the battleship Colorado (BB-45) in World War II, 48-49, 51-52, 56

Brazil
    Shakedown cruise to Rio de Janeiro by the submarine Corsair (SS-435) in 1947, 94-97

Bringle, Vice Admiral William F., USN, (USNA, 1937)
Seventh Fleet commander who sent a message to Long when the fleet flagship ran aground briefly in the late 1960s, 253

Brown, Harold
As Secretary of Defense in the late 1970s, had more interest in technical and programmatic matters than operations and strategy, 306, 330-333; comparison with successor, Caspar Weinberger, 340-341

Budgeting
Role of the Special Projects Office in doing program planning for Polaris in the mid-1960s, 223-232; in the early 1970s, OP-02 became the OpNav sponsor for the submarine budget, 291-293, 295-296; in the 1980s the theater CinCs began having a much greater input to the Defense Department budgeting process than previously, 338-339

Burke, Admiral Arleigh A., USN (USNA, 1923)
Role in establishing the Polaris submarine program in the late 1950s, 165-166; on board the submarine Patrick Henry (SSBN-599) during missile tests in 1960, 195-196; kept long working hours as Chief of Naval Operations, 246

Cambodia
Report in the early 1980s of live Vietnam War missing-in-action personnel still held in Cambodia, 351-352

Carter, President James E. (USNA, 1947)
The readiness of the Navy declined during Carter's term as President in the late 1970s, 305-306, 328-329, 336

Casimir Pulaski, USS (SSBN-633)
Admiral H. G. Rickover on sea trials in 1963, 187-188; Chief Torpedoman's Mate Sam Bledsoe did a fine job as chief of the boat when she went into commission, 210; rapid construction period in 1963-64, 219; was an improved version of the early Polaris submarines, 219, 222

Central Intelligence Agency
In the late 1970s the CIA had difficulty in getting access to U.S. Military information, 332-333, 350; in the 1980s an advisory panel concluded that the intelligence community had problems in both collection and analysis, 333-334

China, People's Republic of
Long's relationship with the nation's minister of defense in the early 1980s, 356; Long discussed U.S.-Sino relations when he visited the nation in 1985, 409-414; travels by Long and his wife Sara through the country, 411-417

Claytor, W. Graham, Jr.
Supportive of the Navy and Marine Corps while serving as Secretary of the Navy in the late 1970s, 307-308

Cochran-Bryan Prep School, Annapolis, Maryland
Before and during World War II, prepared many potential midshipmen for Naval Academy entrance exams, 18-19

Colorado, USS (BB-45)
Commander William Bowers, who served as executive officer during part of World War II, was difficult on subordinates, 48-49, 51-52, 56; gunnery department personnel, 53-57; antiquated equipment during World War II, 57-58; the ship's operational achievements during the second half of the war, 58-60; damage to the Colorado by Japanese shore batteries at Tinian in 1944, 59-60, 71; hit by Japanese kamikazes in November 1944, 64-65; drinking on board, 66-67; operations while the ship was off Okinawa in 1945, 66-68, 78; living conditions for officers and enlisted men, 70; fire while loading 16-inch ammunition at Kerama-retto in 1945, 71-72; resupply of food, fuel, and ammunition, 71-72; communications, 73-74; postwar visit to Japan, 76-77; Magic Carpet rides to return servicemen to the United States, 79

Collisions
The submarine Nautilus (SSN-571) banged into the submarine Sea Leopard (SS-483) at Norfolk in early 1956, 147-150; embarrassing international incident when the submarine George Washington (SSBN-598) collided with and sank the Japanese freighter Nissho Maru in April 1981, 360-362

Communications
Attempts to build a system for extremely low frequency radio transmissions to submarines in the 1970s and 1980s, 281-282; Admiral H. G. Rickover sometimes put too much emphasis on formality in submarine communications, 286-287; joint nature of command, control, and communications architecture, 406-407

Congress, U.S.
Long testified before the Senate on behalf of the Panama Canal treaty in the late 1970s, 314-317; attitude toward the U.S. peace-keeping presence in Lebanon in the early 1980s, 402-403; Long's testimony before Congress in the mid-1980s on the Goldwater-Nichols Bill, 406-408

Conolly, Vice Admiral Richard L., USN (USNA, 1914)
Welcomed students to the Naval War College in 1953 with a facetious remark, 131

Conrad, Dr. William A.
  Naval Academy math professor who was hospitable to midshipmen in the 1940s, 19-20, 33

Corsair, USS (SS-435)
  Commissioned in late 1946, this submarine contained some refinements not in the World War II fleet boats, 90-91; role of the torpedo data computer, 91-92; rundown of the boat's initial officers, 92-93; shakedown cruise to Brazil in 1947, 94-97; tactical ASW work as part of Submarine Development Group Two in the late 1940s, 97-100; administrative chain of command, 100-101; quality of the enlisted crew members, 103-105; the deck gun was used occasionally, 105

Cuban Missile Crisis
  Deployed Polaris submarines increased their readiness conditions and went to sea during the crisis in 1962, 209-210

Cutter, Commander Slade D., USN (USNA, 1935)
  Aggressive style of leadership as a submarine skipper in World War II, 86-88

Cutlass, USS (SS-478)
  Experienced considerable turnover at the top of the command structure in the early 1950s, 117-121; improvement in morale after elimination of Mickey Mouse practices, 121; GUPPY conversions improved the boat's submerged speed and endurance, 122; deployment to the Mediterranean in the early 1950s, 123-127; overhaul at Portsmouth Naval Shipyard, 128-129, 146; network of wives handled things at home when the boat was deployed, 130-131

Daspit, Rear Admiral Lawrence R., USN (USNA, 1927)
  Chewed out subordinates in 1960 for jumping the chain of command with a message about Polaris submarines, 197-198

Davis, Admiral Donald C., USN (USNA, 1944)
  Relationship with CinCPac while serving as CinCPacFlt in the early 1980s, 347-348

Defense Policy Board
  Meetings of in the mid-1980s on the subject of nuclear weapons, 421-422

Deng Xiaoping
  Chinese Deputy Prime Minister with whom Long talked during his visit to China in 1985, 410

Desert One
  Poorly planned operation in April 1980 to rescue U.S. hostages from Iran, 341

Diego Garcia
Unsuitability for operating B-52s in the late 1970s and early 1980s, 366-367

Drugs
In the late 1970s the Navy issued a zero-tolerance policy to deal with the problem of drug abuse, 320

Duncan, Captain Max C., USN (USNA, 1942)
Served in Danang during the Vietnam war, later handled special programs for the Naval Ship Systems Command in the early 1970s, 262-263

Education
Long's high school experience in Kansas City in the late 1930s, 11-12; Long's attendance at Washington University and the University of Missouri before entering the Naval Academy in 1940, 13-18; Long's years at the Naval Academy, 20-42; the importance of military officers receiving education about political, economic, and cultural aspects of other countries, 132-134

Enlisted Personnel
Quality of in the battleship Colorado (BB-45) during World War II, 54-57; in the submarine Corsair (SS-435) in the late 1940s, 103-105; in the submarine Sea Leopard (SS-483) in the mid-1950s, 153-155; in the submarine Patrick Henry (SSBN-599) in the early 1960s, 186, 192-193, 200-201, 209-211; problems with keeping quality officers and enlisted personnel in the Navy with the low pay of the late 1970s, 320

Families of Servicemen
By taking care of children, Navy wives have done a great deal to facilitate their husbands' careers, 129, 156-157; network of wives in the submarine Cutlass (SS-478) in the early 1950s, 130-131

Farzaneh, Vice Admiral Dariusd
Iranian naval officer who was involved in a U.S. shipbuilding program for Iran in the 1970s, 322-323

Felt, Admiral Harry Don, USN (USNA, 1923)
Had a reputation for toughness as Vice Chief of Naval Operations in the late 1950s, later mellowed, 174-175

Fire
On board the battleship Colorado (BB-45) while loading 16-inch ammunition at Kerama-retto in 1945, 71-72

Foley, Admiral Sylvester R., Jr., USN (USNA, 1950)
Relationship with CinCPac while serving as Commander in Chief Pacific Fleet in the early 1980s, 348-349

Fuel Oil
Conversion of U.S. Navy ships from black oil to distillate fuel in the early 1970s, 262, 266

Fuhrman, Commander Albert S., USN (USNA, 1937)
Outstanding as skipper of the submarine Corsair (SS-435) in the mid-1940s, 92-94

Garvey, Lieutenant (junior grade) Richard S., USNR
Boyhood friend of Long's who later served in submarines during World War II, 48

George Washington, USS (SSBN-598)
Embarrassing international incident when the submarine collided with and sank the Japanese freighter Nissho Maru in April 1981, 360-362; commanding officer fired for poor judgment, 361-362

Geraghty, Colonel Timothy, J., USMC
Commanded the Marine amphibious unit devastated by a bomb attack on the Marine barracks at Beirut, Lebanon, in October 1983, 391-392, 402; extremely conscientious commander, 399-401

Goldwater-Nichols Defense Reorganization Act
Law enacted in 1986 had an effect on the operational chain of command in the Department of Defense, 337-338, 342-343; requirement for joint duty to be promoted, 372; Long's testimony before Congress in the mid-1980s on command responsibilities and jointness aspects of the Goldwater-Nichols Bill, 406-408

Gooding, Rear Admiral Robert C., USN (USNA, 1942)
Qualities as vice commander of Naval Ship Systems Command in the early 1970s, 268

Greer, Captain Howard E., USN (USNA, 1944)
Visited Sasebo, Japan, while in command of the aircraft carrier Hancock (CVA-19) in the late 1960s, 258

Gunnery--Naval
Antiquated equipment in the battleship Colorado (BB-45) during World War II, 57-58; damage to the Colorado by Japanese shore batteries at Tinian in 1944, 59-60, 71; antiaircraft fire against kamikazes off Okinawa in the spring of 1945, 67-68, 78

Guns
Removal of deck guns from U.S. submarines after World War II, 105

GUPPY
In the early 1950s GUPPY conversions improved the boat's submerged speed and endurance of submarines, 122; U.S.

ASW forces had difficulty coping with diesel submarines that had the GUPPY improvements, 125-126

Hayward, Admiral Thomas B., USN (USNA, 1948)
Aggressive as Chief of Naval Operations in the late 1970s, 321-322; sometimes his OpNav staff tried to intrude into the operational chain of command, 321, 343-344

Holy Loch, Scotland
Overseas base for the submarine Patrick Henry (SSBN-599) in the early 1960s, 202-204; anti-nuclear protesters in 1961, 202-203

Holloway, Admiral James L. III, USN (USNA, 1943)
As Chief of Naval Operations in the mid-1970s, helped restore stability to the Navy, 296, 319; in 1977 selected Long as VCNO, 304; role on JCS, 313-314; reaction to problems with the Saudi Navy expansion program in the 1970s, 317-318; working style as CNO, 319; investigated the failed hostage rescue operation in Iran in 1980, 388-389

Honolulu, Hawaii
Admiral Long's interaction with the local community when he was serving as Commander in Chief Pacific in the late 1970s and early 1980s, 355-356, 381

Intelligence
Japan bought some sensitive undersea monitoring equipment in the late 1970s to be installed in a Soviet ship, but U.S. agents secretly replaced it beforehand, 308-309; in the late 1970s the Central Intelligence Agency had difficulty in getting access to U.S. Military information, 332-333, 350; in the 1980s an advisory panel concluded that the intelligence community had problems in both collection and analysis, 333-334; intelligence setup on the Pacific Command staff in the early 1980s, 349-350

Investigations
Long headed the commission that investigated the October 1983 bombing of the U.S. Marine barracks at Beirut, Lebanon, 386-405

Iran
U.S. program in the 1970s of building warships for Iran, 322-323; overthrow of the Shah's government in 1979, 323-324; in April 1980 the United States mounted a poorly planned military effort to rescue U.S. hostages from Iran, 341; possibility of using B-52 bombers against, 366-367

Iranian Navy
U.S. program in the 1970s of building warships for Iran, 322-323

Italy
A tender in La Maddalena began supporting Sixth Fleet submarines in the early 1970s, 282

Jamestown, USS (PG-55)
Gunboat used for Naval Academy midshipman cruises on Chesapeake Bay during World War II, 35-39

Japan
Conditions ashore immediately after the U.S. victory in 1945, 76-77; Long and his wife Sara got to know a number of Japanese people when he was based at Sasebo in the late 1960s, 255-257; protests against visits by U.S. nuclear-powered warships in the late 1960s, 257-258; bought some sensitive undersea monitoring equipment in the late 1970s to be installed in a Soviet ship, but it was secretly replaced beforehand, 308-309; military involvement in multinational RimPac training exercises in the early 1980s, 358-359; increased investment in defense forces, 358-359, 362-363; strong ties with the United States in the 1980s, 359-360; possibility of obtaining nuclear weapons, 380-381

Joint Chiefs of Staff
Long was disappointed in the late 1970s when the Joint Chiefs seemed inclined to give only military advice to the President, 306-307

Joint Staff
In the late 1970s the director of the Joint Staff complained that the Navy was not sending its best people to the staff, 310-311

Jones, General David C., USAF
As Chairman of the Joint Chiefs of Staff in the late 1970s and early 1980s, role in chain of command, 341, 343

Kamikazes
Hit the battleship Colorado (BB-45) in November 1944, 64-65; off Okinawa in the spring of 1945, 67-68, 78

Kansas City, Missouri
Political factions in the city and region in the 1920s and 1930s, 4-6

Kelley, General Paul X., USMC
Marine Commandant who testified before Congress in the wake of the October 1983 bombing of the U.S. Marine barracks at Beirut, Lebanon, 403-404

Kerama-retto
Fire on board the battleship Colorado (BB-45) while loading 16-inch ammunition at Kerama-retto in 1945, 71-72

Kerry, John F.
U.S. senator who joined Long on a trip to observe Filipino elections in early 1986, 420-421

Key West, Florida
The price of other real estate went down when the Navy built housing in Key West in the early 1950s, 119

Kidd, Admiral Isaac C., USN (USNA, 1942)
As Chief of Naval Material in the early 1970s came storming after Long concerning submarine systems, 269-271; personality, 269-272

King, Chief Fire Controlman Charles L., USN
Talented enlisted man who ran the F division in the battleship Colorado (BB-45) during World War II, 54-56

Kings Bay, Georgia, Submarine Base
Beautiful facility built in the 1970s to accommodate Trident submarines, 301-302

Kirkpatrick, Jeane D. Jordan
Former U.S. ambassador to the United Nations, in the mid-1980s she chaired a committee on nuclear weapons, 423-426; personality, 426

Korea, North
Pacific Command response to a North Korean attempt to shoot down a U.S. reconnaissance plane in the early 1980s, 342

Korea, South
U.S. Pacific Command response to a coup in the early 1980s, 347; in the early 1980s the former minister of foreign affairs expressed a desire for a continuing U.S. military presence in his country, 363-364

Laboon, Captain John F., Jr., USN (USNA, 1944)
World War II submariner who later became a Catholic priest and Navy chaplain, 46-47, 201

La Maddalena, Italy
A tender in this port began supporting Sixth Fleet submarines in the early 1970s, 282

Laning, Captain Richard B., USN (USNA, 1940)
Imaginative officer who commanded the submarine tender Proteus (AS-19) during Polaris support in the early 1960s, 205

Lebanon
Long headed the commission that investigated the October 1983 bombing of the U.S. Marine barracks at Beirut, 386-405

Leftwich, Lieutenant Colonel William G., Jr., USMC (USNA, 1953)
Aide in the Pentagon in the 1960s, later killed in Vietnam and honored by Ross Perot, 243-244

Lehman, John
Experienced a good deal of autonomy as Secretary of the Navy in the early 1980s, 340-341; had a good start as Secretary but ran into some problems when manipulating selection boards for promotion, 370-371

Long, Charles A.
The son of Robert and Sara Long, he dropped out of college in the 1960s, was drafted into the Army, later was wounded by a land mine in Vietnam, 249-251

Long Commission
Long headed the commission that investigated the October 1983 bombing of the U.S. Marine barracks at Beirut, 386-405

Long, Admiral Robert L. J., USN (Ret.) (USNA, 1944)
Parents of, 1-5, 8-11, 13-14, 27; siblings, 1-2, 5-7, 10-11; childhood, 1-3, 8-11; wife Sara, 8, 43-45, 60-63, 107, 116, 129-130, 156-157, 190, 204, 245, 248, 255-256, 361, 363, 408; education of, 11-18; attended prep school in Annapolis in 1940, 18-19; as a Naval Academy midshipman, 1940-43, 21-42; explanation of having four names, 27-28; met his future wife during an aviation indoctrination trip to Florida in 1943, 43-46; served in the battleship Colorado (BB-45) during the latter part of World War II, 48-60, 63-79; wedding and honeymoon in the summer of 1944, 60-63; as a student at submarine school at New London in 1946, 80-90; duty in the submarine Corsair (SS-435), 1946-49, 90-106; children of, 94, 102, 110-111, 156-157, 184, 249-251; NROTC duty at the University of North Carolina, 1949-51, 106-117; as executive officer of the submarine Cutlass (SS-478), 1951-53, 117-131; student at the Naval War College, 1953-54, 131-138; commanded the submarine Sea Leopard (SS-483), 1954-56, 139-161; served in the Submarine Weapons Readiness Section of OpNav, 1956-58, 161-177; staff of ComSubLant, 1958-59, 177-180; commanding officer of the submarine Patrick Henry (SSBN-599), 1960-63, 185-218; commanding officer of the submarine Casimir Pulaski (SSBN-633), 1963-65, 218-223; in the Special Projects Office, 1965-66, 223-232; aide to the Under Secretary of the Navy, 1966-68, 233-247; selection for rear admiral, 247-249; commanded Service Group Three, 1968-69, 251-260; duty in Naval Ship Systems Command, 1969-72, 261-275; served as ComSubLant, 1972-74, 275-291; as DCNO (Submarine Warfare), 1974-77, 391-304; as Vice Chief of Naval Operations, 1977-79, 304-326, 328-335;

served as Commander in Chief Pacific, 1979-83, 335-385; Secretary of Defense Caspar Weinberger asked Long in 1982 if he would be willing to be Chief of Naval Operations, 382-383; retirement in 1983, 384-385; chaired a commission on the October 1983 bombing of the Marine barracks at Beirut, Lebanon, 386-405; 1985 trip to China, 408-417; post-retirement consulting work, 426

Long, Sara Helms
Met her future husband in Florida in the summer of 1943, 43-45; wedding and honeymoon in the summer of 1944, 60-63; children of, 94, 102, 110-111, 184, 249-251; joined Episcopal church around 1950, 107; took care of the family while her husband was away on duty, 129-130, 156-157, 245, 255-256; accompanied her husband on various travels, 361, 363, 408-417

Lyon, Lieutenant Commander Harvey E., USN (USNA, 1946)
Hard-working, capable officer who was the first executive officer in the gold crew of the submarine Patrick Henry (SSBN-599) in 1960, 214

Lyon, Marge
A real character who was the wife of the first executive officer in the gold crew of the submarine Patrick Henry (SSBN-599) in 1960, 185, 214-215

Mansfield, Michael J.
Strong supporter of the U.S. military while serving as ambassador to Japan in the late 1970s and early 1980s, 359

Marco Polo Club
Prestigious New York City club that made honorary members of the skippers of the early nuclear-powered submarines, 190-191

Marcos, Ferdinand
As President of the Philippines, he had a good relationship with the U.S. Commander in Chief Pacific during the early 1980s, 355, 357-358; his support from his countrymen had waned by the mid-1960s, 419

Marine Corps
Long headed the commission that investigated the October 1983 bombing of the U.S. Marine barracks at Beirut, Lebanon, 386-405

McNamara, Robert S.
As Secretary of Defense in the 1960s, he recruited talented assistants, regardless of political affiliation, 234-235; and the Vietnam War, 239

Meyer, Rear Admiral Wayne E., USN
  Quite effective as program manager for Aegis in the 1970s and 1980s, 334-335

Moreau, Lieutenant Arthur S., Jr., USN (USNA, 1953)
  Talented submarine officer who was not picked by Admiral Hyman Rickover for the nuclear power program in the 1950s but eventually made four-star rank, 211-213

Mountbatten, Captain Louis, RN
  Made a moving speech to the midshipmen during a visit to the Naval Academy in 1941, 33-34

Murray, Robert J.
  Served on the Long Commission that investigated the October 1983 bombing of the U.S. Marine barracks at Beirut, Lebanon, 388-389

NROTC
  Officers assigned to the unit at the University of North Carolina in the late 1940s included Elmo Zumwalt, 107-109, 112; training of midshipmen, 111-117; comparison of NROTC graduates with those from the Naval Academy, 113-114

Nautilus, USS (SSN-571)
  Banged into the submarine Sea Leopard (SS-483) at Norfolk in early 1956, 147-150; capabilities, 148

Naval Academy, U.S., Annapolis, Maryland
  Plebe year in 1940-41, 21-23; academics in the early 1940s, 23-24, 30; daily routine, 25; executive department officers were characters, 26-30; athletics, 30-33; news of the attack on Pearl Harbor in 1941, 33-34; visit by Captain Louis Mountbatten in 1941, 33-34; summer cruises in the early 1940s confined to the Chesapeake Bay, 35-39; midshipman leadership organization, 39-40; social life of midshipmen, 41-42; graduation of the class of 1944, 42-43; comparison of NROTC graduates with those from the Naval Academy, 113-114; Under Secretary of the Navy Robert Baldwin pushed in the 1960s for new buildings, 234

Naval Material Command
  After it was created in the 1960s, it reported directly to the Chief of Naval Operations, 236; relationship to the Naval Ship Systems Command in the early 1970s, 269-270; did not really have an effective role, 270

Naval Ship Systems Command
  Command structure in the late 1960s and early 1970s, 261-262; conversion of the fleet to distillate fuel in the early 1970s, 262, 266; supervision of ship overhauls and repairs in the early 1970s, 263-265; beginning of gas turbine ship propulsion in the Navy in the 1970s,

267-268; relationship to the Naval Material Command in the early 1970s, 269-270

Naval War College, Newport, Rhode Island
President Richard Conolly welcomed students in 1953 with a facetious remark, 131; value in acquainting officers of different services, 131-132; education about political, economic, and cultural aspects of other countries, 132-134; curriculum in the early 1950s, 133-136, 137-138; war games, 135-136; social life of the students, 136-137

Nissho Maru (Japanese Freighter)
Embarrassing international incident when this ship was rammed and sunk by the ballistic missile submarine USS George Washington (SSBN-598) in April 1981, 360-362

Nitze, Paul H.
As Secretary of the Navy in the mid-1960s, demonstrated a thoughtful personality, 233, 244; interest in systems analysis, 237, 239

Nixon, Lieutenant Thomas J. III, USN (Ret.) (USNA, 1937)
Officer who settled with his wife Margaret in Chapel Hill, North Carolina, after being retired because of World War II wounds, 115-116

North Carolina, University of, Chapel Hill
Activities of the Naval ROTC unit in the late 1940s, 107-117

Nuclear Power
Commander Eugene P. Wilkinson, first skipper of the submarine Nautilus (SSN-571), is very knowledgeable on nuclear power, 150-152; training program in the Navy nuclear power program around 1960, 182-185; Admiral H. G. Rickover had so much talent to choose from that he rejected some capable officers for the nuclear training program, 212-213; protests against visits by U.S. nuclear-powered warships to Japan in the late 1960s, 257-258

Nuclear Weapons
Development of the Polaris missile in the late 1950s, 170-171; firing tests on board the submarine Patrick Henry (SSBN-599) in the summer of 1960, 195-198; protesters in Scotland in 1961, 203-203; safeguards in Polaris missile-firing procedures, 207-208; Pacific Command control of theater nuclear weapons in the late 1970s and early 1980s, 378-380; concern about proliferation to other countries, 380; discussed by the Defense Policy Board in the mid-1980s, 422-423; Kirkpatrick Committee on Command and Control of Nuclear Weapons in the 1980s, 423-424

Okinawa
  Operations of battleship <u>Colorado</u> (BB-45) during the campaign for Okinawa in the spring of 1945, 66-68, 78

OpNav
  Within the office of the Chief of Naval Operations, submarine requirements were handled in the late 1950s by OP-311, which included a number of future flag officers, 162-164; a major concern of OP-311 during the late 1950s was the Polaris program, 164-173; OP-311 involvement in North Pole submarine operations in the late 1950s, 174-177; in the early 1970s, OP-02 became the OpNav sponsor for the submarine budget, 291-293, 295-296; OP-02 chaired a wide-ranging program in the mid-1970s to protect ballistic missile submarines from detection, 302-304

Overhaul of Ships
  Portsmouth Naval Shipyard, overhauled the submarine <u>Cutlass</u> (SS-478) in the early 1950s, 128-129, 146; program of complex overhauls initiated in the early 1970s by the Naval Ship Systems Command, 263-265; submarine material maintenance system, 265; attempt to overhaul as close to home port as possible, 273

Owens, Vice Admiral William A., USN (USNA, 1962)
  In 1992 became DCNO with broad responsibility for warfare requirements, 292-293

Pacific Command, U.S.
  As commander in chief in the late 1970s, Long called for the service expertise of staff officers, 294; emphasis on jointness, 311; Long attended a conference at Singapore in the late 1970s about dealing with Soviet expansionism, 326-328; in the late 1970s U.S. strategy called for Pacific forces to move to the Atlantic to support a war against the Soviets in Europe, 330-332, 368; low state of readiness within the command when Long arrived in 1979, 336; increased emphasis on the operational chain of command after Caspar Weinberger became Secretary of Defense in 1981, 336-338; greater input than before on Defense Department budgeting process, 338-339; Pacific Command response to a North Korean attempt to shoot down a U.S. reconnaissance plane in the early 1980s, 342; relationship in the 1970s and 1980s between the theater CinC and his component commanders from the individual services, 345-348; intelligence setup, 349-352; role of staff political adviser, 350; command responsibilities and size of staff, 350-351; relationship with Japan, 358-362; U.S. military role in relation to South Korea, 363-364; Afghanistan became an area of concern for the United States after the Soviet invasion in the late 1970s, 365-366; principal contingency planning had to do with Korea, 378; control of theater nuclear weapons, 378-380

Pacific Fleet, U.S.
In the late 1970s, 25% of the ships in the fleet were not capable of carrying out their missions, 305-306, 329; relationship with CinCPac in the early 1980s, 347-348; long deployments in the Indian Ocean and North Arabian Sea in the early 1980s, 375-377

Panama Canal
Long testified before the Senate on behalf of the Panama Canal treaty in the late 1970s, 314-317

Patrick Henry, USS (SSBN-599)
Equipped with an outboard motor used as a thruster to aid shiphandling, 159; relationship between the blue and gold crews, 167-168; construction and trials, 185-186; enlisted crew members, 186, 192-193, 200-201, 205-206, 209-211; as skipper, Long was invited to make a number of public speeches about the Polaris program, 190-191; deterrent patrols in the early 1960s, 192-194, 215-218; missile firing tests in the summer of 1960, 195-198; based overseas at Holy Loch, Scotland, in the early 1960s, 202-204; safeguards in missile-firing procedures, 207-208; increased readiness condition during the Cuban Missile Crisis in 1962, 208-209; talented officers in the first crew, 211-215; contacts with Soviet submarines, 215-217

Pay and Allowances
Problems with keeping quality officers and enlisted personnel in the Navy with the low pay of the late 1970s, 320

Pendergast, Thomas J.
Political boss who dominated Jackson County, Missouri, in the 1920s and 1930s, 4-6

Perot, H. Ross (USNA, 1953)
Businessman who honored his Naval Academy classmate William Leftwich after he was killed in Vietnam in 1970, 243-244

Philippine Islands
Relationship of the nation's leaders with the U.S. Commander in Chief Pacific during the early 1980s, 355, 357-358; in early 1986 a delegation of Americans acted as observers for Filipino elections, 419-420

Planning
Role of OP-311 in conceptual planning for the Polaris program in the late 1950s, 164-173; planning in the mid-1960s for the continuing operation of the Polaris submarines, 224, 228-230; in the late 1970s U.S. strategy called for Pacific forces to move to the Atlantic to

support a war against the Soviets in Europe, 330-332, 368; in the early 1980s the Pacific Command's principal contingency planning had to do with Korea, 378

Polaris Missile
Development in the late 1950s, 170-171; firing tests on board the submarine Patrick Henry (SSBN-599) in the summer of 1960, 195-198; anti-nuclear protesters in Scotland in 1961, 202-203

Polaris Program
Role of OP-311 in conceptual planning in the late 1950s, 164-173; Rear Admiral William F. Raborn, Jr., was very effective as a salesman for the Polaris program in the late 1950s, 166, 169, 173-174; decision to man each submarine with two crews, 167; from conception to deployment, the Polaris program moved remarkably fast, 169-170; missile development, 170-171; as skipper of the Patrick Henry (SSBN-599), Long was invited to make a number of public speeches about the Polaris program, 190-191; safeguards in missile-firing procedures, 207-208; role of the Special Projects Office, 223-232; planning in the mid-1960s for the continuing operation of the Polaris submarines, 224, 228-230

See also Casimir Pulaski, USS (SSBN-633); Patrick Henry, USS (SSBN-599); Robert E. Lee, USS (SSBN-601); Theodore Roosevelt, USS (SSBN-600)

Polk, Ensign Thomas H., USN (USNA, 1945)
Had a few drinks on board the battleship Colorado (BB-45) in 1945 to celebrate the birth of his first child, 66; attended submarine school in 1946, 81

Portsmouth Naval Shipyard, Kittery, Maine
Overhauled the submarine Cutlass (SS-478) in the early 1950s, 128-129, 146

Prigmore, Becky
As the wife of William Prigmore, an officer in the submarine Corsair (SS-435) in the mid-1940s, she demonstrated a lively sense of humor, 93-94

Prisoners of War
Report in the early 1980s of live Vietnam War missing-in-action personnel still held in Cambodia, 351-352

Promotion of Officers
As Secretary of the Navy in the 1980s John Lehman improperly manipulated selection boards, 370-371; general comments on selection boards, 371-374; quotas for various warfare communities, 373-374; plucking boards picked individuals to retire, 375

Proteus, USS (AS-19)
   Tender that serviced Polaris submarines at Holy Loch, Scotland, in the early 1960s, 202-203, 205

Raborn, Rear Admiral William F., Jr. USN (USNA, 1928)
   Very effective as a salesman for the Polaris program in the late 1950s, 166, 169, 173-174; attended missile firing tests on board the submarine Patrick Henry (SSBN-599) in the summer of 1960, 196-197

Radar
   Replacement of outmoded radar equipment in the battleship Colorado (BB-45) in 1944, 57-58

Religion
   Role in Long's family as he was growing up, 7-8

Retention
   Problems with keeping quality officers and enlisted personnel in the Navy with the low pay of the late 1970s, 320

Rickover, Rear Admiral Hyman G., USN (USNA, 1922)
   Degrading job interview with Long in 1959, 180-181; political power, 182; rode on sea trials of nuclear submarines, 186-188, 288-289; had so much talent to choose from that he rejected some capable officers for the nuclear training program, 212-213; liked to keep trained officers as long as he could, 218; relationship with Levering Smith, 227; Long threatened to use Rickover's name during the Zumwalt people programs of the early 1970s, 283; emphasis on formality in submarine communications, 286-287; stormy personality, 288-290

Rio de Janeiro, Brazil
   Shakedown cruise to Rio by the submarine Corsair (SS-435) in 1947, 94-97

Robert E. Lee, USS (SSBN-601)
   The initial commanding officers, Reuben Woodall and Joe Williams, didn't get along well at first, 206-207

Rogers, General Bernard W, USA (USMA, 1943)
   Served as U.S. Commander in Chief Europe at the time of the October 1983 bombing of the U.S. Marine barracks at Beirut, Lebanon, and the subsequent investigation, 393, 396, 398-399

Rota, Spain
   Served as an overseas base for the submarine Casimir Pulaski (SSBN-633) in the mid-1960s, 220

SR-71 Reconnaissance Aircraft
Pacific Command response to a North Korean attempt to shoot down an SR-71 reconnaissance plane in the early 1980s, 342

Sasebo, Japan
Long and his wife Sara got to know a number of Japanese people when he was based at Sasebo in the late 1960s, 255-257; protests against visits by U.S. nuclear-powered warships in the late 1960s, 257-258; Long and his wife treated warmly on a visit to the city in 1981, 361

Saudi Navy
The U.S. Navy had to replace the program manager when things were not going well in building gunboats for Saudi Arabia in the late 1970s, 317-318

Scotland
Holy Loch was an overseas base for the submarine Patrick Henry (SSBN-599) in the early 1960s, 202-204; anti-nuclear protesters in 1961, 202-203

Sea Leopard, USS (SS-483)
Officers in the mid-1950s, 139-140, 158; work as part of ASW Task Group Alfa in the mid-1950s, 140-146; near-collision with a destroyer, 142-143; capabilities, 146; hit by the USS Nautilus (SSN-571) in early 1956, 147-148; enlisted crew, 153-155; capability of torpedoes, 160

Security
In making public speeches, the skippers of early Polaris submarines had to be careful what they said about capabilities, 191; the Navy initiated a wide-ranging program in the mid-1970s to protect ballistic missile submarines from detection, 302-304; in the mid-1980s Long was part of the Stilwell Commission to investigate security lapses in connection with classified information, 417-418

Selection Boards
See Promotion of Officers

Selin, Ivan
Department of Defense systems analyst who helped plan the Polaris program in the mid-1960s, 224, 228

Service Group Three
Based in the Western Pacific, it provided logistic support to the Seventh Fleet in the Vietnam War in the late 1960s, 252-261

Shannon, Joseph B.
Congressman who appointed Long to the Naval Academy in 1940, 4, 14, 17, 27-28

Shear, Commander Harold E., USN (USNA, 1942)
Served as one of the initial commanding officers when the submarine Patrick Henry (SSBN-599) went into commission in 1960, 167-168, 205-206

Shiphandling
The submarine Nautilus (SSN-571) banged into the submarine Sea Leopard (SS-483) at Norfolk in early 1956, 147-150; the submarine Patrick Henry (SSBN-599) was equipped with an outboard motor used as a thruster to aid shiphandling, 159

Sims, Commander William E., USN (USNA, 1942)
He and his crew in the Theodore Roosevelt (SSBN-600) grew hydroponic vegetables during submerged patrols in the early 1960s, 193

Singapore
Concerns about security have led Singapore to discuss basing U.S. Navy ships there, 326-328

Sirago, USS (SS-485)
When the submarine was in Newfoundland shortly after World War II, one of her junior officers got into fisticuffs with Commander Slade Cutter, 87-88

Sixth Fleet, U.S.
Role of diesel submarines in challenging fleet units for training purposes in the early 1950s, 124-127; new support facilities for submarines in Italy in the 1970s, 282

Smith, Vice Admiral Levering, USN (Ret.) (USNA, 1932)
Had a major role in the development of the Polaris missile in the late 1950s, 170-171; corrected problems following an unsuccessful Polaris missile firing test in the summer of 1960, 195-197; personality, 223, 226-227; work as director of the Special Projects Office in the mid-1960s, 223-228; relationship with Admiral H. G. Rickover, 227; promotion to vice admiral on retired list, 296

Somalia
President Siad Barré in the early 1980s offered to have U.S. forces stationed in his country, 366

Sonar
Role in the tactical work of Submarine Development Group Two in the late 1940s, using submarines against other submarines, 97-98

Sonenshein, Rear Admiral Nathan, USN (USNA, 1938)
Qualities as commander of Naval Ship Systems Command in the early 1970s, 268

Soviet Navy
   Interactions between Soviet submarines and the U.S. submarine <u>Patrick Henry</u> (SSBN-599) in the early 1960s, 215-217; height of expansion was in the late 1970s, 325-326

Spain
   Rota was an overseas base for the submarine <u>Casimir Pulaski</u> (SSBN-633) in the mid-1960s, 220

Special Projects Office
   Role in the Polaris submarine program in the mid-1960s, 223-232

Squash
   Long played the sport from the time he was a midshipman in the 1940s until he was a flag officer in the 1970s, 30-32, 246

Strategic Command, U.S.
   Established in 1992 to control the targeting and use of nuclear weapons, 424-425

Strategy
   In the late 1970s U.S. strategy called for Pacific forces to move to the Atlantic to support a war against the Soviets in Europe, 330-332, 368

Styer, Commander Charles W., Jr., USN (USNA, 1941)
   As commanding officer of the submarine <u>Cutlass</u> (SS-478) in the early 1950s, had difficulty getting a capable exec, 117-120

Submarine Development Group Two
   Tactical antisubmarine warfare work in the late 1940s, using submarines against other submarines, 97-100

Submarine Force, Atlantic Fleet
   Role of Rear Admiral Frederick B. Warder as type commander in the late 1950s, 177-180; rain-drenched change of command ceremony in 1972, 275-276; split of submarines between Atlantic and Pacific fleets in the early 1970s, 277; roles of force commander in the 1970s, 277-279; force commander had operational control in the 1970s, 277-278; logistic support of submarines, 280-281; communications, 281-282; did not fully participate in the Zumwalt people programs of the early 1970s, 283-286; inspection of submarines, 286-287

Submariners
   Enlisted personnel in the submarine <u>Corsair</u> (SS-435) in the late 1940s, 103-105; in the submarine <u>Sea Leopard</u> (SS-483) in the mid-1950s, 153-155; in the submarine

Patrick Henry (SSBN-599) in the early 1960s, 186, 192-193; in the early days of SSBNs most aggressive officers preferred to command nuclear attack submarines rather than the ballistic missile variety, 189-190

Submarines
North Pole submerged operations in the late 1950s, 174-177; in the early 1970s, Long put out a message limited the operating depth of some submarines, 270-271; split of submarines between Atlantic and Pacific fleets in the early 1970s, 277; initiatives in the mid-1970s for use of nuclear submarines in direct support of carrier task groups, 297-298; diesel submarines make sense for other nations but not the United States, 299-300; the Navy initiated a wide-ranging program in the mid-1970s to protect ballistic missile submarines from detection, 302-304

See also Benjamin Franklin, USS (SSBN-640); Casimir Pulaski, USS (SSBN-633); Corsair, USS (SS-435); Cutlass, USS (SS-478); George Washington, USS (SSBN-598); Nautilus, USS (SSN-571); Patrick Henry, USS (SSBN-599); Robert E. Lee, USS (SSBN-601); Sea Leopard, USS (SS-483); Theodore Roosevelt, USS (SSBN-600)

Submarine School, New London, Connecticut
Captain Frederick Warder was the much-admired skipper of the school in 1946, 81; top-notch instructors, 82; training in the techniques of making torpedo approaches, 82-83, 89-90; escape tower training, 85-86

Sugarman, Lieutenant Charles M., USN (USNA, 1932)
Role as a company officer at the Naval Academy in the early 1940s, 26-28

Systems Analysis
Emphasized when Paul Nitze was Secretary of the Navy in the 1960s, 224, 228, 236-237

Tactics
Torpedo approach techniques for U.S. submarines during and after World War II, 89-90; work of Submarine Development Group Two in the late 1940s, using submarines against other submarines, 97-100; work of antisubmarine hunter-killer group, Task Group Alfa, in the mid-1950s, 140-146

Task Group Alfa
Role as hunter-killer antisubmarine group in the mid-1950s, 140-146

Teller, Dr. Edward
Scientist who was impressed by the professionalism of the crew of the submarine Patrick Henry (SSBN-599) when he went on sea trials in 1960, 186

Terrorism
   Long headed the commission that investigated the October 1983 bombing of the U.S. Marine barracks at Beirut, Lebanon, 386-405

Theodore Roosevelt, USS (SSBN-600)
   Crew grew hydroponic vegetables during submerged patrols in the early 1960s, 193

Thresher, USS (SSN-593)
   Lost at sea in April 1963 during a test dive, 221-222

Tinian, Marianas Islands
   Damage to the battleship Colorado (BB-45) by Japanese shore batteries at Tinian in 1944, 59-60, 71

Torpedoes
   The Mark 18 torpedo was used by U.S. submarines in the mid-1950s, 160

Training
   Course at the submarine school in New London in 1946, 82-90; the process by which Long qualified for submarines on board the Corsair (SS-435) in the late 1940s, 101-102; by the NROTC unit at the University of North Carolina, 1949-51, 111-117; training program in the Navy nuclear power program around 1960, 182-185; of submarine crews in the early 1970s, 290; Japanese involvement in multinational RimPac training exercises in the early 1980s, 358-359

Trident Missile
   Offers range advantage over Polaris and Poseidon missiles previously used in ballistic missile submarines, 300-301

Trident Program
   The Trident missile offers range advantage over Polaris and Poseidon missiles previously used in ballistic missile submarines, 300-301; bases built in the 1970s at Bangor, Washington, and Kings Bay, Georgia, 301-302

Turkey
   Received a visit from the submarine Cutlass (SS-478) in the early 1950s, 124

Turner, Admiral Stansfield, USN (USNA, 1947)
   As director of the Central Intelligence Agency in the late 1970s, he had difficulty in having access to U.S. Military information, 332-333

Vietnam War
   Under Secretary of the Navy Robert Baldwin made a fact-finding trip to Vietnam in the mid-1960s, 239-243; Long's

son Charles was wounded by a land mine in Vietnam in the late 1960s, 250-251; U.S. unwillingness to put together a strategy for winning the war, 254; hospital ships took care of wounded from Vietnam, 259; confusion over command relationships in the Pacific theater, 345; report in the early 1980s of live missing-in-action personnel in Cambodia, 351-352

Ward, Rear Admiral Norvell G., USN (USNA, 1935)
Was tough and innovative as commander of the first squadron of Polaris submarines in the early 1960s, 168, 199, 205; attended missile firing tests on board the submarine Patrick Henry (SSBN-599) in the summer of 1960, 196-197; jumped the chain of command by sending suggestions for Polaris directly to the CNO in 1960, 197-198; as Commander Service Group Three in the late 1960s, 251-252, 258

Warder, Captain Frederick B., USN (USNA, 1925)
Much-admired as skipper of the submarine school at New London in 1946, 81; headed the submarine branch, OP-31, of OpNav in the late 1950s, 166, 174-175; as ComSubLant in the late 1950s, 177-180; temperament, 178-179

War Games
At the Naval War College in the early 1950s, 135-136

Warner, John W.
As Under Secretary of the Navy in 1969, told Long he was being reassigned to the Naval Ship Systems Command, 261; as Secretary of the Navy in 1972, attended a rain-drenched ComSubLant change of command ceremony, 275-276

Watkins, Admiral James D., USN (USNA, 1949)
During his tenure as Chief of Naval Operations in the early 1980s his OpNav staff sometimes tried to intrude into the operational chain of command, 321, 343-344; as CinCPacFlt in the early 1980s, 348

Weinberger, Caspar W.
U.S. military capability experienced a resurgence after Weinberger became Secretary of Defense in 1981, 336; developed a closer relationship with the theater CinCs than his predecessors had had and put more emphasis on the operational chain of command, 336-338; style in handling the two major facets of his job, 340-341; personality, 342; asked Long in 1982 if he would be willing to be Chief of Naval Operations, 382-383; got Long to chair the commission that investigated the October 1983 bombing of the Marine barracks at Beirut, Lebanon, 386-387, 394-397

Weir, Margaret
Widow who lived in Scotland in the early 1960s and told ghost stories, 204

Weisner, Admiral Maurice F., USN (USNA, 1941)
  As CinCPac in the late 1970s, did an excellent job of improving rapport with his component commanders, 346

Weiss, Seymour
  Ambassador who in the early 1980s helped overturn the previous U.S. strategic plan of moving forces from the Pacific to Atlantic, 368

Wickham, General John A., Jr., USA (USMA, 1950)
  Had an important role in the Pacific Command during a South Korean coup in the early 1980s, 347

Wilhite, Captain Drewery R., USN (USNA, 1942)
  Commanded a task group of underway replenishment ships in the Western Pacific during the late 1960s, 254-255

Wilkinson, Vice Admiral Eugene P., USN
  As commanding officer of the USS Nautilus (SSN-571), rammed the submarine Sea Leopard (SS-483) at Norfolk in early 1956, 146-150; did a fine job of showing the Nautilus to visitors, 150; characteristics, 149-152; very knowledgeable on nuclear power, 152; relieved by Long as ComSubLant and rain-drenched ceremony in 1972, 275-276

Williams, Commander Joe, Jr., USN (USNA, 1943)
  As first skipper of the gold crew of the USS Robert E. Lee (SSBN-601) in the early 1960s, initially had trouble getting along with his blue counterpart, 206; Navy wife Marge Lyon wrote a poem for Williams's 50th wedding anniversary, 214

Woodall, Commander Reuben F., USN (USNA, 1943)
  As first skipper of the blue crew of the USS Robert E. Lee (SSBN-601) in the early 1960s, initially had trouble getting along with his gold counterpart, 206

Woolsey, R. James, Jr.
  Imaginative individual who was Under Secretary of the Navy in the late 1970s, 308-309

Xu-Yimin
  Chinese general who served as a host for the Longs when they visited his country in 1985, 411-412

Yew, Lee Kuan
  Singapore President who in the late 1970s expressed concern about Soviet expansionism, 326-327

Yom Kippur War
  During this Middle East War in the autumn of 1973, U.S. submarines were ready to deploy on short notice, 279-280

Zumwalt, Lieutenant Elmo R., Jr., USN (USNA, 1943)
As NROTC instructor at the University of North Carolina in the late 1940s, 107-110; when he was Commander Naval Forces Vietnam in the late 1960s, he tried to get Long's son Charles to visit his father in Saigon, 250-251; the Atlantic Fleet Submarine Force did not fully participate in the Zumwalt people programs of the early 1970s, 283-286; attempts as CNO to diminish parochialism in warfare specialties, 293

www.ingramcontent.com/pod-product-compliance
Lightning Source LLC
Chambersburg PA
CBHW080624170426
43209CB00007B/1512